I0199156

www.ingramcontent.com/pod-product-compliance
Lightning Source LLC
Chambersburg PA
CBHW060800100426

42813CB00004B/890

* 9 7 8 1 9 3 4 1 5 2 6 4 5 *

The

PRACTICAL

TANYA

Also by Chaim Miller

The Kol Menachem Chumash – Gutnick Edition

The Kol Menachem Chumash (Hebrew) – Leviev Edition

Rambam: Principles of Faith – Slager Edition

The Kol Menachem Haggadah – Slager Edition

The Kol Menachem Megillah – Slager Edition

The Five Books of Moses, Lifestyle Books – Slager Edition

Prayers for Friday Night, Lifestyle Books – Slager Edition

The Kol Menachem Tehillim – Schottenstein Edition

Turning Judaism Outward: A Biography of Rabbi Menachem Mendel Schneerson

The Practical Tanya Part One: The Book for Inbetweeners

The Practical Tanya Part Two: Gateway to Unity and Faith

THE SLAGER EDITION

The

PRACTICAL
TANYA

PART THREE
LETTER ON REPENTANCE

RABBI
SHNEUR
ZALMAN of LIADI

ADAPTED BY

CHAIM MILLER

GUTNICK LIBRARY
OF JEWISH CLASSICS

ISBN-13: 978-1-934152-64-5 | ISBN-10: 1-934152-64-1

© Copyright 2018 by Chaim Miller

Published and distributed by: Kol Menachem, 827 Montgomery Street, Brooklyn, NY 11213.

1-888-580-1900 | 1-718-951-6328 | 1-718-953-3346 (Fax)

www.kolmenachem.com | orders@kolmenachem.com

Contact the author at: chaimmiller@gmail.com | rabbichaimmiller.com

First Edition — 2018.

All rights reserved. No part of this book may be reproduced in any manner whatsoever without written permission from the copyright holder, except in the case of brief quotations in reviews for inclusion in a magazine, newspaper or broadcast.

Praise for *The Practical Tanya*

"An astonishing accomplishment... and suitable for anyone... even those who do not read in Hebrew and are not familiar with esoteric texts."

—Rabbi Moshe Wolfson, *Mashgiach Ruchani Yeshivas Torah Ve-Da'as.*

"It is wonderful that this sacred text has now been clarified in a way that anyone can benefit from it."

—Rabbi Gavriel Zinner, author *Nitei Gavriel,* Rav of Congregation *Nitei Gavriel.*

"An important contribution... makes the flow of the *Tanya* very clear for all who study.

—Rabbi Yehuda Leib Schapiro, *Yeshiva Gedola* Rabbinical College of Greater Miami.

"With a masterful command of the English language, Rabbi Miller has managed to open up the *Tanya* to the wider public... not an easy task!"

—Rabbi Nochum Kaplan, Director, *Merkos* Office of Education.

"A lucid and scholarly translation... will undoubtedly assist multitudes."

—Rabbi Moshe Bogomilsky, *halachic* authority, author of *Vedibarta Bam* series.

"Brings the warmth, genius, and inspiration of the *Tanya* to life.... This work will certainly help inspire souls."

—Rabbi Zev Reichman, Director, Mechina Program, Yeshiva University.

"Rabbi Chaim Miller has made it accessible to everyone.... This book will awaken, inspire, and challenge you."

—Daniel Matt, translator of *The Zohar: Pritzker Edition.*

"Quite simply the best version in the English language."

—Rabbi Dov Greenberg, Chabad of Stanford University.

"A wonderful work which makes the *Tanya* accessible and understandable to a whole new generation of spiritual explorers... beautifully written."

—Rabbi Mark Wildes, Director, *Manhattan Jewish Experience.*

"A new classic.... Practical and relevant in the fast-moving, rapidly-changing technological era in which we live."

—Rabbi Mendel Lew, Stanmore & Canons Park Synagogue, U.K.

"Rabbi Chaim Miller's crisp, lucid and contemporary translation promises... concrete strategies for personal spiritual growth."

—Henry Abramson, Dean, Touro College, Brooklyn.

UPPER TESHUVAH

INTRODUCTION

ROLE OF FASTING

LOWER TESHUVAH

TRANSLATOR'S INTRODUCTION

THE THIRD BOOK OF TANYA

The *Tanya* was first published in 1796 as a single volume containing two separate works, *The Book for Inbetweeners* (*Sefer shel Beinonim*), and *Gateway to Unity and Faith* (*Sha'ar Ha-Yichud Ve-Ha-Emunah*).[1] These have been translated and elucidated in volumes one and two of this series.[2] The present work, *Letter on Repentance* (*Igeres Ha-Teshuvah*), appeared as a third section in later printings of the *Tanya*, and was the final section of the work to appear in the author's lifetime.[3]

While *Letter on Repentance* did not appear in the first published edition of the *Tanya*, it had already been in circulation in manuscript form for a number of years. The author had begun publicly distributing hand-written copies of the *Tanya* as early as 1792, and surviving manuscripts from this period speak of the "Small Tanya," a reference to the *Letter on Repentance* before it was formally named.[4]

After its initial publication in 1796, in Slavita, Ukraine, the *Tanya* was published for a second time in 1799 in Zolkiva (Zhovkva), Galicia, by R' Ya'akov son of Rabbi Naftali Hertz of Brod.

1. For bibliographic details see Rabbi Yehoshua Mondshine, *Torath Habad: Bibliographies of Habad Hasiduth Books,* volume 1, (Brooklyn: Kehos, 1981, Hebrew), pp. 15-16.

2. Rabbi Chaim Miller, *The Practical Tanya, Part One: The Book for Inbetweeners* (Brooklyn: Kol Menachem, 2016), and *Part Two: Gateway to Unity and Faith* (Brooklyn: Kol Menachem, 2018). For biographical information on the *Tanya's* author, a history of its composition and printing, the origin of the *Tanya's* teachings and its methodology, see my "Translator's Introduction" in Part One. I will only add here additional information pertinent to this volume.

3. A later printing, published posthumously by the author's sons in 1814, included a fourth part, *Sacred Letter* (*Igeres Ha-Kodesh*) containing various scholarly letters written by the author; and a fifth part, *Final Tract* (*Kuntres Acharon*), containing material which the author had composed at the same time the original *Tanya* was being written.

4. Since the *Letter*, too, begins with the Hebrew word *Tanya*, and it is a much shorter work. For details of the early circulation of *Tanya* manuscripts see my "Translator's Introduction" to Part One, p. xiii.

R' Ya'akov was an active publisher during the 1790s and 1800s, and was instrumental in the printing of a variety of works, including volumes of *Midrash, Musar* and *Halacha* and even one other Chasidic work.[5]

R' Ya'akov's second printing of the *Tanya*, in 1799, clearly violated the five year ban against any further publication, pronounced in the Rabbinic approbations to the original 1796 edition.[6] In his Publisher's Forward, R' Ya'akov stated that his community in Galicia did not have open trade for Jewish books with Ukraine, where the *Tanya* had appeared, apparently defending his printing of the work during the five year period.

> *"I have received many requests to publish this holy book which was printed in another country, whose doors are closed and locked. For this reason this work has not reached our country, and, as far as I have seen, not one copy is to be found in the city."*[7]

R' Ya'akov had obtained a manuscript copy of the "Small Tanya," and published it for the first time in his 1799 edition. He introduced the work with the following note.

> *"In my possession is a fine pearl from the esteemed author, a handwritten pamphlet which discusses matters relating to repentance, and for the benefit of the public it is being published here."*[8]

The work was not yet named *Letter on Repentance,* and simply bore the title *"Tanya Part Three: an explanation of matters pertaining to repentance."* It was also not divided into chapters.

The third section of *Tanya* was not printed in the author's homeland for almost a decade after the appearance of the initial two parts, first appearing in the 1806 Shklov edition. During the interim period, the author, Rabbi Shneur Zalman, had been imprisoned and released twice, in 1798 and 1800, and had subsequently relocated to Liadi. After his release, the length,

---

5. In 1799 R' Ya'akov re-published *Igeres Ha-Kodesh* of Rabbi Menachem Mendel of Vitebsk (Rabbi Shneur Zalman's senior colleague and teacher), which had first appeared in 1794. For an overview of the publishing activity of R' Ya'akov see Rabbi Ephraim Grossberger, "The Publisher R' Ya'akov ben Rav Naftali Hertz from Brod," in *Ohr Yisrael,* issue *27,* (Monsey, 2002), pp. 206-210.

6. *The Practical Tanya, Part One,* pp. 6, 8.

7. Publisher's Forward of R' Ya'akov son of Rabbi Naftali Hertz of Brod to the 1799 edition of *Tanya,* p. 74b, (reproduced in Mondshine, p. 40). The point is reiterated in the Rabbinic approbations which R' Ya'akov received (ibid. p. 42).

8. 1799 Edition, p. 67a, Mondshine, p. 39.

depth, and sophistication of Rabbi Shneur Zalman's discourses increased noticeably.

It is therefore significant that, during this period of intensification of his teachings, the author carried out a major revision of the third part of *Tanya* before its publication. While the first and second parts of the printed version of *Tanya* also differ from their earlier manuscript form, the changes are minimal when compared with the editing and reworking of the third part, that appeared in 1806.[9] The Fifth Lubavitcher Rebbe, Rabbi Shalom Dov Ber Schneersohn noted that *Letter on Repentance, "was rewritten by the Rebbe after (his imprisonment in) Petersburg in a different style.... We see that several passages, when revised the second time, are expanded upon, with more profound scholarship."*[10] In a similar vein, the Seventh Lubavitcher Rebbe, Rabbi Menachem Mendel Schneerson, observed: "*In Letter on Repentance the discussions of Kabbalah, Chasidus and classical sources are more developed than in the rest of the Tanya."*[11]

The 1806 version has became the standard edition, forming the basis of subsequent printing and study.[12] It also formally named the work as *Letter on Repentance.*

While a relatively small book of just twelve chapters, *Letter on Repentance* is far longer than one would expect from a "letter," (it also does not appear to ever have been sent as a letter). The name therefore invites some interpretation.

In one of his talks, the Rebbe offered two insightful explanations. Practically, the *Letter* is a guide to *spiritual recovery*, the restitution from a state of sin. Recovery is not supposed to be a permanent activity: you recover, and then you move on. Therefore the work was named a "letter," to emphasize its *temporary status,* for, unlike a book, one generally disposes of a letter after use.

The mystical dynamic of *teshuvah* is a process of reinventing oneself through drawing on transcendent energies. In the language of Kabbalah, *teshuvah* is powered by *Binah,* the Divine "womb," from which the energies

---

9. The first edition is printed in *Likutei Amarim First Versions, Based on Earliest Manuscripts* (Kehos, 1981). Rabbi Shneur Zalman's hand written edits, used to produce the second edition, have survived. For a facsimile, see Mondshine p. 19.

10. Rabbi Shalom Dov Ber Schneersohn, *Toras Shalom* (Kehos, 1947), p. 55.

11. Rabbi Menachem Mendel Schneerson, *Toras Menachem,* vol. 60 (Lahak, 2017), p. 195.

12. There were, however, a few subsequent printings of the first edition. See Mondshine p. 16, note 55. As noted in Part One of the *Practical Tanya,* this work is based on the text of the 1900 Vilna edition, which contains the "second edition" of *Igeres Ha-Teshuvah.*

that conduct the universe are "born." *Teshuvah* brings a person to be "re-born" by channeling fresh transcendent energies from *Binah*.[13]

A letter has the specific connotation of content that has been *sent from one place to another*. *Teshuvah*, the Rebbe suggested, resembles a "letter" which "sends" healing energies from a distant, transcendent place (*Binah*), down to the penitent on earth.[14]

TESHUVAH IN JEWISH MYSTICAL SOURCES

The third part of *Tanya* is a discussion of the theory and practice of *teshuvah* (repentance), both from a legal/Talmudic and a mystical perspective. The *Letter* builds on a vast Rabbinic and Kabbalistic literature on the topic,[15] and seeks to guide the reader on a path of *teshuvah* that is fitting for the emerging Chasidic movement.

One of the major innovations of the Kabbalah's treatment of *teshuvah* is an emphasis on the spiritual damage caused by sin and the corresponding healing properties of *teshuvah*.

The Zohar teaches:

> "'If a man opens a pit or if a man digs a pit (and does not cover it, and an ox or a donkey falls into it)' (*Exodus* 21:33). What is written next? 'The owner of the pit shall make restitution...' (ibid., 34). If such is the case in this situation, all the more so with one who harms the world by his sins! ... Teshuvah restores everything—repairing above, repairing below, mending oneself, mending the whole world.'"[16]

---

13. See *Zohar, Raya Mehemna*, 3, 122a.

14. See Rabbi Menachem Mendel Schneerson, *Sichos Kodesh* 5731, vol. 2, pp. 21-24. The Rebbe also notes that the first two parts of *Tanya* correspond to the lower energies of *Zeir Anpin* (*Sefer Shel Beinonim*), and *Malchus* (*Sha'ar Ha-Yichud Ve-Ha-Emunah*). Presumably this is because the first book of *Tanya* is aimed at *emotional management*, reflecting *Zeir Anpin*, the realm of emotions; and the second book of *Tanya* is aimed at achieving *awareness of G-d's presence* in the world, an expression of *Malchus*, the Divine power of manifestation.

15. For a good review in English of *teshuvah* in classical Jewish sources see Shimon Shokek, *Kabbalah and the Art of Being: The Smithsonian Lectures* (London and New York: *Routledge*, 2001), pp. 127-147. For a list of important Rabbinic works on *teshuvah* see idem., p. 160, n. 4.

16. *Zohar* 3, 122a (Daniel Matt trans., *The Zohar, Pritzker Edition*, volume 8, (Stanford University Press, 2014), pp. 290-1).

The principle is explained beautifully by Rabbi Eliyahu de Vidas in his *Reishis Chochmah.*

> "The word teshuvah refers to the intention to restore previous levels and repair them to their original status. This can be compared to the removal of water flowing from a fountain, in order to nourish various gardens, orchards, fields, and vineyards; along comes some fool who diverts the (channel of) water toward the trash, or to some empty place where it will serve no purpose. The owner of the fountain will be angry at him, first because he caused this watering of his fine gardens to be stopped, and secondly because he spoiled and broke the (original) channel."

> "The consequences of actual sin are much more grave than in this case. For if one spoils the channels of the divine flow from coming to their appropriate places, by diverting them, he has angered the King, the G-d of Hosts; he takes holiness and diverts it to impurity; he causes a place that should be dry and barren (of support) and waters and saturates it.... Teshuvah repairs the broken channels, restores the flow to its proper place, everywhere according to the flaw within him."[17]

The *Zohar* develops this theme further, depicting sin as causing a fragmentation in G-d's name, the Tetragrammaton. Specifically, it is the letter *hei* that becomes detached from the other three letters of the name, a defect which is restored by *teshuvah.* Following this insight, the word *teshuvah* can be read as *tashuv-hei,* "return the *hei.*"

In one key passage, the Zohar delineates different levels of *teshuvah.*

> "There are many types of teshuvah a person can do, all good, but not all are identical in character."

> "One person may have been a complete rasha (wicked human) all his life, transgressing many prohibitions, but subsequently he regrets his actions and confesses them. Afterward he does neither good (acts of kindness and charity), nor bad (transgressions). Such a person will certainly be forgiven by the Blessed Holy One, but he will not merit 'upper teshuvah.'"

---

17. Rabbi Eliyahu De Vidas, *Reishis Chochmah, Sha'ar ha-Teshuvah,* ch. 2, sect. 2. The translation here is from Daniel M. Horwitz, *A Kabbalah and Jewish Mysticism Reader* (Jewish Publication Society, 2016), p. 221.

> *"Another person, after repenting of his sins and achieving atone-ment, will follow in the path of the commandments and devote him-self with all his abilities to revere and love the Blessed Holy One. Such a person will merit 'lower teshuvah,' called (returning the) hei (of the Tetragrammaton). This is 'lower teshuvah.'"*

> *"Then there is the person, who after regretting his sins and re-penting, studies the Torah with reverence and love of the Blessed Holy One, not with the expectation of reward."*

> *"Such a person will merit the letter vav, (of the Tetragrammaton) who is the 'son' of yud-hei (of the Tetragrammaton. Then the vav) is called the son of Binah (since Binah is composed of the word ben, 'son,' plus the letters yud and hei). And this person will cause vav to return to (the first) hei (of the Tetragrammaton)."*

> *"And that is why the word 'teshuvah' means return ('tashuv,') the vav to hei."*[18]

Letter on Repentance is largely built on this passage from the *Zohar*. Rabbi Shneur Zalman seeks to clarify the meaning of these two levels of "upper" and "lower" *teshuvah*, both in terms of the mystical processes the Zohar indicates, and their practical implementation as states of con-sciousness. Chapters four to seven expound upon 'lower *teshuvah*,' and chapters eight to twelve focus on "upper *teshuvah*."

THE ROLE OF FASTING

The first three chapters of *Letter on Repentance* are devoted to the ques-tion: Is fasting a necessary component of *teshuvah*?

Some historical context is in order here. The *Talmud*, in its various dis-cussions of *teshuvah*, does not stipulate fasting as a requirement for re-pentance. Maimonides, in his codification of *Talmudic* law, states simply, *"What is teshuvah? That the sinner stops the sin, removing it from his thoughts, deciding in his heart not to do it again."*[19]

While this establishes *teshuvah* as a purely mental process, in subse-quent centuries, a demanding regimen of fasting became the norma-tive prescription in Rabbinic literature for those seeking to repent. This was largely a result of the literature of the *Chasidei Ashkenaz*, a group

18. *Zohar, Raya Mehemna, 3, 123a.*

19. *Rambam, Mishneh Torah, Laws of Teshuvah 2:2; see below pp. 19, 27.*

of pietists active in German Rhineland during the 12th and 13th centuries.[20] While the *Chasidei Ashkenaz* were a relatively fringe group, their approach to *teshuvah* proved to be extremely influential after being adopted extensively by the mainstream Halachic responsa in the 12th-15th centuries. As a result *teshuvah* came to mean, in the eyes of many people, a mental process that had to be accompanied by a Rabbinically advised penitential schedule, (which usually included fasting).[21]

This unique development of medieval Ashkenazi Judaism was not an organic development of earlier practice. *Letter on Repentance* makes this clear in chapter one, and stresses the *Talmudic/Maimonidean* model: *"The mitzvah of teshuvah, from the Torah is: just the decision to stop sinning."*[22] In other words, no fasting at all is technically required.

This discouragement of fasting accords with the popular characterization of the *Ba'al Shem Tov's* Chasidic movement as a form of pietism that rejected asceticism. For the *Besht*, *devekus* (Divine consciousness and emotional connection) was paramount, and self-mortification was likely to lead to sadness, a mood which compromises the capacity for *devekus*.

The following statement, by early Chasidic Master, Rabbi Ze'ev Wolf of Zhitomir is typical:

> *"I have heard that in the days of the Besht there was such a person who engaged in self-mortification... and the Besht said that in the world to come they are laughing at him. For the truth is that all of this is not necessary, particularly when one's heart is lacking in the essential worship, namely, devekus."*[23]

The *Besht* likewise similarly wrote to his disciple Rabbi Ya'akov Yosef of Polonye:

---

20. The penance literature of the *Chasidei Ashkenaz* was authored by Rabbi Shmuel *Ha-Chasid* of Speyer, his son Rabbi Yehudah *Ha-Chasid* of Speyer/Regensburg and by Rabbi Yehudah's disciple, Rabbi Elazar of Worms. The two innovations in this literature about *teshuvah* are: 1. that the sinner must go to a Rabbi in order to receive a prescription for penance; 2. that this prescription would invariably require fasting and other modes of physical suffering. For an exhaustive discussion see Emese Kozma, *The Practice Of Teshuvah (Penance) In The Medieval Ashkenazi Jewish Communities* (Phd dissertation, Eötvös Loránd University, Budapest, 2012).

21. See below pp. 23-24.

22. See below, p. 17-23.

23. Rabbi Ze'ev Wolf of Zhitomir, *Ohr ha-Meir*, p. 43b.

"You write that you are forced to fast, and my innards grew angry from what I read."

"I hereby add by a most holy oath... that you must not endanger yourself in this way for this is a depressing and sad act. G-dliness will not rest where there is depression, but rather, where there is the joy of a mitzvah."[24]

However, as *Letter on Repentance* subsequently demonstrates, the notion that Chasidism rejected the approach of fasting is an oversimplification.

First, Rabbi Shneur Zalman does not reject outright the literature of the *Chasidei Ashkenaz.* His point is that fasting is not an *intrinsic* or *necessary* part of the *teshuvah* process and can therefore be dispensed with. He does, however, concur that penitential fasting could (in certain circumstances) assist with atonement, the Divine forgiveness that follows *after* a person's *teshuvah.*[25]

There is another body of pietistic, penitential literature, which in many ways resembles the works of the *Chasidei Ashkenaz,* though was composed independently from it—the texts from the school of Rabbi Yitzchak Luria, (*Arizal,* 16th century). Basing himself on Kabbalistic *gematria* (numerology), *Arizal* recommended a rigorous scheme of fasting for a variety of different transgressions, often along with accompanying meditations.[26]

This material was accepted more enthusiastically, though not unreservedly, by Rabbi Shneur Zalman. In principle, he writes, the fasts recommended by *Arizal* should be carried out, but only if they will not be injurious to health, in which case they can be substituted by charitable donations. For those who are able to carry out the fasts, certain *halachic* leniencies are encouraged, to ease the process.[27]

---

24. *Shivchei Ha-Besht* p. 105.

25. For the distinction between *teshuvah* and atonement, see the extensive discussions in Chapter One.

26. These are reproduced in Rabbi Meir Poppers (ed.), *Sha'ar Ha-Yichudim, Sha'ar Tikunei Avonos;* Rabbi Emmanuel Chai Ricchi, *Mishnas Chasidim, Maseches Teshuvah;* Rabbi Naftali Hertz Bacharach, *Eimek Ha-Melech, Sha'ar Tikunei Avonos.*

27. These are discussed in Chapter Three. Rabbi Shneur Zalman frames this activity (in Chapter Two), not as a means of securing atonement, but in the spirit of the sacrifices brought in Temple times, as a post-atonement "gift" to G-d, so as to be pleasing again in His eyes.

XVII | THE PRACTICAL TANYA

Beshtian Chasidism, then, at least in the *Tanya's* formulation, did not reject fasting outright; it followed a more nuanced approach. Early Chasidism, it turns out, was somewhat encouraging of fasting, and saw great spiritual benefits to the activity, in those cases where it would not compromise health.[28]

Needless to say, the *Letter on Repentance* does not constitute an exhaustive treatment of the topic of *teshuvah,* a theme which is expanded upon greatly in the later discourses of Rabbi Shneur Zalman and his successors.[29] The Seventh Lubavitcher Rebbe made *teshuvah* a central theme of both his public discourse and communal work, and he vigorously encouraged the study of *Letter on Repentance,* often advising that it be studied before the other parts of *Tanya.*[30]

COMMENTARIES ON THE THIRD BOOK OF TANYA

The third book of *Tanya, Letter on Repentance,* has been the subject of significant commentary and analysis. Some of the commentaries on books one and two also discuss book three, so I will recap these first. Since they have already been described in the "Translator's Introduction" to book one, I will mention them just briefly here.

> The Lubavitcher Rebbe, Rabbi Menachem Mendel Schneerson, *Notes on Tanya*[31] and various *sichos* (talks).[32]

28. Today, however, the recommendations of *Arizal* appear to be rarely, if ever, practiced in the Chasidic community.

29. For a comparative survey of *teshuvah* in the writings of the Chabad leaders see Dov Schwartz, *Chabad Thought: From Beginning to End* (Heb). (Bar Ilan, 2011), chapter 5.

30. See Rabbi Menachem Mendel Schneerson, *Igros Kodesh,* volume 17, pp. 46, 107; volume 21, p. 413.

31. Rabbi Menachem Mendel Schneerson, *Notes and brief comments to Sefer Shel Beinonim* (Brooklyn: Kehos, 2014). I refer to this work here as "*Notes on Tanya.*"

32. While the Rebbe quotes all parts of the *Tanya* extensively throughout his vast corpus of published talks, *Letter on Repentance* is unique in that it merited a sustained, systematic treatment from him. These lectures, delivered during the years 1969-1970, have been reprinted a number of times; the best and most recent versions are found in *Likutei Sichos* volume 39 (Brooklyn: Kehos, 2001), pp. 121-160 (talks edited by the Rebbe); and in *Toras Menachem, Hisvaduyos* vols. 56-61 (Brooklyn: Lahak, 2016-2018), see index "Talks on *Letter on Repentance*" (talks transcribed by students and not edited by the Rebbe). The Rebbe also offered extensive commentary on his father's Kabbalistic notes to *Letter on Repentance* (*Likutei Sichos* ibid. pp. 51-159). For the Kabbalistic notes themselves see: *Likutei Levi Yitzchak, Ha'aros al Sefer Ha-Tanya* (Brooklyn: Kehos, 1970).

Rabbi Aharon Chitrik ed., *Likutei Amarim Tanya, Igeres Ha-Teshuvah, Be-Tziruf Ma'arei Mekomos, Likut Perushim, Shinui Nuscha'os,* (Brooklyn: Kehos, 1986), an anthology of comments on the *Tanya* found in the discourses of Chabad Rebbeim. This material is complex, and is, generally speaking, not aimed at clarifying the literal meaning of the text.

Rabbi Alexander Sender Yudasin (d. 1982), *Ha-Lekach Ve-Ha-Libuv* (Kfar Chabad, 1968), the second volume of this series contains commentary on *Igeres Ha-Teshuvah.*

Rabbi Yehoshua Korf (1905-2007), *Likutei Biurim Be-Sefer Ha-Tanya* (Brooklyn, 1968-1980), 2 vols.

Rabbi Yosef Wineberg (1917-2012), *Shiurim Be-Sefer Ha-Tanya, Igeres Ha-Teshuvah* (Brooklyn: Kehos, 1984, Yiddish); Rabbis Levy Wineberg and Shalom B. Wineberg (trans.), *Lessons in Tanya,* volume 3 (Brooklyn: Kehos, 1989, English).

Rabbi Yoel Kahn (b. 1930), (Rabbi Eliyahu Avraham Kirshenbaum ed.), *Igeres Ha-Teshuvah im biurei Ha-Rav Yoel Kahn* (Jerusalem: Mayanosecha, 2009). This is the best in-depth Hebrew commentary available.[33]

Rabbi Yekusiel Green, *Tanya im Maskil Le-Eitan, Igeres Ha-Teshuvah* (Kfar Chabad, 1987, Hebrew).

Rabbi Levi Yitzchak Ginsberg, *Peninei Ha-Tanya, Igeres Ha-Teshuvah* (Kfar Chabad: Ufaratzta 1994).

Rabbi Adin Steinsalz *Biur Tanya,* (Jerusalem: Sifrei Milsa, 1997); one volume of this series is devoted to *Igeres Ha-Teshuvah.*

Rabbi Avraham Alashvili *Sha'ar Ha-Yichud Ve-Ha-Emunah ve-Igeres ha-Teshuvah in Perush Katzar* (Brooklyn: Kehos, 2015), is an expanded version of the author's *Tanya Mevuar* (Nachlas Har Chabad: Nachlas Sefer, 1998), and is the best short treatment of *Sha'ar Ha-Yichud Ve-Ha-Emunah.*

33.　Rabbi Kahn's commentary on *Igeres Ha-Teshuvah* has also been adapted by Rabbi Moshe Link in his series, *Likutei Amarim Tanya im Biurim u-Peninim,* (Israel: Machon Ma'or She-be-Torah, 2013-4), but the adaptation of Kirshenbaum in this case is by far the superior work.

Rabbi Moshe Yehudah Kroll et. al, *Sefer Likutei Amarim Tanya* (Bnei Brak: Pe'er Mikdashim, 2014).

In addition to the above, *Letter on Repentance* has merited the following treatment devoted exclusively to this section of the *Tanya*.

Rabbi Yosef Yitzchak Katz, *Talelei Teshuvah* (2007), an exhaustive, in depth analysis of the text.

ACKNOWLEDGMENTS

First and foremost I extend my gratitude to David and Lara Slager whose outstanding generosity has made this book possible, as well as most of my other works throughout the last decade. The Slager family have set an example to the Jewish community, both in their personal lives and with their outstanding philanthropic efforts towards an impressive array of causes across the globe. I wish David, Lara, and their precious children Hannah and Sara Malka, all the abundant blessings that they deserve.

I extend my heartfelt wishes to Rabbi Meyer Gutnick, co-founder and director of Kol Menachem publishing, who had the courage to invest in an unknown author, and since then has been an unfailing source of material support and moral encouragement for my work. Motivated by a great love for the Rebbe, and recognizing the urgency of spreading his Torah teachings, Rabbi Gutnick has chosen to invest his own natural talent at "getting things done" into a very worthy cause. In the merit of this, and all his many other impressive philanthropic efforts, may G-d bless him, together with his dear wife Shaindy, and all their wonderful children and grandchildren, with *chasidishe nachas* and only revealed and open goodness.

I am grateful to my father-in-law, Rabbi Yeremi Angyalfi for scrutinizing the entire text and offering many helpful corrections and comments. For assistance with proofreading I thank Chanan Maister.

To my parents, Trevor and Denise Miller, for their love, for investing in my education and for supporting me in becoming a rabbi, even if they would have preferred I had become a doctor.

And finally, to my greatest support, my wife Chani, and to my wonderful children: Leah, Mendel, Mushka, Levi, Esther Miriam, Ariella and Menucha, my greatest pride and joy.

Chaim Miller

Rosh Chodesh Sivan 5778

ליקוטי אמרים חלק שלישי

AUTHOR'S TITLE PAGE

This brief introductory section of Part Three of *Tanya* was written by the author to formally name this work.

לִיקוּטֵי אֲמָרִים — The book *"An Anthology of Teachings"* (*Likutei Amarim*).

Parts One, Two and Three of the *Tanya* are collectively named "An Anthology of Teachings." The *Tanya* is not an "anthology" in the sense of a "cut-and-paste" selection from other works; it's more a *synthesis* of various teachings the author had received, both written and oral, that he then enlarged upon and adapted for practical implementation in daily life.

The collected sermons of Rabbi Dov Ber of Mezritch (d. 1772), Rabbi Shneur Zalman's teacher, were published in 1781 with the same title, *Likutei Amarim,* and it is surely no coincidence that the *Tanya* (first published in 1796), was given the same name. While Rabbi Shneur Zalman undoubtedly put much of his own creative input into the pages of the *Tanya,* he chose to emphasize the direct continuity of his work with Rabbi Dov Ber's ideas by giving it the same name as his master's work.

Despite the author's choice of title, this book came to be generally known by the public as *"Tanya,"* the Hebrew word with which the book begins. (This name had been in common use before the *Tanya* was printed, when it had circulated in manuscript form). Already in the second printing of the work in 1799, the title *Tanya* formally appears, and has since become a permanent fixture.

חֵלֶק שְׁלִישִׁי — **Part Three.**

The first printed edition of the *Tanya* contained two parts. Part One, *The Book of the Inbetweeners* (*Sefer Shel Beinoinim*)*,* is a psychologically orientated guide to worship. Part Two, *Gateway to Unity and Faith* (*Sha'ar Ha-Yichud ve-ha-Emunah*) focuses on the esoteric philosophy which forms the foundation of Chasidic thought.

(Though we cannot be certain, it appears that Rabbi Shneur Zalman had originally composed *Gateway to Oneness and Faith* as Part One of the book, but later made the decision to place the more practical *Book of the Inbetweeners* at the beginning of his published work.)

הנקרא בשם אגרת התשובה

The second printing of the *Tanya*, in 1799, included a third section, later entitled *Letter on Repentance* (*Igeres Ha-Teshuvah*), which had already been in broad circulation in manuscript form since the summer of 1792.

The complete *Tanya,* as it was published in the author's lifetime therefore consisted of these three sections. *Igeres Ha-Teshuvah* is the culmination and completion of the book.

A later printing, published posthumously by the author's sons in 1814, included a fourth part, *Sacred Letter* (*Igeres Ha-Kodesh*) containing various scholarly letters written by the author; and a fifth part, *Final Tract* (*Kuntres Acharon*), containing material which the author had composed at the same time the original *Tanya* was being written.

הַנִּקְרָא בְּשֵׁם אִגֶּרֶת הַתְּשׁוּבָה — Part Three of the *Tanya* is **called by the name,** **"Letter on Repentance"** (*Igeres Ha-Teshuvah*).

The "Letter on Repentance" is a relatively brief work discussing the theory and practice of *teshuvah*. The term *teshuvah* has two connotations: a.) *repentance*, and b.) *return*, a devotional re-attachment to G-d where the soul is "handed back" to its Creator. Both themes are explored at length by the author.

The content of "Letter on Repentance" is exceptionally rich. The author presents a rigorous analysis of classical, Talmudic sources deeply integrated with themes from Jewish mysticism (Kabbalah and Chasidus).

In many ways, the rigorousness of this work surpasses the previous two parts of *Tanya*. This reflects the fact that "Letter on Repentance" was the only section of the *Tanya* which was significantly revised by the author as a second edition. (The first two parts were also revised before publication, but to a lesser extent).

The first printed edition of "Letter on Repentance" in 1799, closely resembled the earlier manuscript version which had been circulating since 1792. After Rabbi Shneur Zalman's two imprisonments in 1797 and 1800, his teachings underwent a significant maturation, and it was during this later period that he composed the second edition of the "Letter." The second edition was first published in 1806, as the third section of *Tanya*. At this time the work was formally named "Letter on Repentance"; previously it had been known as the *"small Tanya,"* since, like the first section of the book, it begins with the word "*Tanya*".

The text presented here is the second edition which is the version included in virtually all editions of the *Tanya* since its first appearance. (The first edition, which does not appear in this volume, is available in Hebrew, published by Kehos in 1981 as *Likutei Amarim First Versions, Based on Earliest Manuscripts.*)

CHAPTER 1

THE DEFINITION OF TESHUVAH

SECTION ONE: ATONEMENT

In this chapter the *Tanya* will construct a very precise, rigorous definition of *teshuvah,* what feelings and activities it includes, and what it does not.

Before we begin our in depth definition of *teshuvah,* in Section Two, the *Tanya* first presents us with a discussion of *atonement.*

Teshuvah represents *your efforts* for G-d to forgive you for a sin. Atonement is *G-d's response*, as He forgives you and cleanses you from any remnant of your sin.

Atonement is therefore the *goal* and *outcome* of *teshuvah.*

תָּנְיָא בְּסוֹף יוֹמָא — **We learn at the end of** Tractate *Yoma* (86a):

שְׁלוֹשָׁה חִלּוּקֵי כַּפָּרָה הֵם — *There are three different categories of atonement.*

From a Chasidic perspective atonement is an experience of *reconnection*. The sin separates your soul from G-d; the atonement restores it. The sin causes negative forces to attach to your soul; the atonement washes them away.

While any sin will separate you from G-d, they do not do so equally. The extent of disconnection can be deduced from the level of atonement that is required. If a sin requires more atonement, it's because the sin has disconnected you more from G-d.

So we begin with a discussion from the *Talmud* about levels of atonement, and this will soon lead us to understand the spiritual dynamic of reconnection.

וּתְשׁוּבָה עִם כָּל אֶחָד — *Repentance (teshuvah) must accompany each one* of the three different categories of atonement.

A sin is a rebellion against G-d. To repair that, every sin without exception requires repentance (*teshuvah*), a term we will define later on in this chapter.

The different categories of atonement will help us to fathom *to what extent* a disconnect has occurred. But, ultimately, a disconnect is a disconnect. "Repen-

עַל מ"ע וְשָׁב אֵינוֹ זָז מִשָּׁם עַד שֶׁמּוֹחֲלִין לוֹ עָבַר עַל
מל"ת וְשָׁב תְּשׁוּבָה תּוֹלָה וְיוה"כ מְכַפֵּר. (פי' דאע"ג

tance must accompany each" type of atonement, because it is repentance that
establishes the re-connection.

The *Talmud* will now specify the "three different categories" in detail.

The first category is:

עָבַר עַל מִצְוַת עֲשֵׂה וְשָׁב — *"For failing to observe a positive command* of the
Torah," as soon as **the person repents,** אֵינוֹ זָז מִשָּׁם עַד שֶׁמּוֹחֲלִין לוֹ — *"he is forgiven immediately, before he even moves from where he is standing."*

The Torah contains 613 commands, some phrased as "dos" and others as
"don'ts" (prohibitions). The "dos" are called "positive commands" since they are
an instruction to actively do something, such as, for example, to eat *matzah* on
the first night of Passover, or to give charity.

In this first category, the *Talmud* informs us that for failure to observe a positive command, once repentance has been carried out, no further activity is
necessary. Atonement is effective *immediately*, "before he even moves from
where he is standing."

The second category is:

עָבַר עַל מִצְוַת לֹא תַעֲשֶׂה וְשָׁב— *"If a person violates a prohibition and then repents,"* repentance alone is not sufficient to secure atonement, as was the case
with failing to observe a positive command.

Rather, in this case:

תְּשׁוּבָה תּוֹלָה וְיוֹם הַכִּפּוּרִים מְכַפֵּר — *"The repentance suspends* any negative
consequences of the sin, *until the Day of Atonement brings full atonement."*

In the case of prohibitions, repentance merely *initiates* the atonement process, but does not *complete* it. Repentance gives the sinner a temporary allevi-
ation from any punishment or negative repercussion that would have resulted
from the sin; but repentance alone is not sufficient to restore the person to his

A CHASIDIC THOUGHT

"There can be no question that *teshuvah* is effective in every case and whatever the transgression, for *teshuvah* is one of G-d's commandments, and G-d does not require of us the
impossible."

(From a Letter of the Rebbe, Erev Shavuot 5716)

דלענין קיום מ"ע גדולה שדוחה את ל"ת. היינו משום
שע"י קיום מ"ע ממשיך אור ושפע בעולמות עליונים

innocent, pre-sin status, or to cleanse his soul fully from the effect of the sin. For that, the additional power of the Day of Atonement is required. (Below we will clarify why this is the case).

We have so far cited two of the "three different categories of atonement" mentioned in Tractate *Yoma*. Before mentioning the third category, the *Tanya* will first address (at some length) a concern that the educated reader may have, from another *Talmudic* principle which seems to be at odds with what we have learned.

[פֵּרוּשׁ דְּאַף עַל גַּב דְּלְעִנְיָן קִיּוּם מִצְוַת עֲשֵׂה גְּדוֹלָה — **This means that even though** in terms of general *mitzvah* **observance, a positive command is superior** to a prohibition, nevertheless, in terms of atonement, it is less severe.

Tractate *Yoma's* ruling that the violation of a prohibition requires *more* atonement than the failure to observe a positive command, seems to fly in the face of the conventional wisdom that *"a positive command is superior."* This contradiction requires clarification.

First, however, the *Tanya* will cite a proof for the superiority of a positive command.

שֶׁדוֹחָה אֶת לֹא תַעֲשֶׂה — The proof being that when they both coincide, a positive command *"overrides a prohibition"* (*Talmud, Yevamos* 3b).

For example, it is prohibited to wear a garment made of a mixture of wool and linen (*shatnez*). However, if a person wears a *tallis* made of *shatnez*, there is no violation involved, because the positive command of wearing the *tallis* overrides the prohibition of *shatnez* (*Yevamos* ibid., from *Deuteronomy* 22:11-12).

So we need to explain the apparent contradiction between a.) the legal *superiority* of a positive command over a prohibition; and b.) the fact that failing a positive command requires *less* atonement than the violation of a prohibition.

To clarify this point, the *Tanya* will teach us the difference between a positive command and a prohibition in terms of their *spiritual ramifications*.

הַיְנוּ מִשּׁוּם שֶׁעַל יְדֵי קִיּוּם מִצְוַת עֲשֵׂה מַמְשִׁיךְ אוֹר וְשֶׁפַע בְּעוֹלָמוֹת עֶלְיוֹנִים מֵהֶאָרַת אוֹר אֵין סוֹף בָּרוּךְ הוּא — **This is because,** spiritually speaking, **the observance of a**

PRACTICAL LESSONS

Teshuvah **represents your request and efforts to ask G-d to forgive you for a sin.**

Atonement is *G-d's response,* **as He forgives you and cleanses you from any remnant of your sin.**

מהארת אור א"ס ב"ה (כמ"ש בזהר דרמ"ח פקודין

positive command causes a shining of Divine **"light"** (and **flow**), **from the Infinite Light of G-d into the upper worlds.**

A fundamental cornerstone of Kabbalistic thought is that human worship in the physical world causes an improved alignment of energies in the Divine realm. Works of the Kabbalah, most notably the writings of *Arizal*, describe in detail how this alignment occurs, but for our purposes here the *Tanya* offers a general summary: a flow occurs *"from the Infinite Light of G-d into the upper worlds."*

It might seem odd, at first glance, that the "upper worlds" are lacking anything. In reality though, the "upper worlds" is a cluster of energies, and like any system, it is only as strong as its weakest link. The energies of the "upper worlds" also have distinct forms, and sometimes clash with each other. These deficiencies are healed by the flow of Infinite Light from above, restoring elasticity, harmony and flow to the upper worlds.

The *Tanya* notes here that this flow *only occurs with positive commands.*

In the case of prohibitions, there is no substantive activity involved in worship: you simply *refrain* from a prohibited act. So there is no actual deed that might "stimulate" the upper worlds.

Only with positive commands, where *distinct human activity* is present, is the cause-and-effect relationship between the physical world and its spiritual mirror fully engaged. Positive commands alone cause *"a shining of Divine 'light'... from the Infinite Light of G-d into the upper worlds."*

While such a goal may seem abstract and almost irrelevant to us here on earth, it is, in fact, of tremendous importance. Everything that happens in our universe is a result of the flow of Divine energy. When we rectify that flow in its source, things improve for us, our surroundings, and ultimately for all humanity. Nothing is actually more important or more beneficial than bringing *"the Infinite Light of G-d into the upper worlds"!*

And that is the inner reason why the *Talmud* teaches that a positive command overrides a prohibition: The opportunity to bring Infinite Light into the upper worlds is crucial for the universe and must not be missed.

(כְּמוֹ שֶׁכָּתוּב בַּזֹּהַר דְּרְמַ"ח פְּקוּדִין אִינּוּן רְמַ"ח אֵבָרִין דְּמַלְכָּא) — **As the *Zohar* states, that the 248 positive commands are the 248** *"organs of the King"* (*Tikunei Zohar* 74a; see *Tanya,* Part One, p. 256).

Here the *Tanya* addresses a potential problem with the above explanation. Our assumption that prohibitions do not provide any human activity to stimu-

אינון רמ"ח אברין דמלכא) וגם על נפשו האלקית כמ"ש

late the "upper worlds" is, in fact, an oversimplification. When you choose not to violate a prohibition, it is a form of action, just a passive one. And since, at a certain level, you did some worship "activity," there will be some mirroring and improved alignment in the spiritual worlds.

So we appear to be back to square one. What is the difference between positive commands and prohibitions if both cause Infinite Light to flow to the upper worlds?

To clarify the subtle distinction, the *Tanya* cites *Tikunei Zohar:* "The 248 positive commands are the 248 'organs of the King.'"

PRACTICAL LESSONS

With positive commands, the cause-and-effect relationship between the physical world and its spiritual mirror is fully engaged.

That is why a positive command overrides a prohibition: The opportunity to bring Infinite Light into the upper worlds is crucial for the universe and must not be missed.

Obviously G-d does not have an actual body or "organs." The point of this metaphor is to describe the phenomenon of *spiritual embodiment*. Flow reaches us from the Divine realm because infinite, *formless* "lights" become contained and "embodied" in finite (spiritual) "vessels," which *possess form*. This is the crucial metaphysical bridge between an infinite G-d and His finite creations. It is a totally spiritual process, but it resembles physical embodiment since "light" entering "vessel" shares some similarities with the phenomenon of the soul entering the body.

On earth, *embodied worship* only occurs when a positive command is observed through *tangible activity*. The passive worship of avoiding transgression may be an activity, but lacks the crucial component of embodiment.

Since the spiritual realm mirrors the physical world, only the embodied worship of a positive command is capable of bringing about embodiment of energies in the upper worlds, *i.e.,* of "light" entering and inhabiting "vessels," bringing *tangible* flow to the universe. That is why the positive commands are referred to as "organs" by the *Tikunei Zohar,* to indicate their unique power of spiritual embodiment.

In summary: A positive command overrides a prohibition since it benefits the universe more by stimulating the embodiment of energies in the upper worlds, resulting in a more tangible flow to us.

וְגַם עַל נַפְשׁוֹ הָאֱלֹקִית — And this light also flows **to the Divine soul** of the person observing the command.

אשר קדשנו במצותיו. אבל לענין תשובה אף שמוחלין
לו העונש על שמרד במלכותו ית' ולא עשה מאמר

The sequence is:

1.) Human worshiper observes a positive command.

2.) Infinite Light enters finite vessels in the Divine realm, rendering it more tangible and accessible.

3.) Light flows down into the universe, especially through the soul of the human worshiper who initiated it.

כְּמוֹ שֶׁאוֹמְרִים אֲשֶׁר קִדְּשָׁנוּ בְּמִצְוֹתָיו — **As we say** in the blessing recited before performing a commandment, *"who has sanctified us (KiDiSHanu) with His commandments."*

This phrase, recited before the performance of a positive command, expresses the intimate union with the Divine which is achieved by the worshiper. As the *Tanya* has already taught us, *kidishanu* can also be translated as "married," like a man that marries (*meKaDeSH*) a woman (Part One, chapter 46).

"A man marries a woman to be one with her, in a complete union, as the verse states, "a man... clings to his wife and they become one flesh" (Genesis 2:24), and in exactly the same way, but with infinitely more intensity, is the union of the Divine soul with the Blessed Infinite Light, when it observes Torah and mitzvos, which is united along with the energizing Animal Soul and its 'garments'" (ibid. p. 597-8).

We have now clarified the teaching from Tractate *Yevamos* that a positive command is superior to a prohibition, and can therefore overrides it (because it brings about spiritual embodiment). Now we are left to explain the contradictory teaching from Tractate *Yoma,* that failing to observe a positive command is less severe than violating a transgression and requires less atonement. Surely if a positive command is more important, failing to observe it should be a greater "crime"?

PRACTICAL LESSONS

A *mitzvah* is an act of intimacy with G-d resembling the intimacy of husband and wife.

אֲבָל לְעִנְיַן תְּשׁוּבָה — **However,** this importance of the positive command is only true in general, but **in regard to *teshuvah*,** the process of atonement is easier.

The *Tanya* clarifies a basic reason why the atonement is easier.

אַף שֶׁמּוֹחֲלִין לוֹ הָעֹנֶשׁ עַל שֶׁמָּרַד בְּמַלְכוּתוֹ יִתְבָּרֵךְ — **For while,** as we learned in Tractate *Yoma,* **the person is** immediately **spared punishment for defying G-d's authority,** as soon as he repents, and does not have to wait until the Day of Atonement, וְלֹא עָשָׂה מַאֲמַר הַמֶּלֶךְ — this is not because failing to observe a

המלך. מ"מ האור נעדר וכו' וכמארז"ל ע"פ מעוות לא
יוכל לתקן זה שביטל ק"ש של ערבית או וכו'. דאף

positive command is less serious, rather because it is *passive*, **"he did not observe the King's word"** (*Esther* 1:15).

As we have seen, the most metaphysical power is carried by *tangible activity*. Failing to observe a positive command is a *passive* rebellion against G-d, there was no deed involved. (The *Tanya* stresses this point by citing the verse, *"he did not observe the Kings word"*; the words *"he did not observe"* indicate a passive failure to observe, rather than an active violation). That is why the required atonement is less.

מִכָּל מָקוֹם נֶעְדָּר וְכוּ' — **Nevertheless,** when a person fails to observe a positive command **the** flow of Divine **light** which would have resulted from the positive command **is lacking,** *etc.*

In any instance, the *level of atonement* only gives us part of the picture: it just indicates *the extent of active rebellion*. It does not bring to light the crime of omission, *the extent of missed opportunity*.

For example, in terms of criminal law, who is the worse villain: a.) one who mugs an innocent bystander, causing them serious injury, or b.) a person who sees another person drowning and doesn't jump in to save them?

Person 'a' is definitely a criminal; person 'b' is probably not. Person 'a,' on the other hand caused some injuries that will soon heal; person 'b' has the loss of an entire life on his hands.

Violating a transgression is like person 'a.' It requires more atonement because the crime was active and tangible. Failing to observe a positive command is like person 'b': you are less culpable, technically speaking, but your crime of omission has resulted in a greater loss for the universe.

The *Tanya* cites a *Talmudic* teaching which highlights this point.

וּכְמַאֲמַר רַז"ל עַל פָּסוּק מְעֻוָּת לֹא יוּכַל לְתַקֵּן — **As our Sages taught, commenting on the verse,** *"a crookedness that cannot be fixed"* (*Ecclesiastes* 1:15), זֶה שֶׁבִּטֵּל קְרִיאַת שְׁמַע שֶׁל עַרְבִית אוֹ וְכוּ' — *"this refers to the* failure **to recite the** *Shema in the evening or* morning" (*Talmud, Berachos* 26a).

The *Shema* is a series of scriptural passages, opening with a declaration of faith in one G-d. We are required to recite the *Shema* twice daily, in the evening and in the morning, *"when you go to sleep and when you get up"* (*Deuteronomy* 6:7). Since the requirement is time-bound, if it is missed, that one particular window of opportunity to recite the *Shema* will never arise again. Therefore it is *"a crookedness that cannot be fixed."*

שֶׁנִּזְהַר מֵעַתָּה לִקְרוֹת ק"ש שֶׁל עַרְבִית וְשַׁחֲרִית לְעוֹלָם
אֵין תְּשׁוּבָתוֹ מוֹעֶלֶת לְתַקֵּן מַה שֶּׁבִּטֵּל פ"א. וְהָעוֹבֵר

G-d can *forgive* the omission, but you can never fully *compensate* for the omission, since you cannot go back in time and correct it.

דְּאַף שֶׁנִּזְהָר מֵעַתָּה לִקְרוֹת קְרִיאַת שְׁמַע שֶׁל עַרְבִית וְשַׁחֲרִית לְעוֹלָם — **For even if you** repent fully, meaning that you **are now forever careful to read the** *Shema* **each evening and morning,** אֵין תְּשׁוּבָתוֹ מוֹעֶלֶת לְתַקֵּן מַה שֶּׁבִּטֵּל פַּעַם אַחַת — **your repentance will not help to fix the** void of Divine light which is now lacking **since you failed to observe** the *mitzvah* **on that one occasion.**

Each "unit" of time and space was created by G-d to be sanctified with Divine consciousness and Torah observance. Since time is irreversible, a failure to sanctify a particular moment cannot be rectified, even through repentance.

We have discussed at some length the metaphysical power of a positive command. Now we will turn to the deeper significance of violating a prohibition.

וְהָעוֹבֵר עַל מִצְוַת לֹא תַעֲשֶׂה — **When a person violates a prohibition,** עַל יְדֵי שֶׁנִּדְבַּק הָרַע בְּנַפְשׁוֹ — in additional to the rebellion against G-d, there are negative spiritual repercussions too, **as negative forces become attached to his soul** (see *Zohar* 1, 73b).

A sin has two different effects: 1.) It compromises your relationship with G-d, and 2.) it spiritually damages the universe, especially your soul.

Failing to observe a positive command compromises your relationship less (as it is just a crime of omission), but it harms the universe more (by starving it of light). Violating a prohibition compromises your relationship more (since it is an active crime), but the damage it causes can be repaired (through atonement).

Nevertheless, the *Tanya* informs us that even in the case of violating a prohibition, there is significant damage. The failure to observe a positive command may harm the "upper worlds" by *depriving* them of the light they need to flow properly; but violating a prohibition, on the other hand, works in the opposite direction, by *attracting* negative forces.

The *Tanya* stresses that these negative forces become attached *to the soul* of the sinner. This marks a contrast with the failure to observe a positive command, which starves the *upper world* of light. The soul of the sinner, on the other hand, is found down here, in the sinner's body within the lower world, and that is where the negative forces are initially drawn through transgression.

(According to the Kabbalah, negative forces are not to be found in the highest of the spiritual worlds. That seems, at first glance, to be the reason why the

על מל"ת ע"י שנדבק הרע בנפשו עושה פגם למעלה
בשרשה ומקור חוצבה (בלבושי' די"ס דעשי' כמ"ש

Tanya stresses that the negative forces are drawn to the sinner's soul, because they cannot reach the highest world).

Are we to conclude, then, that failing with a positive command damages the upper worlds, whereas a transgression does not?

The *Tanya* clarifies now that this is not the case.

עוֹשֶׂה פְּגָם לְמַעְלָה בְּשָׁרְשָׁה — And when the negative forces become attached to the sinner's soul below in this world, **this causes damage to his soul's source above,** וּמְקוֹר חָצְבָה — and it thereby damages **the source from which** the soul **was carved.**

The spiritual realm is characterized by *interconnectedness.* When an embodied soul is damaged down here, the spiritual root of that soul in the "upper worlds" is also damaged. And when a soul's spiritual root is damaged, the entire "location" from which the soul was "carved" suffers damage.

PRACTICAL LESSONS

Each unit of time and space was created by G-d to be sanctified with Divine consciousness and Torah observance. Since time is irreversible, a failure to sanctify a particular moment cannot be rectified, even through repentance.

(The Kabbalah teaches that only a small portion of your soul enters the body. Most of the soul remains bound to its source, and communicates with the portion that has been embodied. This provides a pathway for damage in the lower world to reach the higher world.)

In a parenthetical note, the *Tanya* now informs us of the precise spiritual "location" of the soul's source, which is damaged by a transgression.

(בִּלְבוּשִׁים דְּעֶשֶׂר סְפִירוֹת דַּעֲשִׂיָּה — A transgression damages the soul's source in the external aspect **of the ten *sefiros* of** the World of **Asiyah,** which are called its **"garments"** by *Tikunei Zohar.*

A transgression only damages the lowest part of the soul (the level of *nefesh*) which is the most exposed to the negative forces. The source of this lowest part is the ten *sefiros* (energies) of the lowest spiritual world, *Asiyah* (*Notes on Tanya*). In fact, within the *sefiros* themselves, only the most external part (the "garments") are damaged.

Nevertheless, the matrix of *sefiros* is deeply enmeshed and interconnected. Even damage to the external aspect of the lowest world affects the entire system (*Ha-Lekach Ve-Ha-Libuv*).

בת"ז לבושין תקינת לון דמנייהו פרחין נשמתין לב"נ
וכו') לכך אין כפרה לנפשו ולא למעלה עד יוה"כ
כמ"ש וכפר על הקדש מטומאות בנ"י ומפשעיהם וכו'
לפני ה' תטהרו לפני ה' דייקא ולכן אין ללמוד מכאן

כְּמוֹ שֶׁכָּתוּב בְּתִקּוּנֵי זֹהַר לְבוּשִׁין תְּקִינַת לוֹן דְּמִינַיְיהוּ פָּרְחִין נִשְׁמָתִין לִבְנֵי נָשָׁא וְכו') — As *Tikunei Zohar* (17a) states, *"You made garments from which souls fly forth for humans, etc."*

The text of *Tikunei Zohar* demonstrates that the source of human souls is the "garments" (*sefiros*) from which the souls "fly forth."

לְכָךְ אֵין כַּפָּרָה לְנַפְשׁוֹ — **Therefore,** even after a person has repented from a violating a prohibition, **his soul is not atoned,** וְלֹא לְמַעְלָה — **nor** the damage he has caused **above** fixed, עַד יוֹם הַכִּפּוּרִים — **until the Day of Atonement.**

Atonement is a process of repairing spiritual damage. If you fail to observe a positive command, it leaves a huge spiritual void, but relatively little damage. Therefore atonement occurs immediately with *teshuvah*.

Violating a prohibition brings about a more profound damage to your soul and to the spiritual worlds. Repentance alone is not sufficient to repair it and only *"Yom Kippur brings full atonement,"* as we learned in Tractate *Yoma*, cited at the opening of our chapter.

The *Tanya* quotes a scriptural support for the power of the Day of Atonement.

כְּמוֹ שֶׁכָּתוּב וְכִפֶּר עַל הַקֹּדֶשׁ מִטֻּמְאֹת בְּנֵי יִשְׂרָאֵל וּמִפִּשְׁעֵיהֶם וְכו' לִפְנֵי ה' תִּטְהָרוּ — **As** the verse states, *"And he shall atone over the sacred zone for the impurities of the Israelites and for their sins... before G-d (Havayah) you shall be cleansed"* (*Leviticus* 16:16, 30).

לִפְנֵי ה' דַּיְיקָא — **The emphasis here is,** *"before Havayah."*

As we shall learn later on, the Tetragrammaton (*Havayah*), is symbolic of the energetic structure of the Divine realm, the web of *sefiros*. Since transgressions damage this structure, an even higher energy is required to repair it. That is the inner reason why the verse describes the Day of Atonement as being "before *Havayah*": the day provides an energy which transcends (is "before") the Tetragrammaton, and is therefore able to repair any damage caused to its structure through transgression.

Sins damage *Havayah,* so to speak, so the healing energy must be "before *Havayah*."

וְלָכֵן אֵין לִלְמֹד מִכָּאן שׁוּם קַל וָחֹמֶר וְשָׁלוֹם בְּמִצְוֹת עֲשֵׂה — **Therefore,** based on the above discussion it should be clear that **one cannot infer from** the easier

שׁוּם קוּלָא ח"ו במ"ע וּבפרט בת"ת. ואדרבה ארז"ל
ויתר הקב"ה על ע"ז וכו' אף שהן כריתות ומיתות

process of atonement for (omitted) **positive commands, any leniency in** their observance, **G-d forbid.**

The *Talmud* (in Tractate *Yoma*) has taught us that atonement for the failed observance of a positive command is easier than the atonement for a transgression. So one might come to the conclusion that Jewish law values the prohibitions as more important that the positive commands. Perhaps, then, one could be more lenient with the latter?

PRACTICAL LESSONS

Atonement is a process of *repairing spiritual damage*. If you fail to observe a positive command, it leaves a huge spiritual void, but relatively little damage. Therefore atonement occurs immediately with *teshuvah*.

Violating a prohibition brings about a more profound damage to your soul and to the spiritual worlds. Repentance alone is not sufficient to repair it and only *Yom Kippur* brings full atonement.

The *Tanya* has, however, clarified that the failure to observe a positive command is spiritually *worse* than a transgression (in terms of the missed opportunity to cause *"a shining of Divine "light"... from the Infinite Light of G-d into the upper worlds"*). Practically speaking, this should deter us from any leniency in the observance of positive commands.

וּבִפְרָט בְּתַלְמוּד תּוֹרָה — **Especially** the command to **study Torah.**

The legal requirement to study Torah is constantly in force at every available moment (see Part One, Chapter One, p. 32), and is therefore very easy to neglect. The *Tanya* warns us here to be honest about such a failing, and not to rationalize the constant requirement to study Torah as impractical or lacking in importance.

אָמְרוּ רַז"ל וִתֵּר הַקָּדוֹשׁ בָּרוּךְ — **On the contrary,** וְאַדְרַבָּה הוּא עַל עֲבוֹדָה זָרָה וְכו' — **our Sages said, "***The Blessed Holy One forgave*** Israel even for** ***idol worship, adultery and murder,*** אַף שֶׁהֵן כְּרֵתוֹת וּמִיתוֹת בֵּית דִּין (**even though these transgressions warrant** the most serious punishments of ***kareis*** **"soul cutting," and the death penalty),"** וְלֹא וִתֵּר עַל בִּטּוּל תַּלְמוּד תּוֹרָה — **"***but*

for neglecting Torah study, **G-d** *never forgave them"* (*Jerusalem Talmud, Chagigah* 1:7).

The violation of a Torah prohibition carries a stated penalty. The most severe of these are a (Divinely imposed) "cutting" (*kareis*) of the soul, and the (humanly executed) death sentence. The *Talmud* informs us that G-d "forgave" Israel for even the most heinous sins that carry these punishments, *"but for neglecting Torah study, G-d never forgave them."*

ב"ד ולא ויתר על ביטול ת"ת). עבר על כריתות ומיתות
ב"ד תשובה ויוה"כ תולין ויסורין ממרקין (פי'
גומרין הכפרה והוא מלשון מריקה ושטיפה לצחצח
הנפש. כי כפרה היא לשון קינוח שמקנח לכלוך
החטא) שנאמר ופקדתי בשבט פשעם ובנגעים עונם.

Our chapter opened with a quote from the *Talmud* of *"three different categories of atonement."* Before citing the third category, the author devoted several
lines to clarify the inner meaning of the first two. Now, we return to the quote,
and are informed of the third category.

עָבַר עַל כְּרֵתוֹת וּמִיתוֹת בֵּית דִּין — *"For transgressions punishable by kareis
or the death penalty, administered by the court,"* תְּשׁוּבָה וְיוֹם הַכִּפּוּרִים תּוֹלִין
— *"repentance and the Day of Atonement suspend the full negative consequences of the sin,"* וְיִסּוּרִין מְמָרְקִין —*"and suffering* on the other days of the
year *effects cleansing"* (*Yoma* ibid.).

The *Tanya* translates the last phrase:

(פֵּרוּשׁ) — *"Effects cleansing"* (memarkin) *means,* גּוֹמְרִין הַכַּפָּרָה — that it completes atonement.

וְהוּא מִלְשׁוֹן מְרִיקָה וּשְׁטִיפָה לְצַחְצֵחַ הַנֶּפֶשׁ — Memarkin is an expression of "soul
cleansing," implied by the Hebrew term *merikah,* which means "scrubbing."

כִּי כַּפָּרָה הִיא לְשׁוֹן קִנּוּחַ — For the level of atonement (*kaparah*), which precedes *merikah,* implies a more superficial type of "cleaning," שֶׁמְּקַנֵּחַ לִכְלוּךְ
(הַחֵטְא) — where the "dirt" of a sin is cleaned off.

Sins which carry the punishment of *kareis* or the death penalty inflict more
spiritual damage than other transgressions. In such a case, even the power
of *Yom Kippur* may not be sufficient to complete atonement, and the process
could require the sinner to experience suffering.

The *Tanya* concludes its quote from Tractate *Yoma* with the verse (that the
Talmud cites) to illustrate the third category of atonement:

שֶׁנֶּאֱמַר וּפָקַדְתִּי בְשֵׁבֶט פִּשְׁעָם וּבִנְגָעִים עֲוֹנָם — *"As the verse states, 'I will requite
their crime with the rod, and with plagues, their wrongdoing'"* (*Psalms* 89:33).

Here we see that G-d will sometimes cause a sinner to suffer, in order to
achieve atonement (*Rashi* to *Yoma* ibid.).

עַד כָּאן לְשׁוֹן הַבָּרַיְיתָא — This concludes our citation from Tractate *Yoma*.

SECTION TWO: THE MITZVAH OF TESHUVAH

8TH TAMMUZ REGULAR | 12TH TAMMUZ LEAP

The previous section focused on atonement, the Divine forgiveness and cleansing of the soul which is the *goal* and *outcome* of *teshuvah*.

Now we turn to the issue of *teshuvah* itself, the process of repentance.

וְהִנֵּה מִצְוַת הַתְּשׁוּבָה מִן הַתּוֹרָה — Let us first define **the** *mitzvah* **(commandment) of** *teshuvah,* **from the Torah.**

The *Tanya* classifies *teshuvah* as a "*mitzvah* from the Torah." This definition is challenging to understand both textually and rationally.

Textually it is a problem since *Rambam* omits any mention of *teshuvah* from the exhaustive list of the 613 *mitzvos* in his *Book of Commandments*. He merely states that "*we are commanded to confess our sins that we have done before G-d, and verbalize them when we do teshuvah*" (ibid., positive command 73). A careful reading of this line suggests that only the *verbal confession* (*vidui*) of sin is an actual *mitzvah*, whereas the *teshuvah* itself is not.

Minchas Chinuch (commandment 364) compares this to the law of a *get* (bill of divorce). It is certainly not a *mitzvah* to divorce one's spouse, but *if one chooses to do so,* one must write a *get*. Similarly, *Minchas Chinuch* argues, it is not a *mitzvah* to do *teshuvah* (according to *Rambam*)*,* but if one does so, sins must be confessed verbally.

Rationally speaking, the position that *teshuvah* is not a *mitzvah* seems to make more sense. [For example, imagine that you had offended one of your co-workers, and your employer instructed you to apologize. The apology would probably lack sincerity because you had been *commanded* to do it by an authority]. A true apology must come from within, without any coercive force.

So, for *teshuvah* to be real, surely it *cannot* be a commandment?

This would also seem to be the case from a spiritual perspective. As we have learned above, the 613 commandments each form a connection with G-d, which is severed by sin. (Below the *Tanya* will compare this to a rope of 613 strands). How does *teshuvah* repair that damage? Because each *mitzvah* represents a *particular* connection with G-d. *Teshuvah*, on the other hand, represents your *general* connection that transcends those particulars.

To put it in other words, the connection through *mitzvos* is bounded and limited by the laws that define it. But *teshuvah* is unbounded and unlimited—you can always do *teshuvah* however far you have strayed.

So, if *teshuvah* would indeed be a *mitzvah,* how could it do its job? *Teshuvah* has to transcend the commander/subject relationship to provide the opportunity for: a.) genuine remorse; and b.) a spiritual healing power that is greater than any particular *mitzvah.*

Nevertheless, the *Tanya* is unequivocal that *teshuvah* is a "*mitzvah* from the Torah." How are we to understand this position?

The author of *Tanya* would answer: *both are true. Teshuvah* transcends the particular trappings of a *mitzvah,* but it is *also* a *mitzvah.*

Everything we have argued above is correct; *teshuvah* is indeed higher than a *mitzvah.* But the *Tanya* chose specifically to stress the other side of the coin, that of *teshuvah-as-mitzvah,* to give the reader a certain practical direction and emphasis.

To understand why this is the case we need to probe the position of *teshuvah-as-mitzvah* more deeply.

We need to clarify:

1.) If *teshuvah* is a *mitzvah,* why was it omitted by *Rambam* in his codification of the *mitzvos*?

2.) Rationally and spiritually speaking, if *teshuvah* must transcend the commander/subject relationship, how do we understand *teshuvah* as a (limited) *mitzvah?*

The following could be argued:

1.) *Rambam* viewed the *mitzvah* of *teshuvah* in a very similar way to how he perceived the *mitzvah* of prayer. Prayer has two components: a.) the mental/emotional experience (*kavanah*); and, b.) the verbalization of prayer. Obviously, the mental/emotional component is more important, for that is what prayer really is. Nevertheless, when codifying the *mitzvah* from the point of view of Jewish law, *Rambam* emphasizes verbalization. Apparently, *Rambam* maintained that when a commandment has two components, one mental/emotional and the other verbal, Jewish Law must stress the latter. But that does not mean to say that the former is less important; in fact, the opposite is true. (A similar scenario exists in the case of the *mitzvah* of Torah study: the main component is the comprehension, but Jewish law emphasizes the verbalization).

Similarly, in the case of *teshuvah:* though *Rambam* stresses the verbal component of confession, he certainly deemed its mental/emotional component—the *teshuvah* itself—to be the more important component.

2.) *Teshuvah-as-mitzvah* is not an *alternative position* to *Teshuvah-transcends-mitzvos;* it is a *second phase.*

היא עזיבת החטא בלבד (כדאי' בגמ' פ"ג דסנהדרין

For *teshuvah* to be real, it must be totally autonomous and not "coerced" in any way by Divine command. As a first phase, *teshuvah* must transcend the status of *mitzvah* and be an act of human agency alone.

The *Tanya* emphasizes here that *teshuvah* is *also* a *mitzvah* to teach us that there must be a second phase. *Teshuvah* is a necessary rupture from the past, a retreat from one's former lifestyle, but it must be followed by a re-entry into normative observance. When, for example, Rabbi Elazar ben Durdia did such a profound *teshuvah* that his soul expired and he died (*Talmud, Avodah Zara* 17a), that second phase was lacking. The fact that *teshuvah* is a *mitzvah* sends us the message that its purpose is not merely the escape and retreat from the past, but to be forwardly orientated, invigorating all subsequent *mitzvah* observance (Based on *Likutei Sichos* volume 38, pp. 18-25).

הִיא עֲזִיבַת הַחֵטְא בִּלְבַד — The *mitzvah* of *teshuvah*, from the Torah **is: just** the decision **to stop sinning.**

PRACTICAL LESSONS

Teshuvah is a necessary rupture from the past, a retreat from one's former lifestyle, but it must be followed by a re-entry into normative observance.

As *Rambam* writes, *"What is teshuvah? That the sinner stops the sin, removing it from his thoughts, deciding in his heart not to do it again"* (*Laws of Teshuvah* 2:2).

While *Rambam* does not state which verse "from the Torah" this *mitzvah* is derived, the source would appear to be: *"And you shall circumcise the foreskin of your heart, nor shall you show a stiff neck any more"* (*Deuteronomy* 10:16). The stress that negative behavior (such as sin) should not persist *"any more,"* implies that it has *occurred already*, and the prescribed solution is *"you shall circumcise the foreskin of your heart,"* i.e., decide not to do it again (*Likutei Sichos, ibid.* p. 18).

The *Tanya's* emphasis that the *mitzvah* of *teshuvah* is "just" to stop sinning is surprising, as it seems to exclude other activities which are traditionally deemed to be part of the *teshuvah* process such as: remorse, confession, and asking G-d for forgiveness (for an extended list see *Chovas Ha-Levavos, Sha'ar Ha-Teshuvah* chapter 4).

The *Tanya* does not wish to imply that these are not *teshuvah* related activities; rather, its message is that *they are not the essence of teshuvah*. If you simply decide to stop sinning and do nothing more, you have done *teshuvah* "from the Torah."

ובח"מ ססי' ל"ד לענין עדות) דהיינו שיגמור בלבו בלב

What, then, is the role of remorse, confession and asking for forgiveness? And why are these activities not deemed to be the essence of *teshuvah?*

The *mitzvah* of *teshuvah* from the Torah is *forward looking.* It is "just the decision to stop sinning," *in the future.*

Remorse, confession and requesting forgiveness all relate to the past. You are remorseful about your earlier sinful activity and you confess to G-d about it. Then you pray that He will atone and cleanse your soul from what happened *in the past.*

Further proof that atonement is not central to the *mitzvah* of *teshuvah* is that it is not a guaranteed outcome: G-d will not necessarily forgive you for your sin. But that does not mean that you have failed in the *mitzvah* of *teshuvah,* whose essence is *"just the decision to stop sinning."*

In this sense the *mitzvah* of *teshuvah* is similar to the *mitzvah* of prayer. It is a *mitzvah* from the Torah to pray to G-d, asking him to fulfill your needs; and that *mitzvah* is applicable regardless of whether G-d listens and fulfills your request or not!

Likewise, it is a *mitzvah* to do *teshuvah* and stop sinning, regardless of whether G-d will subsequently forgive you and grant you atonement. *Teshuvah* is your obligation; atonement is G-d's business (Based on *Likutei Sichos* vol. 17, pp. 197-201).

The *Tanya* now brings a proof that *"the mitzvah of teshuvah, from the Torah is just the decision to stop sinning."*

PRACTICAL LESSONS

The *mitzvah* of *teshuvah* from the Torah is *forward looking.* It is just the decision to stop sinning, in the future.

Remorse, confession and requesting forgiveness all relate *to the past.*

כִּדְאִיתָא בַּגְּמָרָא פֶּרֶק ג' דְּסַנְהֶדְרִין וּבְחֹשֶׁן מִשְׁפָּט סוֹף סִימָן) עֵדוּת לְעִנְיַן ד"ל) — As indicated by the law about the acceptability (of a dice gambler as a **witness** initially stated in the *Talmud, Sanhedrin chapter three* (25b), and later recorded in the Code of Jewish Law, **Choshen Mishpat, end of chapter thirty-four,** par 29).

The *Talmud* states: *"The following are disqualified to be witnesses... one who gambles with dice.... When is their repentance accepted? Once they destroy their dice"* (Sanhedrin 24b, 25b).

The professional dice-player is guilty of the sin of gambling and is therefore unacceptable as a witness in court. Once he repents from this sin, he can once again be accepted as a witness. The *Talmud* rules that all the gambler has to

שלם לבל ישוב עוד לכסלה למרוד במלכותו
ית' ולא יעבור עוד מצות המלך ח"ו הן במ"ע הן

do for his repentance to be validated is to destroy his dice, an act which proves intent on the part of the gambler to stop sinning. *There is no requirement for the gambler to express remorse or confess his sin.* This is proof for the *Tanya's* position that *"the mitzvah of teshuvah from the Torah is just the decision to stop sinning,"* and no more (Based on *Sichos Kodesh* 5729, p. 190).

The *Tanya* now defines in more detail what *"the decision to stop sinning"* means.

דְּהַיְינוּ שֶׁיִגְמֹר בְּלִבּוֹ בְּלֵב שָׁלֵם לְבַל יָשׁוּב עוֹד לְכִסְלָה — *"The decision to stop sinning"* **means that a person resolves with a full heart not to "return to foolishness"** (see *Psalms* 85:9), and do the sin again, לִמְרֹד בְּמַלְכוּתוֹ יִתְבָּרֵךְ — that he will not **rebel against G-d's authority,** וְלֹא יַעֲבֹר עוֹד מִצְוַת הַמֶּלֶךְ חַס וְשָׁלוֹם **— and that he will no longer transgress the King's command, G-d forbid,** הֵן בְּמִצְוֹות עֲשֵׂה הֵן בְּמִצְוֹות לֹא תַעֲשֶׂה **— both positive commands and prohibitions.**

The decision contains three elements:

1.) Not to perform this particular sin again (*"not to 'return to foolishness'"*).

2.) To fix the *underlying cause* of the sinful activity, by re-accepting G-d's authority (*"he will not again rebel against G-d's authority"*).

3.) In fixing the "rebellion" that occurred through this one sin, he now accepts G-d's authority regarding all *mitzvos* in the future, (*"that he will no longer transgress the King's command, G-d forbid"*).

Element '1' is *Rambam's* core definition, cited above.

Elements '2' and '3' are innovations of the *Tanya* here.

PRACTICAL LESSONS

Even one single sin inevitably includes a rejection of G-d's authority *in general.*

Therefore *teshuvah* even for one sin must fix the underlying cause through re-accepting G-d's authority.

The *Tanya* understood that the particular rebellion of one violation inevitably includes a rejection of G-d's authority *in general.* (That is why, as we learned in Part One, Chapter One, *"the moment when a person transgresses, he is classified as a total rasha,"* p. 31).

Therefore, the *Tanya* understood, while *"the mitzvah of teshuvah from the Torah is just the decision to stop sinning,"* it must also include a restoration of the general rebellion against G-d which has taken place. This is the necessity for elements '2' and '3' (Based on *Likutei Sichos* vol. 39, p. 123, note 14).

במל"ת. וזהו עיקר פי' לשון תשובה לשוב אל ה'
בכל לבו ובכל נפשו לעבדו ולשמור כל מצותיו
כמ"ש יעזוב רשע דרכו ואיש און מחשבותיו וישוב

Based on this interpretation, that to repent from one sin you must re-orientate your relationship with G-d in general, we will be able to understand the term *teshuvah* more deeply.

וְזֶהוּ עִקַּר פֵּרוּשׁ לְשׁוֹן תְּשׁוּבָה — This clarifies **the principle meaning of the term** *teshuvah,* which literally means "return," לָשׁוּב אֶל ה' בְּכָל לִבּוֹ וּבְכָל נַפְשׁוֹ — **to return to G-d, with all your heart and with all your soul,** לְעָבְדוֹ וְלִשְׁמֹר כָּל מִצְוֹותָיו — **to worship Him and carefully observe all His commandments.**

Though *teshuvah*, in its most basic sense, is "just the decision to stop sinning," that decision is inevitably the result of a certain internal process. As we have learned, "the *mitzvah*... from the Torah" does not technically require remorse for the past, but it does necessitate a reorientation with regard to the future: to accept G-d's authority again and direct that energy towards future *mitzvah* observance.

That is why the term *"teshuvah"* implies not only repentance, "the decision to stop sinning," but also the internal process which accompanies that decision, *"to return to G-d, with all your heart and with all your soul."*

"Return" is a *literal* translation of the word *teshuvah* itself, from the root *shav*. *Teshuvah*, while defined as the external re-orientation with regard to one sin, is named after the internal recalibration that occurs to the person's relationship with G-d in general. This is the *"principle meaning"* of the term *teshuvah*.

To prove this point, that an internal "returning" to G-d is required in order "to stop sinning," the *Tanya* cites a scriptural source.

כְּמוֹ שֶׁכָּתוּב יַעֲזֹב רָשָׁע דַּרְכּוֹ וְאִישׁ אָוֶן מַחְשְׁבֹתָיו וְיָשֹׁב אֶל ה' וְכוּ' — **As the verse states, "Let the wicked forsake his way, and the unrighteous man his thoughts, and let him return to G-d, etc.,"** (Isaiah 55:7).

A CHASIDIC THOUGHT

"*Teshuvah,* as interpreted in Chasidus, does not mean "repentance" (which is only one aspect of it), but — as the word indicates — a return of the soul to its 'source and root.' The 'return' referred to here is not the return of the soul to its Maker at the end of its allotted years on earth, but its return to its true essence."

(From a Letter of the Rebbe, 1st Day of Chanukah, 5730)

אל ה' וכו'. ובפ' נצבים כתיב ושבת עד ה' אלקיך
ושמעת בקולו וכו' בכל לבבך וכו' שובה ישראל עד
ה' אלקיך וכו' השיבנו ה' אליך וכו'. ולא כדעת

Here the decision to stop sinning (*"Let the wicked forsake his way etc.,"*) is stated alongside the phrase *"let him return to G-d."* The implication is that merely to "stop sinning" is not enough; there must also be a re-evaluation of one's entire relationship with G-d, *"let him return to G-d."*

Isaiah 55:7 is the basic proof of this association. The *Tanya* now cites three more verses which highlight this meaning of the term "return." The verses are cited in the order that they appear in *Tanach*, and contain one citation from each of Torah, Prophets and Writings.

And in — וּבְפָרָשַׁת נִצָּבִים כְּתִיב וְשַׁבְתָּ עַד ה' אֱלֹקֶיךָ וְשָׁמַעְתָּ בְקֹלוֹ וְכוּ' בְּכָל לְבָבְךָ וְכוּ' **the Torah portion of *Niztavim,* the verse states,** *"And you shall return to G-d your G-d and listen to His voice... with all your heart etc.,"* (*Deuteronomy* 30:2).

From this verse we see that returning to G-d must be "with all your heart."

שׁוּבָה יִשְׂרָאֵל עַד ה' אֱלֹקֶיךָ וְכוּ' — *"Return, Israel, to G-d your G-d, etc.,"* (*Hosea* 14:2).

הֲשִׁיבֵנוּ ה' אֵלֶיךָ וְכוּ' — *"O G-d, return us to You, etc.,"* (*Eichah* 25:2).

(For an explanation why the *Tanya* cites four verses here, see *Likutei Sichos* vol. 39, pp. 171-6).

SECTION THREE: THE ROLE OF FASTING AND SUFFERING

In the 12th and 13th centuries, the *Chasidei Ashkenaz,* a group of pietists in the German Rhineland, introduced a set of very demanding recommendations for a penitent to achieve atonement. These included physical self-mortification through extensive fasting, other painful acts, and even public rituals of humiliation. While the *Chasidei Ashkenaz* were a relatively small group, their writings were influential, and the mainstream Ashkenazic Rabbinic literature (and courts) adopted their methods.

However, these harsh methods of penance were not an organic development from the *Talmud* (or the writings of the Ge'onim, who were active after the *Talmud's* completion). As we have seen above, the *Talmud* stresses *teshuvah* exclusively as a psychological process, which does not require any self-mortifying penitential act.

וְלֹא כְּדַעַת הֶהָמוֹן — The above definition of *teshuvah* **refutes the popular mis-**

ההמון שההתשובה היא התענית. ואפי' מי שעבר על
כריתות ומיתות ב"ד שגמר כפרתו היא ע"י יסורים.
היינו שהקב"ה מביא עליו יסורים (וכמ"ש ופקדתי
בשבט וכו' ופקדתי דייקא) והיינו כשתשובתו רצויה

conception, שֶׁהַתְּשׁוּבָה הִיא הַתַּעֲנִית — **that** in addition to "the decision to stop sinning *etc.*," a necessary part of *teshuvah* **is fasting.**

In the previous section, the *Tanya* has given us a precise definition of *teshu-vah*, which does not include any requirement to fast.

The *essence* of *teshuvah* includes only: 1.) the decision to stop sinning; 2.) the acceptance of G-d's authority; 3.) the acceptance of all 613 commandments. The *full expression* of *teshuvah*, through atonement, requires: confession, remorse over the past and asking G-d for forgiveness.

The *Tanya* now addresses a potential challenge to this position (that fasting is not part of *teshuvah*) from the *Talmudic* passage we learned above: *"For transgressions punishable by kareis or the death penalty... suffering effects cleansing."* Perhaps, part of this "suffering" is to be achieved by fasting?

The *Tanya* explains why this is not the case:

וַאֲפִלּוּ מִי שֶׁעָבַר עַל כְּרֵתוֹת וּמִיתוֹת בֵּית דִּין — **And even a person who has committed a transgression punishable by *kareis* or the death penalty,** שֶׁגְמַר כַּפָּרָתוֹ הִיא עַל יְדֵי יִסּוּרִים — **for which the complete atonement is only achieved through "suffering,"** as we learned above, הַיְינוּ שֶׁהַקָּדוֹשׁ בָּרוּךְ הוּא מֵבִיא עָלָיו יִסּוּרִים — **this however means that G-d will bring suffering upon him,** not that he must bring the suffering on himself, through fasting.

The fact that G-d will bring the suffering, and not man, is indicated by *Rambam's* formulation of the law: *"For transgressions punishable by kareis or the death penalty... the suffering which **comes upon** the person completes atonement"* (*Laws of Teshuvah* 1:4). *Rambam* makes clear that the suffering which completes atonement is not self-imposed, but rather, *"comes upon the person."*

The *Tanya* quotes a proof of this point from Scripture.

(וּכְמוֹ שֶׁכָּתוּב וּפָקַדְתִּי בְשֵׁבֶט וְכוּ' — **As the verse states, *"I will requite their crime with the rod,"*** (וּפָקַדְתִּי דַּיְיקָא — the use of the first person, **"I will requite" is a reference** to G-d personally bringing the suffering of "the rod" on a sinner.

The *Tanya* explains the significance of the suffering which is imposed by G-d in such a case.

וְהַיְינוּ כְּשֶׁתְּשׁוּבָתוֹ רְצוּיָה לְפָנָיו יִתְבָּרֵךְ — **This means that when a person carries out a *teshuvah* that is acceptable to G-d,** בְּשׁוּבוֹ אֶל ה' בְּכָל לִבּוֹ וְנַפְשׁוֹ מֵאַהֲבָה —

לְפָנָיו ית' בְּשׁוּבוֹ אֶל ה' בְּכָל לִבּוֹ וְנַפְשׁוֹ מֵאַהֲבָה אֲזַי
בְּאִתְעֲרוּתָא דִּלְתַתָּא וּכְמַיִם הַפָּנִים וְכוּ' אִתְעֲרוּתָא

since the person has returned to G-d with all his heart and soul, out of love, G-d will return the love by visiting suffering on the person to cleanse his or her soul.

Suffering is imposed from above as a *kindness* from G-d, to achieve complete atonement and spiritual cleansing for the penitent's soul. This occurs through a process of Divine mirroring: the person returns to G-d "out of love," and G-d sends "love" back, in the form of penitential suffering. (The *Tanya* will dwell more on this point at the end of this chapter and in chapters 11-12.)

Interestingly, this means that even the suffering that G-d sends a person for the sake of complete atonement *is under the person's control*. The mirror always works: When you send G-d love, He returns it. So if a person returns to G-d *"with all his heart and soul, out of love,"* G-d will definitely return that love, in the form of the necessary suffering (*Notes on Tanya*).

The *Tanya* cites sources that indicate the principle of Divine mirroring.

אֲזַי בְּאִתְעֲרוּתָא דִּלְתַתָּא וְכַמַּיִם הַפָּנִים וְכוּ' אִתְעֲרוּתָא דִּלְעֵילָא — Then *"with an awakening from below, there is a (corresponding) awakening from Above"* (*Zohar* 2, 135b), *"As face reflects face in water, so the heart of man to man"* (*Proverbs* 27:19).

As we have learned in Part One of *Tanya,* this verse in *Proverbs* describes the process of emotional mirroring. As *Metzudas David* explains: *"Just as water reflects back a face similar to the one gazing into it—a happy face reflects a happy one, a sad face reflects a sad one—the same is true with a person's heart. If a person's heart is good to his friend, his friend's heart will be good to him too. If it's nasty, he'll be nasty too."*

A CHASIDIC THOUGHT

"The difficulties, trials, and tests of life are themselves the means by which we are to attain our ultimate objective—that the soul achieve the lofty spiritual level it once possessed before it descended into the body, *'The soul that you have given me is pure'* (Morning Liturgy). The purpose of life is for the soul to regain that level of original 'purity' and even transcend it—for *'one hour of teshuvah and good deeds in this world is worth more than all the lifetime of the spiritual World to Come.'"*

(From a Letter of the Rebbe, 24th Adar II 5711)

דלעילא לעורר האהבה וחסד ה' למרק עוונו ביסורים
בעוה"ז וכמ"ש כי את אשר יאהב ה' יוכיח וכו'. ולכן
לא הזכירו הרמב"ם והסמ"ג שום תענית כלל במצות
התשובה אף בכריתות ומיתות ב"ד. רק הוידוי

In Part One we were advised to use this principle to generate love *for* G-d: If you contemplate how G-d has shown love for you, you will inevitably feel love back for Him (Part One, pp. 590*ff.*). Here the *Tanya* applies the same dynamic in the other direction: To evoke love *from* G-d. When a person returns to G-d out of love, G-d will return that love, "as face reflects face in water," sending any necessary suffering.

This idea is also expressed in the *Zohar's* teaching, *"an awakening from below, there is a (corresponding) awaking from Above."*

The *Tanya* cites scriptural support for the idea that suffering is an expression of Divine love.

לְעוֹרֵר הָאַהֲבָה וְחֶסֶד ה' — When a person returns out of love to G-d, it **awakens the love and kindness of G-d,** לְמָרֵק עֲווֹנוֹ בְּיִסּוּרִים בָּעוֹלָם הַזֶּה — **to cleanse** the person's **sin through suffering in this world,** וּכְמוֹ שֶׁכָּתוּב כִּי אֶת אֲשֶׁר יֶאֱהַב ה' יוֹכִיחַ וְכוּ' — **as the verse states,** *"For the one whom G-d loves, He rebukes, etc.,"* (*ibid.* 3:12).

In conclusion: Fasting is not a component of *teshuvah,* nor is it a requirement for atonement-through-suffering, which is always imposed by G-d.

וְלָכֵן לֹא הִזְכִּירוּ הָרַמְבַּ"ם וְהַסַּמַ"ג שׁוּם תַּעֲנִית כְּלָל בְּמִצְוַת הַתְּשׁוּבָה — **Therefore there is no mention of fasting as a component of the *mitzvah* of *teshuvah* in the codifications of *Rambam*** (*Book of Commandments,* positive command 73) **or in *Sefer Mitzvos Gadol*** (positive command 16), אַף בִּכְרֵתוֹת וּמִיתוֹת בֵּית דִּין — **even for** the most severe transgressions **punishable by *kareis* or the death penalty.**

PRACTICAL LESSONS

Suffering is imposed from above as a *kindness* from G-d, to achieve complete atonement and spiritual cleansing for your soul.

This occurs through a process of Divine mirroring: when you return to G-d out of love, G-d sends back love, in the form of penitential suffering.

The fact that fasting is not an essential part of the *mitzvah* of *teshuvah* is proven by its omission from these definitive texts.

רַק הַוִּדּוּי וּבַקָּשַׁת מְחִילָה — **The only** additional requirements mentioned in these texts **are: 1.)** verbal **confession and 2.) requesting forgiveness** from G-d for one's sins.

ובקשת מחילה כמ"ש בתורה והתודו את חטאתם

As *Rambam* writes in his *Book of Commandments* (ibid.):*"We are command-ed to verbally acknowledge the sins we have before G-d... and request for-giveness for this (transgression) with all the eloquence at one's command."*

"Verbal confession" is a requirement codified by all authorities, since it is stated explicitly in the Torah (see below). "Requesting forgiveness" is required, in addition to *Rambam*, by: *Sefer Ha-Chinuch, mitzvah* 364, *Sefer Yereim* sec. 363, *Chovas Ha-Levavos, Sha'ar Ha-Teshuvah* chapter 4; *Meiri, Chibur Ha-Te-shuvah* 1:8, *Sa'adia Ga'on, Book of Beliefs and Opinions* 5:5.

Above, the *Tanya* taught us that the *"mitzvah of teshuvah from the Torah is just the decision to stop sinning,"* (which inevitably involves accepting G-d's au-thority and re-committing to *mitzvah* observance). Our definition of the *mitzvah* of *teshuvah* did not include "verbal confession" or "requesting forgiveness." How, then, are we to understand these requirements?

PRACTICAL LESSONS

Verbal confession and requesting forgiveness secure atonement, contributing to the full expression of *teshuvah*; but they do not constitute the essential *mitzvah* of *teshuvah* itself.

The *Tanya's* view is that while "verbal confession" and "requesting forgiveness" are part of the *overall te-shuvah process,* they are not the *essence of teshuvah.* They are a means of ensuring personal *atonement.*

Teshuvah and *atonement* exist in a cause-and-effect relationship: full atonement indicates that the process of *teshuvah,* including its desired outcome, has been completed. So atonement is the *outcome* of perform-ing the essential *mitzvah of teshuvah.*

"Verbal confession" and "requesting forgiveness," which secure atonement, contribute to the full expres-sion of *teshuvah;* but they do not constitute the essen-tial *mitzvah* itself. That is because, as we have learned, the essential *mitzvah* itself relates to the future, not to sin again, whereas atonement relates to the past, that earlier wrongs should be forgiven.

The *Tanya* cites the Torah source for the requirement of confession.

כְּמוֹ שֶׁכָּתוּב בַּתּוֹרָה וְהִתְוַדּוּ אֶת חַטָּאתָם וְכוּ' — **As the Torah states,** *"They shall confess their sins etc.,"* (*Numbers* 5:7).

Rambam (ibid.) explains the method of confession: "*This 'confession' means to say: 'O G-d, I have sinned, I have committed iniquity, I have transgressed and done [name of sin].'"*

וכו'. ומ"ש ביואל שובו עדי בכל לבבכם בצום ובבכי כו' היינו לבטל הגזרה שנגזרה למרק עון הדור ע"י

The *Tanya* raises a challenge from Scripture to our above conclusion, that fasting is not part of the *mitzvah* of *teshuvah*.

וּמַה שֶּׁכָּתוּב בְּיוֹאֵל שֻׁבוּ עָדַי בְּכָל לְבַבְכֶם וּבְצוֹם וּבְבְכִי כוּ' — **And as for what is written in the** Book of **Joel, "Return to Me with all your heart, and with fasting, and with weeping, etc.,"** (*Joel* 2:12).

The verse appears to connect *teshuvah* (*"return to Me"*) directly with fasting.

Why did the *Tanya* stress that this is a verse "in the Book of Joel"? It is uncharacteristic for the author to specify the sources of his scriptural citations?

Joel was a *Ba'al Teshuvah* (penitent). We can discern this from the fact that Joel was the son of Shmuel (1 *Shmuel* 8:2), and we are told that Shmuel's sons, *"did not follow his ways. They turned aside after dishonest gain and accepted bribes and perverted justice"* (ibid. 3). Nevertheless, since Joel later merited to become a prophet, we see that he must have returned to G-d in *teshuvah*!

The *Tanya's* question is therefore strengthened by stressing that its citation is from "the Book of Joel": The plea to *"Return to Me... with fasting,"* was not only a call to *teshuvah*, it was said by a *Ba'al Teshuvah*. This makes the apparent connection between "fasting" and *teshuvah* even stronger (*Sichas Purim* 5729, sec. 60).

The *Tanya* responds:

הַיְינוּ לְבַטֵּל הַגְּזֵרָה שֶׁנִּגְזְרָה לְמָרֵק עֲוֹון הַדּוֹר — The fasting, requested by Joel, was not an act of *teshuvah* to atone for past sins, but rather, to convince G-d **to annul a decree** of suffering **which had been issued** from heaven, **to cleanse the sin of the generation,** עַל יְדֵי יִסּוּרִים בָּאַרְבֶּה — namely, a decree **of** future **suffering** through starvation (after **a plague of locusts).**

The Book of Joel (chaps 1-2) presents a graphic depiction of an unprecedented locust plague, which ravaged the food supply of the people, leaving them to starve. The lack of rain prevented any further crops from growing. The prophet encouraged the people to beseech G-d's mercy through repentance, fasting, and prayer. The people responded and rain followed, saving the crops for the year.

From this we see that the fasting was to avert the *future* effects of the decree of starvation, and was clearly not an act of *teshuvah* which is carried out for *past* sins.

יְסוּרִי' בָּאַרְבֶּה. וְזֶהוּ הַטַּעַם בְּכָל תַּעֲנִיּוֹת שֶׁמִּתְעַנִּין עַל
כָּל צָרָה שֶׁלֹּא תָבֹא עַל הַצִּבּוּר וּכְמ"ש בִּמְגִלַּת אֶסְתֵּר.

וְזֶהוּ הַטַּעַם בְּכָל תַּעֲנִיּוֹת שֶׁמִּתְעַנִּין עַל כָּל צָרָה שֶׁלֹּא תָבוֹא עַל הַצִּבּוּר — **And this is the reason for all** public **fasts which are performed to avert a misfortune falling upon the community.**

Public fasts are often carried out to avert misfortune falling on the community. These are not part of the *mitzvah* of *teshuvah*.

וּכְמוֹ שֶׁכָּתוּב בִּמְגִלַּת אֶסְתֵּר — **As stated in the Book of Esther.**

This is *not* a reference to the well known fast requested by Esther: *"Go and assemble all the Jews found in Shushan and fast for me. Don't eat nor drink for three days, night and day. I and my girls will also fast the same. Then I*

PRACTICAL LESSONS

Public fasts are carried out, not as acts of *teshuvah*, but to avert misfortunes from occurring in the future.

will violate the law and go to the king—and if I am going to perish, then I will perish" (*Esther* 4:16). This verse clearly indicates a fast to avert a misfortune occurring *personally* to Esther ("fast *for me*"), upon her unannounced arrival at the court of the king. The *Tanya*, however, refers specifically to "fasts which are performed to avert a misfortune falling *upon the community.*"

The *Tanya*'s mention here of "the fasts... stated in the Book of Esther," refers to the public fasts mentioned in the verse: *"To uphold these days of Purim in their appointed times, as Mordechai the Jew and Esther the queen had urged them, in the same vein that they had accepted various fasts and their laments upon themselves and their descendants"* (ibid. 9:31; *Sichas Purim* 5729, sec. 53).

In conclusion: Public fasts are carried out, not as acts of *teshuvah,* but to avert misfortunes from occurring in the future.

Below, in Section Four, we will learn of a type of fast which *is* carried out in connection with *teshuvah,* namely a fast which is *"to speed up the complete atonement of a person's soul."* Why did the *Tanya* reject this as a possible rationale for the public fasts mentioned in this section?

Because, as the *Talmud* rules, *"G-d does not despise the prayers of the public"* (*Berachos* 8a). G-d does not reject the public prayer for atonement, so no fast would be required *"to speed up the complete atonement"* of the public (*Toras Menachem, Hisvaduyos,* 5729, vol. 2, pp. 350-1).

ומ"ש בספרי המוסר ובראשם ספר הרוקח וס' חסידים
הרבה תעניות וסיגופים לעובר על כריתות ומיתות 91B
ב"ד וכן למוציא זרע לבטלה שחייב מיתה בידי שמים
כמ"ש בתורה גבי ער ואונן ודינו כחייבי כריתות לענין

SECTION FOUR: FASTS CONNECTED WITH TESHUVAH

In the previous section, the *Tanya* presented proof that *public* fasts are not associated with *teshuvah*. Now the *Tanya* will discuss the issue of *personal* fasts, raising a challenge to our earlier conclusions from advice given in ethical (*Mussar*) texts.

וּמַה שֶּׁנִּמְצָא בְּסִפְרֵי הַמּוּסָר — **As for what is found in ethical (*Mussar*) manuals,** וּבְרֹאשָׁם סֵפֶר הָרוֹקֵחַ וְסֵפֶר חֲסִידִים — **most notably in** the writings of *Chasidei Ashkenaz,* Rabbi Elazar of Worms (c. 1176–1238), **Sefer Rokeach** (*Laws of Teshuvah*), **and** Rabbi Yehudah *ha-chasid* of Regensburg (1150–1217), **Sefer Chasidim** (par. 167), הַרְבֵּה תַּעֲנִיּוֹת וְסִגּוּפִים — the advice to carry out **multiple fasts and acts of self-inflicted pain** for one's sins, these too are not an intrinsic part of *teshuvah,* as we shall see.

The *Tanya* offers an example of the serious transgressions for which these texts recommend "multiple fasts and acts of self inflicted pain."

לָעוֹבֵר עַל כְּרֵתוֹת וּמִיתוֹת בֵּית דִּין — **These fasts are advised by** *mussar* **texts for someone who commits a transgression punishable by** *karais* **or the death penalty,** וְכֵן לַמּוֹצִיא זֶרַע לְבַטָּלָה — **or for spilling seed in vain,** שֶׁחַיָּב מִיתָה בִּידֵי שָׁמַיִם כְּמוֹ שֶׁכָּתוּב בַּתּוֹרָה גַּבֵּי עֵר וְאוֹנָן — **which is punishable by "death through the agency of heaven," as the Torah states in reference to Er and Onan** (*Genesis* 38:6-7), וְדִינוֹ כְּחַיָּבֵי כְּרֵתוֹת לְעִנְיָן זֶה — **and, in this respect,** spilling seed in vain **is treated like a violation punishable by** *karais.*

The usual period of fasting recommended by these texts for serious transgressions was forty days, one or more times. In some extreme cases, periods of one or more years of fasting were decreed. (This was often to be accompanied by self-flagellation each day with additional corporal self-tortures in summer and winter).

The *Tanya* responds with three answers:

הַיְנוּ כְּדֵי לְנַצֵּל מֵעֹנֶשׁ יִסּוּרִים שֶׁל מַעְלָה חַס וְשָׁלוֹם — **This** fasting advised by *Mussar* texts: 1.) **Is not connected with the *mitzvah* of *teshuvah* at all but to avert punishment by suffering inflicted from Heaven, G-d forbid.**

זה. היינו כדי לינצל מעונש יסורי' של מעלה ח"ו.
וגם כדי לזרז ולמהר גמר כפרת נפשו. וגם אולי אינו
שב אל ה' בכל לבו ונפשו מאהבה כ"א מיראה:

In this answer, the personal fasts recommended by the *Mussar* texts resemble the public fasts mentioned in the Book of Joel and the Book of Esther: The fasts are purely to prevent any pending suffering which has been decreed by heaven.

PRACTICAL LESSONS

Public fasts are never associated with teshuvah or atonement. They are aimed purely at averting negative heavenly decrees.

The personal fasts recommended by *Mussar* texts may also serve this purpose.

There is, however, the possibility that personal fasts may be associated with teshuvah in a tertiary fashion, to ensure that atonement will take place or to speed up its completion.

In the remaining two answers, the *Tanya* will suggest that the personal fasts recommended by the *Mussar* texts *do* have some connection to *teshuvah;* but they are nevertheless not an *intrinsic* part of the *teshuvah* process (*Sichas Purim* 5729, sec. 55).

וְגַם כְּדֵי לְזָרֵז וּלְמַהֵר גְּמַר כַּפָּרַת נַפְשׁוֹ — **Also,** one could answer that the fasts recommended by the *Mussar* texts are intended: 2.) **To speed up the complete atonement of a** person's **soul,** by G-d.

As we have learned, atonement (forgiveness) is a *result* of *teshuvah,* but it is not crucial to *teshuvah.* One possible role of personal fasting is to "speed up" the atonement process, so the penitent does not have to wait for G-d to send the suffering necessary for atonement.

In this sense, fasting has a tertiary association with *teshuvah*: fasting speeds up atonement, which is a secondary effect of *teshuvah.*

The *Tanya's* third and final answer also connects personal fasting with the process of atonement.

וְגַם אוּלַי אֵינוֹ שָׁב אֶל ה' בְּכָל לִבּוֹ וְנַפְשׁוֹ מֵאַהֲבָה — **Also,** one could answer that the fasts recommended by the *Mussar* texts are because: 3.) **Perhaps** the person **did not return to G-d with all his heart and soul, out of love,** כִּי אִם מִיִּרְאָה — **rather out of fear,** and therefore G-d will not send him atonement.

As we have learned, G-d sends suffering to a person for complete atonement as an act of love. But G-d does this only when the penitent's *teshuvah* is also carried out with love.

If the *teshuvah* is motivated by fear, G-d will not mirror back the love of suffering/atonement. Fasting is therefore a further act which may be carried out to encourage G-d to complete a full atonement (with or without suffering).

In a similar fashion to the second answer, this third answer also frames fasting as having a tertiary association with *teshuvah*. Fasting is aimed at achieving atonement, which itself is a secondary effect of *teshuvah*.

פרק ב אך   כל זה לענין כפרה ומחילת העון
שנמחל לו לגמרי מה שעבר על
מצות המלך כשעשה תשובה שלימה ואין מזכירין לו
דבר וחצי דבר ביום הדין לענשו ע"ז ח"ו בעוה"ב

CHAPTER 2

THE ROLE OF FASTING

SECTION ONE: A POST-ATONEMENT "GIFT" TO G-D

9TH TAMMUZ REGULAR | 13TH TAMMUZ LEAP

In the previous chapter the *Tanya* discussed the connection between fasting and *teshuvah,* arguing that fasting has either no role at all in *teshuvah*, or a mere tertiary connection, of assisting atonement.

In this chapter we will discuss another aspect of fasting, which has a closer, secondary connection to *teshuvah*.

First, however, we will discuss the status of a person after *teshuvah* and atonement has been achieved. As we shall see, a further step is still required to find favor in G-d's eyes.

אַךְ כָּל זֶה לְעִנְיַן כַּפָּרָה וּמְחִילַת הֶעָוֹן — **However, all the above concerns atonement and forgiveness for sin,** שֶׁנִּמְחַל לוֹ לְגַמְרֵי מַה שֶּׁעָבַר עַל מִצְוַת הַמֶּלֶךְ כְּשֶׁעָשָׂה — **that you are completely forgiven for transgressing the "king's command"** only **when you carry out complete repentance.** תְּשׁוּבָה שְׁלֵמָה

As we learned in Chapter One, there is the *essence* of *teshuvah* (the decision to stop sinning, and re-acceptance of G-d's authority); and there is the *complete expression* of *teshuvah*, atonement (as a result of confession, remorse for the past, asking G-d for forgiveness, and receiving penitential suffering, if necessary). The *Tanya* speaks here of the stage where atonement is complete, the person is considered to have carried out "complete repentance" and is "completely forgiven" by G-d.

The *Tanya* defines what "forgiveness" means.

וְאֵין מַזְכִּירִין לוֹ דָּבָר וַחֲצִי דָּבָר בְּיוֹם הַדִּין לְעָנְשׁוֹ עַל זֶה חַס וְשָׁלוֹם בָּעוֹלָם הַבָּא — **And then,** when you are completely forgiven by G-d, **no charges whatsoever will be made against you in the world-that-is-coming, on judgment day, to punish you**

וְנִפְטָר לְגַמְרֵי מִן הַדִּין בָּעוֹהַ"ב. אָמְנָם שֶׁיִּהְיֶה לְרָצוֹן
לִפְנֵי ה' וּמְרוּצֶה וְחָבִיב לְפָנָיו ית' כְּקוֹדֶם הַחֵטְא לִהְיוֹת
נַחַת רוּחַ לְקוֹנוֹ מֵעֲבוֹדָתוֹ. הָיָה צָרִיךְ לְהָבִיא קָרְבָּן
עוֹלָה אֲפִי' עַל מ"ע קַלָּה שֶׁאֵין בָּהּ כָּרֵת וּמִיתַת ב"ד

for that sinful act, **G-d forbid, הַבָּא** — **and you will be completely exempt from judgment in the next world.**

"Complete atonement" and "forgiveness" means that you are totally free of any pending punishment.

Still, there is something lacking, even after complete atonement.

אָמְנָם שֶׁיִּהְיֶה לְרָצוֹן לִפְנֵי ה' — **However, in order that you should be** *desirable* **to G-d,** **וּמְרוּצֶה וְחָבִיב לְפָנָיו יִתְבָּרֵךְ כְּקוֹדֶם הַחֵטְא** — **as pleasing and cherished to Him as you were before the sin,** **לִהְיוֹת נַחַת רוּחַ לְקוֹנוֹ מֵעֲבוֹדָתוֹ** — **bringing satisfaction to your Maker through worshiping Him,** a further step is necessary.

Even when a sin has been atoned, meaning that your soul has been completely "cleansed" from it, your history of sin still tarnishes your relationship with G-d. He has forgiven you, but that does not mean to say you are *as pleasing and cherished to Him as you were before the sin.*"

הָיָה צָרִיךְ לְהָבִיא קָרְבָּן עוֹלָה — **To achieve this com**plete reconciliation **it was necessary** in Temple times **to bring a** sacrificial **Burnt Offering, אֲפִלּוּ עַל מִצְוַת עֲשֵׂה קַלָּה שֶׁאֵין בָּהּ כָּרֵת וּמִיתַת בֵּית דִּין** — **even for** transgressing **a basic positive command, that is not punishable by** *kareis* **or death (by the court).**

We learned in Chapter One that for failing to observe a positive command, as soon as the person repents, *"he is forgiven immediately, before he even moves from where he is standing."*

Nevertheless, we learn here that, in Temple times, the person would still bring a sacrifice.

What is the need for a sacrifice for someone who has already been forgiven for his sin?

The *Tanya* explains that it is *"in order that you should be desirable to G-d, as pleasing and cherished to Him as you were before the sin."*

PRACTICAL LESSONS

"Complete atonement" and "forgiveness" means that you are totally free of any pending punishment.

But even then, your history of sin still tarnishes your relationship with G-d.

That is why in Temple times a Burnt Offering was brought, as a post-atonement "gift."

כְּמוֹ שֶׁדָּרְשׁוּ רַזַ"ל בת"כ ע"פ וְנִרְצָה לוֹ וכדאיתא בגמ'
פ"ק דזבחים דעולה מכפרת על מ"ע והיא דורון לאחר
שעשה תשובה ונמחל לו העונש. וכאדם שסרח

The *Tanya* will now cite two sources to prove: a.) the requirement to bring a sacrifice even for transgressing a basic positive command, that is not punishable by *kareis* or death; and, b.) the role of this sacrifice in restoring Divine favor.

כְּמוֹ שֶׁדָּרְשׁוּ רַזַ"ל בְּתוֹרַת כֹּהֲנִים עַל פָּסוּק וְנִרְצָה לוֹ — **As our Sages expounded in** *Toras Kohanim* on the verse, *"He shall lay his hand on the head of the Burnt Offering, and **it will be accepted for him** to atone for him"* (*Leviticus* 1:4).

In *Toras Kohanim,* a legal *Midrash* on the Book of *Leviticus*, we are taught:

"For which sins (will the Burnt Offering) 'be accepted for him'?"

"If you would argue that the verse refers to sins which carry the penalty of kareis, the death penalty through the court, the death penalty administered by heaven or lashes — this cannot be the case since these sins have their own stated punishments (which are required for their atonement)."

"So (this Burnt Offering) is surely 'accepted' only for failing to observe a positive commandment (which has no stated punishment)" (1:31).

Here we see that the Burnt Offering is:

a.) Brought for transgressing a basic positive command that is not punishable by *kareis* or death;

b.) It is associated with being "accepted" by G-d, even after full atonement has taken place.

We now turn to a second source for these ideas, which will explain the role of the Burnt Offering with a helpful analogy.

וּכְדְאִיתָא בִּגְמָרָא פֶּרֶק קַמָּא דִּזְבָחִים — **And as the *Talmud* states in** Tractate *Zevachim,* **chapter 1** (7b), דְּעוֹלָה מְכַפֶּרֶת עַל מִצְוַת עֲשֵׂה — **that a Burnt Offering "atones" fo**r the failure to perform a **positive command,** וְהִיא דּוֹרוֹן לְאַחַר שֶׁעָשָׂה תְּשׁוּבָה וְנִמְחַל לוֹ הָעֹנֶשׁ — but this "atonement" is not meant literally, rather the *Talmud* explains it as a post-atonement **"gift"** to G-d, **after a person's *teshuvah*,** after he has been fully atoned **and forgiven from punishment.**

The *Talmud* proves that the Burnt Offering is a "gift" brought *after* complete atonement, as follows.

Rava said: "A Burnt Offering is a (post-atonement) 'gift.' For in what scenario could it possibly atone? If the person has not repented, then it falls into the category of 'The sacrifice of the wicked is an abomination' (Proverbs 21:27; i.e., it is ineffective). If, on the other hand, the person has repented, then we have

בְּמֶלֶךְ וּפִיְּיסוֹ עַ"י פְּרַקְלִיטִין וּמָחַל לוֹ. אעפ"כ שׁוֹלֵחַ
דּוֹרוֹן וּמִנְחָה לְפָנָיו שֶׁיִתְרֲצֶה לוֹ לִרְאוֹת פְּנֵי הַמֶּלֶךְ

learned, 'For failing to observe a positive command of the Torah, as soon as the person repents, he is forgiven immediately, before he even moves from where he is standing,' (without making a sacrifice)! Clearly, then, the Burnt Offering is a (post-atonement) 'gift'" (Zevachim ibid.).

The *Talmud* and *Rashi* (ibid.) elaborate on the significance of this "gift":

וּכְאָדָם שֶׁסָּרַח בַּמֶּלֶךְ וּפִיְּיסוֹ עַל יְדֵי פְּרַקְלִיטִין וּמָחַל לוֹ — **This is comparable to a person who angered the king, and then appeased him through a mediator, and was forgiven by** the king, אַף עַל פִּי כֵן שׁוֹלֵחַ דּוֹרוֹן וּמִנְחָה לְפָנָיו שֶׁיִתְרַצֶּה לוֹ לִרְאוֹת פְּנֵי הַמֶּלֶךְ — **nevertheless, he still sends the king a gift/present so that the king will be pleased to see him again.**

The "mediator" here is the Sin Offering brought for (inadvertent) violation of a transgression. The Sin Offering(s) must be brought *before* the Burnt Offering, because the former actually bring about atonement ("appeasing the king") an act which must precede any post-reconciliatory "gift" (see *Zevachim* ibid.).

PRACTICAL LESSONS

A post-atonement "gift" represents a *general reconciliation* with G-d, enabling you to appear before the King and satisfy Him with your worship

While the "gift" is indeed post-atonement, it is nevertheless not unrelated to the *teshuvah* process. We learned in chapter one that the "*mitzvah* of *teshuvah* from the Torah" contains three elements:

1.) Not to perform this particular sin again ("*he will not return to foolishness*").

2.) To fix the *underlying cause* of the sinful activity, by re-accepting G-d's authority ("*he will not again rebel against G-d's authority*").

3.) One accepts G-d's authority regarding all *mitzvos* in the future, ("*that he will no longer transgress the King's command, G-d forbid*").

Element '1' fixes the *particular* rebellion against G-d for this one sin. But since any one sin also represents a *general* rebellion against G-d's authority, elements '2' and '3' are also required.

Atonement is a full expression of element '1.' G-d has completely forgiven you for your sin, and you will not be punished for it.

The "gift" (of a Burnt Offering) is the full expression of elements '2' and '3,' the *general* reconciliation with G-d, enabling you to appear before the King and satisfy Him with your worship (Based on *Likutei Sichos* volume 32, p. 9).

(ולשון מכפרת וכן מ"ש בתורה ונרצה לו לכפר עליו
אין זו כפרת נפשו אלא לכפר לפני ה' להיות נחת
רוח לקונו כדאי' שם בגמ' וכמ"ש תמים יהי' לרצון).

The *Tanya* now addresses a problem with the *Talmud's* choice of wording.

וּלְשׁוֹן מְכַפֶּרֶת) — When the *Talmud* states that the Burnt Offering **"atones,"** וְכֵן מַה שֶּׁכָּתוּב בַּתּוֹרָה וְנִרְצָה לוֹ לְכַפֵּר עָלָיו — **and likewise when the Torah states,** *"It will be accepted for him to atone for him"* (*Leviticus* 1:4), אֵין זוֹ כַּפָּרַת נַפְשׁוֹ — this does not mean that the Burnt Offering *literally* atones for the soul, כִּדְאִיתָא שָׁם בִּגְמָרָא — as the *Talmud* (ibid.) clarifies.

As we have seen, the *Talmud* proves unequivocally that the "gift" can only be offered *after* atonement has been granted. It is therefore confusing that the *Talmud* itself (and likewise *Leviticus* 1:4) repeatedly refers to the *"atonement* of a Burnt Offering." Why call it "atonement," when it is not?

The *Tanya* answers:

אֶלָּא לְכַפֵּר לִפְנֵי ה' — In this context, the "atonement" of the Burnt Offering does not mean forgiveness for sin, **rather, it has a different connotation of atonement** *before G-d,* לִהְיוֹת נַחַת רוּחַ לְקוֹנוֹ — to bring *"satisfaction to one's Maker"* (*Rashi* to *Zevachim* 6b) in the future, through worship.

The "atonement" we discussed in Chapter One is a personal relief from punishment and a cleansing of the soul. It is a state achieved *within the sinner himself.* The "atonement" described here is "atonement *before G-d,"* i.e., not a personal change, but a restoration of the person's *relationship with G-d.* Now he can appear before the King, and please Him in worship.

(The *Tanya* here follows the view of *Rashi* to *Zevachim* 7b, *s.v. olah*. For a different interpretation see *Ibn Ezra* and *Ramban* to *Leviticus* 1:4).

In this context, the term *kaparah* ("atonement") resembles the term used by Jacob when sending a gift of appeasement to his brother Esau, *"Let me placate (achaparah) him with the gift that goes before me"* (*Genesis* 32:21; Rabbi Adin Steinsaltz).

The *Tanya* cites another verse to demonstrate that an offering is associated with winning "good will" from G-d.

וּכְמוֹ שֶׁכָּתוּב תָּמִים יִהְיֶה לְרָצוֹן) — **And as the verse states** in reference to the Peace Offering, which is not brought to atone for sins, *"Perfect it shall be to be accepted"* (*Leviticus* 22:21).

In the phrase, *"It will be accepted for him to atone for him"* (*Leviticus* 1:4), said in reference to the Burnt Offering, "atone for him" does not mean atonement from punishment, but rather, *"atonement before G-d, to bring satisfaction to*

ועכשיו שאין לנו קרבן להפיק רצון מה' התענית הוא
במקום קרבן כמ"ש בגמרא שיהא מיעוט חלבי ודמי
שנתמעט כאלו הקרבתי לפניך וכו'. ולכן מצינו

one's Maker." The proof of this is that both *Leviticus* 1:4 and 22:21 contain the same phrase, "be accepted," indicating an identical role. The *Tanya's* argument is: Just as the Peace Offering is certainly not brought as atonement for sins, that must be true also for the Burnt Offering (*Notes on Tanya*).

SECTION TWO: FASTS CONNECTED WITH TESHUVAH

In the current era, when we do not have the opportunity to give a post-atonement "gift" to G-d in the form of a Burnt Offering, how is a full restoration of our relationship with G-d achieved after *teshuvah* and atonement?

The *Tanya* will argue that fasting can fulfill this role.

'וְעַכְשָׁו שֶׁאֵין לָנוּ קָרְבָּן לְהָפִיק רָצוֹן מֵה — **And now,** after the Temple's destruction, **when we do not have** the opportunity to offer **a sacrifice, "to elicit favor from G-d"** (see *Proverbs* 8:35), הַתַּעֲנִית הוּא בִּמְקוֹם קָרְבָּן — **fasting replaces the sacrifice.**

In Chapter One, the *Tanya* presented elaborate proofs that fasting is not an intrinsic part of the *teshuvah* process. At the end of the chapter we learned that fasting can sometimes have a tertiary *teshuvah*-related function, in assisting with atonement. Here we learn another role of fasting which is more closely related to the *teshuvah* process: After *teshuvah* and atonement are complete, fasting can fulfill the role of a post-atonement "gift," similar to the Burnt Offering in Temple times.

The *Tanya* proves from the *Talmud* that a fast can substitute for a sacrifice.

שֶׁיְּהֵא מִעוּט חֶלְבִּי וְדָמִי שֶׁנִּתְמַעֵט כְּאִלּוּ — As the *Talmud* states, כְּמוֹ שֶׁכָּתוּב בִּגְמָרָא הִקְרַבְתִּי לְפָנֶיךָ וְכו' — **"My diminished fat and blood** (from fasting) **should be considered as a sacrifice to You etc,"** (*Berachos* 17a).

The *Talmud* (ibid.) relates:

When Rav Sheishes would sit fasting, after he had prayed, he would say the following: "Master of the Universe! You know that when the Holy Temple stood, a person who had sinned would bring an offering (of an entire animal). The priests would only offer up its fat and blood, yet (that was enough for) atonement to be granted to the person. Now I have been sitting and fasting, and so my fat and blood have diminished. May it be pleasing before you that my diminished fat and blood (from fasting) should be considered as a sacrifice to You on the altar and may I find favor in Your eyes!"

בכמה תנאים ואמוראי' שעל דבר קל היו מתענים
תעניות הרבה מאד כמו ראב"ע שהי' מתיר שתהא
92A פרה יוצאה ברצועה שבין קרניה בשבת וחכמים
אוסרי' ופ"א יצאה כן פרתו של שכנתו ולא מיחה
בה והושחרו שיניו מפני הצומות על שלא קיים דברי

Having clarified the role of a fast as a post-atonement "gift" we can explain a number of other statements in the *Talmud*.

וְלָכֵן מָצִינוּ בְּכַמָּה תַּנָּאִים וַאֲמוֹרָאִים שֶׁעַל דָּבָר קַל הָיוּ מִתְעַנִּים תַּעֲנִיּוֹת הַרְבֵּה מְאֹד — That is why we find that many early and later *Talmudic* sages **would carry out multiple fasts even for a small matter.**

A "small matter" certainly does not require atonement, so the fasts carried out by the *Talmudic* sages could not have been in the context of our discussion at the end of Chapter One (to assist with atonement). And since fasting is not a core element of the *teshuvah* process, that cannot have been their motivation either. But now we have clarified that a fast acts as a "gift" to G-d to become favorable in His eyes after a sin, we can understand why this would motivate a person to fast "even for a small matter."

PRACTICAL LESSONS

Nowadays, fasting can replace the post-atonement "gift" of a Burnt Offering rendering you as desirable to G-d, as pleasing and cherished to Him as you were before your sin.

The *Tanya* gives us examples of sages who *"would carry out many fasts even for a small matter."* (We are offered three examples of minor violations in the areas of thought, speech and action.)

כְּמוֹ רַבִּי אֶלְעָזָר בֶּן עֲזַרְיָה שֶׁהָיָה מַתִּיר שֶׁתְּהֵא פָרָה יוֹצְאָה בִּרְצוּעָה שֶׁבֵּין קַרְנֶיהָ בַּשַּׁבָּת — Such as **Rabbi Elazar ben Azaryah, who permitted a cow to go out on the Sabbath with a strap between its horns,** וַחֲכָמִים אוֹסְרִים — **whereas the other Sages prohibited it.**

On the Sabbath, it is prohibited to carry in the public domain, or to use your animal to carry for you. Wearing clothing and jewelry are, however, permitted. The sages argued whether a strap worn between a cow's horns was considered an item worn, and therefore permitted, or carried, and therefore forbidden. Rabbi Elazar ben Azaryah deemed it to be acceptable, whereas the other Sages did not (see *Shabbos* 54b; *Beitza* 23a).

וּפַעַם אַחַת יָצְאָה כֵּן פָּרָתוֹ שֶׁל שְׁכֶנְתּוֹ וְלֹא מִחָה בָּהּ — **On one occasion** Rabbi Elazar ben Azaryah's **neighbor's cow went out** carrying a strap and Rabbi Elazar ben Azaryah **did not protest,** וְהֻשְׁחֲרוּ שִׁנָּיו מִפְּנֵי הַצּוֹמוֹת עַל שֶׁלֹּא קִיֵּם עַל דִּבְרֵי חֲבֵרָיו —

חביריו. וכן ר' יהושע שאמר בושני מדבריכם ב"ש
והושחרו שיניו מפני הצומות. ורב הונא פעם אחת
נתהפכה לו רצועה של תפילין והתענה מ' צומות.
וכהנה רבות. ועל יסוד זה לימד האריז"ל לתלמידיו
עפ"י חכמת האמת מספר הצומות לכמה עוונות

and for failing to support his colleagues' position, Rabbi Elazar ben Azaryah **fasted until his teeth went black** (*Jerusalem Talmud, Beitzah* 2:8).

It is a *mitzvah* to protest your friend's sinful behavior (see Part One, Chapter 32). But what do you do in a situation where you don't consider the behavior to be sinful, but others do? Rabbi Elazar ben Azaryah ruled that his neighbor's cow wasn't violating the Sabbath and therefore did not protest. Later he realized he had committed another oversight, that of "failing to support his colleagues' position" and therefore he fasted. This is "a small matter" since, according to Rabbi Elazar ben Azaryah, no Sabbath violation had actually occurred.

The *Tanya* cites two more examples of Sages who fasted over "a small matter."

וְכֵן רַבִּי יְהוֹשֻׁעַ שֶׁאָמַר בּוֹשַׁנִי מִדִּבְרֵיכֶם בֵּית שַׁמַּאי — **Likewise, Rabbi Yehoshua who said, "I am ashamed of your words, School of Shammai!"** וְהֻשְׁחֲרוּ שִׁנָּיו מִפְּנֵי הַצּוֹמוֹת — **fasted until his teeth went black** (*Talmud, Chagigah* 22b).

וְרַב הוּנָא פַּעַם אַחַת נִתְהַפְּכָה לוֹ רְצוּעָה שֶׁל תְּפִלִּין — **And Rav Huna, after finding his *tefilin* strap had flipped over,** וְהִתְעַנָּה אַרְבָּעִים צוֹמוֹת — **fasted forty times** (*Mo'ed Katan* 25a).

The *tefilin* straps are painted black on one side, which must be kept facing outwards (*Rashi* ibid; see *Shulchan Aruch Ha-Rav, Orach Chaim* 27:19). Clearly, such an oversight is a very "small" violation of the law.

וְכָהֵנָּה רַבּוֹת — **And there are many other such examples** (see, for example, *Bava Metzia* 33a; *Nazir* 52b).

Practically speaking, how many fasts are we to carry out nowadays as a post-atonement "gift" to G-d, in place of the Burnt Offering?

The *Tanya* cites a precedent from the writings of 16th century Kabbalist, Rabbi Yitzchak Luria (*Arizal*).

וְעַל יְסוֹד זֶה — **On this foundation,** that fasting is a substitute for the post-atonement "gift" of a Burnt Offering, לִמֵּד הָאֲרִיזַ"ל לְתַלְמִידָיו עַל פִּי חַכְמַת הָאֱמֶת מִסְפַּר הַצּוֹמוֹת לְכַמָּה עֲווֹנוֹת וַחֲטָאִים — ***Arizal* would advise his students, based on Kabbalah, a specific number of fasts for various different sins** (see *Sha'ar Ha-Yichudim, Sha'ar Tikunei Avonos*; *Mishnas Chasidim, Maseches Teshuvah*).

וחטאים אף שאין בהן כרת ולא מיתה בידי שמים
כמו על הכעס קנ"א תעניות וכו'. ואפי' על איסור
דרבנן כמו סתם יינם יתענה ע"ג תעניות וכו' וכן על

By stressing that these are *Arizal's* teachings *"to his students, based on Kab-balah,"* the *Tanya* appears, at first glance, to have rendered this practice irrel-evant to its readership. *Arizal* taught an elite group of elevated mystics, whose piety and mystical consciousness far outstripped the average reader to whom the *Tanya* was pitched. What was the author's intention here?

The *Tanya* was troubled by a problem arising from our above discussion, (that fasting acts a post-atonement "gift" to G-d in place of the Burnt Offering). It is true that this principle is firmly based on the *Talmud's* teachings in Trac-tates *Zevachim* and *Berachos*, as we have established; but why is there no mention of this idea in the later legal codes, in *Rambam's* legal writings, or in the *Shulchan Aruch?*

Responding to this concern, the *Tanya* states: *"On this foundation, Arizal would advise his students, based on Kabbalah."*

"On this foundation," meaning to say that the *basic foundation* of this prac-tice is found in the *Tractates Zevachim* and *Berachos;* but it was never expand-ed upon by the codes, because its practical application is "based on Kabbalah."

In stressing that this was something *"Arizal would advise his students, based on Kabbalah,"* the *Tanya* does not wish to imply that this information is not rele-vant to us. Rather, the author is offering us his explanation as to why these facts have taken so long to reach mainstream awareness (Based on *Likutei Sichos,* volume 39, pp. 190-1).

אַף שֶׁאֵין בָּהֶן כָּרֵת וְלֹא מִיתָה בִּידֵי שָׁמַיִם — *Arizal* advised this scheme of fasts **even for sins which were not punishable by *kareis* or the death penalty,** since they were not intended to achieve atonement, but as a post-atonement "gift," similar to the Burnt Offering in Temple times.

The *Tanya* offers some examples of *Arizal's* advice:

כְּמוֹ עַל הַכַּעַס קנ"א תַּעֲנִיּוֹת וְכו' — **Such as for anger,** *Arizal* advised **151 fasts, etc.,** (*Sha'ar Tikunei Avonos*, Chapter 6).

The number 151 is the numerical value of the word for "anger" in Hebrew, spelled *caf* (20), *ayin* (70), *samech* (60), plus one for the value of the word itself (ibid.).

וַאֲפִלּוּ עַל אִסּוּר דְּרַבָּנָן — *Arizal* would advise such a schedule of fasts **even for transgressing** a minor **Rabbinic law,** כְּמוֹ סְתָם יֵינָם יִתְעַנֶּה ע"ג תַּעֲנִיּוֹת וְכו' — **such as** for consuming **Rabbinically forbidden wine** (see *Avodah Zarah* 36b), **73 fasts, etc.**

ביטול מ"ע דרבנן כמו תפלה יתענה ס"א תעניות וכו'
ודרך כלל סוד התענית היא סגולה נפלאה להתגלות
רצון העליון ב"ה כמו הקרבן שנא' בו ריח ניחוח לה'.

The number 73 is the numerical value of the word for "wine" in Hebrew, spelled *yud* (10), *yud* (10), *nun* (50), plus one for each letter of the word (*Mishnas Chasidim*, *Maseches Teshuvah* 10:2).

וְכֵן עַל בִּטוּל מִצְוַת עֲשֵׂה דְּרַבָּנָן — *Arizal* would also advise such a schedule of fasts **for neglecting a positive Rabbinic command,** כְּמוֹ תְּפִלָּה — **such as** neglecting the times of daily **prayer,** יִתְעַנֶּה ס"א תַּעֲנִיוֹת וְכוּ' — *Arizal* **would recommend 61 fasts,** *etc.*

The number 61 is the numerical value of the word for "I" (*ani*) in Hebrew, spelled *alef* (1), *nun* (50), *yud* (10). In the Kabbalah the word *ani* hints to *Malchus*, the Divine feminine, which is the energy of prayer (ibid. Chapter 11).

SECTION THREE: THE "SECRET" OF FASTING

Up to this point we have learned a number of roles of fasting:

1.) Public and personal fasts which are not connected with *teshuvah* and are carried out to avert negative decrees (Chapter One).

2.) Personal fasts carried out to assist atonement, the full expression of *teshuvah* (Chapter One).

3.) Personal fasts carried out as a post-atonement "gift," to find favor in G-d's eyes (Chapter Two).

Now we will learn a fourth role of fasting.

וְדֶרֶךְ כְּלָל סוֹד הַתַּעֲנִית — **And, in general, there is a secret** power **of fasting.**

The above three roles for fasting were sourced in the *Talmud*. (Even *Arizal's* advice, "based on the Kabbalah" had its "foundation" in the *Talmud*). The fourth role, which we are about to learn, is a total "secret," that we know only from Jewish mystical texts and not from the exoteric sources of *Talmud etc.* (*Toras Menachem, Hisvaduyos* 5729, volume 2, p. 353-4).

הִיא סְגֻלָּה נִפְלָאָה לְהִתְגַּלּוּת רָצוֹן הָעֶלְיוֹן בָּרוּךְ הוּא — Namely, that fasting **is a wonderfully effective ritual (***segulah***) to bring about a revelation of blessed, supernal, Divine favor (***ratzon ha-elyon***).**

Above we learned that the post-atonement Burnt Offering (or the fast which replaces it), is *"to elicit **favor (ratzon)** from G-d."*

וכמ"ש בישעי' הלזה תקרא צום ויום רצון לה' מכלל
שהצום הנרצה הוא יום רצון:

Here, as we learn the "secret power of fasting," the *Tanya* discloses that an even higher level can be reached, that of *"the blessed, **supernal Divine favor.**"*

What is the difference between "Divine favor" and "*supernal* Divine favor"?

A sin does not only damage your soul, it also has a negative effect on the spiritual worlds (even the highest world of *Atzilus, "*Emanation*"*). This damage is repaired by "Divine favor," achieved through atonement and post-atonement "gifts" to G-d.

"Supernal Divine favor" is something even higher than that. It is a Divine energy which transcends both the damage caused by sin and the "favor" needed to repair it. "*Supernal* Divine favor" is a light so powerful it could never be "damaged" in the first place.

The "secret of fasting" is that it has the power to draw this "supernal" light into our lives (*Toras Menachem,* ibid.).

PRACTICAL LESSONS

The mystical "secret" of fasting is that it brings "supernal Divine favor" into the world.

כְּמוֹ הַקָּרְבָּן שֶׁנֶּאֱמַר בּוֹ רֵיחַ נִיחוֹחַ לַה' — In this sense a fast is **like a sacrifice, which causes** *"A spirit of satisfaction to G-d"* (*Leviticus* 1:9).

Rashi (ibid.) interprets this verse to mean that G-d says: *"It gives Me satisfaction, that I spoke and My will (ratzon) was fulfilled!"*

From this we see that a sacrifice is also associated with the level of *ratzon* (Divine will/favor).

וּכְמוֹ שֶׁכָּתוּב בִּישַׁעְיָה הֲלָזֶה תִּקְרָא צוֹם וְיוֹם רָצוֹן לַה' — **As the verse states in Isaiah, "Will you call this a fast, a day of favor to G-d"?** (58:5), מִכְּלָל שֶׁהַצוֹם הַנִּרְצֶה הוּא יוֹם רָצוֹן — **which implies that an acceptable fast is a "day of favor."**

The "secret" of fasting, that it brings "supernal Divine favor" into the world, is hinted by the words of Isaiah, who describes a fast as "a day of favor (*ratzon*)."

The *Tanya* stresses that this verse was said by Isaiah whose visions of the Divine "chariot" were unsurpassed (see *Chagigah* 3b), from which we can conclude that he was uniquely empowered among the prophets to perceive the sublime energy of "supernal Divine favor" (*Toras Menachem,* ibid.).

פרק ג הנה חכמי המוסר האחרונים נחלקו במי
שחטא חטא א' פעמים רבות. דיש
אומרים שצריך להתענות מספר הצומות לאותו חטא
פעמים רבות כפי המספר אשר חטא. כגון המוציא

CHAPTER 3

REDEEMING YOUR SOUL

SECTION ONE: THREE VIEWS OF FAST CALCULATION

10TH TAMMUZ REGULAR | 14TH TAMMUZ LEAP

In Chapter Two we learned that while fasting is not an intrinsic part of the *teshuvah* process, it can act as a substitute for the Burnt Offering (brought in Temple times). This was a post-atonement "gift" to G-d, *"in order that you should be desirable to G-d, as pleasing and cherished to Him as you were before the sin, bringing satisfaction to your Maker through worshiping Him."*

We also learned that *Arizal* offered a series of guidelines as to how to carry out these fasts practically, identifying the number of fasts that are advisable for various different sins.

In this chapter the *Tanya* will clarify a doubt regarding the recommendations of *Arizal*.

וְהִנֵּה חַכְמֵי הַמּוּסָר הָאַחֲרוֹנִים נֶחְלְקוּ בְּמִי שֶׁחָטָא חֵטְא אֶחָד פְּעָמִים רַבּוֹת — Now the later scholars of *Mussar* were divided over the question of a person who transgressed the same sin several times.

In such a case, is the number of fasts recommended by *Arizal* sufficient for *multiple* violations of the same sin, or not?

דְיֵשׁ אוֹמְרִים שֶׁצָּרִיךְ לְהִתְעַנּוֹת מִסְפַּר הַצּוֹמוֹת לְאוֹתוֹ חֵטְא פְּעָמִים רַבּוֹת כְּפִי הַמִּסְפָּר אֲשֶׁר חָטָא — Some scholars were of the more stringent opinion that you must carry out the number of fasts recommended for that sin *multiplied by* the number of times you committed it (see *Responsa Chut ha-Sheni*, sec. 47; *Yesod Yosef* chap. 11).

The *Tanya* illustrates this view with an example.

כְּגוֹן הַמוֹצִיא זֶרַע לְבַטָּלָה — For example, take the sin of emitting seed in vain, **שֶׁמִּסְפַּר הַצּוֹמוֹת הַמְפֹרָשׁ בְּתִקּוּנֵי תְּשׁוּבָה מֵהָאֲרִיזַ"ל הֵן פ"ד תַּעֲנִיּוֹת** — which in *Arizal*'s guidelines for repentance requires 84 fasts (*Mishnas Chasidim, Maseches Teshuvah*, chapter 10).

זרע לבטלה שמספר הצומות המפורש בתיקוני תשובה
מהאריז"ל הן פ"ד תעניות ואם חטא בזה עשר או
עשרים פעמים עד"מ צריך להתענות עשר או עשרים
פעמים פ"ד וכן לעולם. דומיא דקרבן חטאת שחייב
להביא על כל פעם ופעם. ויש מדמין ענין זה לקרבן
עולה הבאה על מ"ע דאפי' עבר על כמה מ"ע
מתכפר בעולה אחת כדאי' בגמ' פ"ק דזבחים. והכרעה

וְאִם חָטָא בָּזֶה עֶשֶׂר אוֹ עֶשְׂרִים פְּעָמִים עַל דֶּרֶךְ מָשָׁל — **If a person would commit this sin ten or twenty times, for example,** צָרִיךְ לְהִתְעַנּוֹת עֶשֶׂר אוֹ עֶשְׂרִים פְּעָמִים פ"ד — then according to the more stringent opinion of the later *Mussar* scholars **he would have to carry out ten or twenty times 84 fasts,** a total of 840 or 1680 fasts respectively, וְכֵן לְעוֹלָם — **and so too** with all **subsequent** violations.

The *Tanya* provides a source supporting this stringent view.

דּוּמְיָא דְּקָרְבַּן חַטָּאת — In this stringent view, the fasting **is comparable to** the law of **the Sin Offering,** שֶׁחַיָּיב לְהָבִיא עַל כָּל פַּעַם וּפַּעַם — **which would be offered for every single transgression** (*Zevachim* 6a; see *Shaloh, Sha'ar Osios,* letter *kuf*).

וְיֵשׁ מְדַמִּין עִנְיָן זֶה לְקָרְבַּן עוֹלָה הַבָּאָה עַל מִצְוַת עֲשֵׂה — **Other** scholars of *Mussar* were more lenient, and compared multiple transgressions of the same sin **to the Burnt Offering, brought for** failing to carry out **a positive command,** דַּאֲפִלּוּ עָבַר עַל כַּמָּה מִצְווֹת עֲשֵׂה מִתְכַּפֵּר בְּעוֹלָה אַחַת — **where** the law states **that even the repeated neglect of a positive command is atoned with just** *one* **Burnt Offering,** כְּדְאִיתָא בִּגְמָרָא פֶּרֶק קַמָּא דְּזְבָחִים — **as the** *Talmud* **teaches in the first chapter of** *Zevachim* (5b).

According to this lenient view, a person need only carry out 84 fasts for any number of violations of emitting seed in vain.

What is the rationale underlying the lenient and stringent views?

The 613 commandments each correspond to different parts of the body as well as the portion of the soul which energizes that body part. The lenient view's concern is: how do we spiritually heal *that particular body part* (and its portion of the soul) once a sin has occurred?

This helps us understand why the lenient view only requires one round of fasts, even for multiple violations of the same sin. After one violation, the associated body part becomes *completely* contaminated. Further violations do no further significant spiritual harm. One round of fasting is therefore sufficient to atone for multiple violations, because, in essence, we only really need to heal the first infraction.

92B הַמְקוּבֶּלֶת בָּזֶה לְהִתְעַנּוֹת ג"פ כְּפִי מִסְפַּר הַצּוֹמוֹת
דְּחַטְא זֶה. דְּהַיְינוּ רנ"ב צוֹמוֹת עַל הוֹצָאוֹת שז"ל וְכֵן
בִּשְׁאָר חֲטָאִים וַעֲווֹנוֹת. וְהַטַּעַם הוּא עפ"י מ"ש בַּזוֹה"ק
ס"פ נֹחַ כֵּיוָן דְּחַב ב"נ קַמֵּי קוֹדְב"ה זִמְנָא חֲדָא עָבִיד
רְשִׁימוּ כוּ' זִמְנָא תְּלִיתָאָה אִתְפַּשַּׁט הַהוּא כִּתְמָא מִסִּטְרָא
דָּא לְסִטְרָא דָּא כוּ'. לָכֵךְ צָרִיךְ מִסְפַּר הַצּוֹמוֹת ג"כ

The stringent view has a different concern. While a sin's strongest effects are upon one particular body part, nevertheless, there is also a seepage of contamination into the rest of the body (and soul). This has no limit: every time you repeat that sin, further seepage occurs. Therefore the stringent view requires a round of fasting for *every violation*, to spiritually heal the further seepage caused on each occasion (Based on *Likutei Sichos* volume 39, pp. 124-5).

The *Tanya* now cites an intermediate position, between the stringent and lenient views.

וְהַכְרָעָה הַמְקוּבֶּלֶת בָּזֶה — **The consensus which has been accepted** and transmitted to us by our teachers is somewhere between the two positions, לְהִתְעַנּוֹת ג' פְּעָמִים כְּפִי מִסְפַּר הַצּוֹמוֹת דְּחַטְא זֶה — namely **to fast *three times* the number of fasts required for a particular sin,** even if many more than three violations occurred (see *Bris Menuchah* to *Sefer Chasidim* sec. 394; *Divrei Chachamim, Sha'ar ha-Teshuvah* chap. 12).

דְּהַיְינוּ רנ"ב צוֹמוֹת עַל הוֹצָאוֹת שִׁכְבַת זֶרַע לְבַטָּלָה — **For example, in the above case of emitting seed in vain, this would total** three times 84 which equals **252 fasts for** any number of violations, וְכֵן בִּשְׁאָר חֲטָאִים וַעֲווֹנוֹת — **and** the calculation would be **the same for other sins and violations.**

The *Tanya* explains the logic behind the intermediate position.

וְהַטַּעַם הוּא עַל פִּי מַה שֶׁכָּתוּב בַּזֹהַר הַקָּדוֹשׁ סוֹף פָּרָשַׁת נֹחַ — **The reason for** the multiple of three here **is based on a statement of the holy *Zohar*, at the end of *Parshas Noach*,** כֵּיוָן דְּחָב בַּר נַשׁ קַמֵּי קוּדְשָׁא בְּרִיךְ הוּא זִמְנָא חֲדָא — **"When a person sins before the Blessed Holy One once,"** עָבֵיד רְשִׁימוּ כוּ' — **"it makes an impression...,"** זִמְנָא תְּלִיתָאָה — **"on the third occasion,"** אִתְפַּשַּׁט הַהוּא כִּתְמָא — מִסִּטְרָא דָּא לְסִטְרָא דָּא כוּ' — **"the stain spreads from one side to the other etc.,"** (*Zohar* 1, 83b).

לְכָךְ צָרִיךְ מִסְפַּר הַצּוֹמוֹת גַּם כֵּן ג' פְּעָמִים וְכוּ' — **On this basis, the number of fasts** recommended by the intermediate position **is three times, etc.**

The first three violations of a sin are particularly damaging as they cause negative energy to spread "from one side to the other" of the particular body part (and its soul energy) associated with that sin.

ג"פ וכו'. אכן כל זה באדם חזק ובריא שאין ריבוי

Above we explained (in our discussion of the lenient view) that a body part (and its soul energy) becomes *completely* contaminated upon the first violation of the sin associated with it. How are we to understand the *Tanya's* teaching here that three violations are required?

Every body part has its own independent identity, but it is also part of the bigger system of the body as a whole. Any system is built on *interconnectedness:* each part of the system is connected with, and "contains," all the other parts.

The lenient view's concern was the body part's *independent identity.* That indeed becomes completely contaminated upon the first violation of the sin associated with it.

The intermediate position is concerned also with the body part's *systemic identity,* how all the other parts of the body (system) are included *within* that particular body part. It was about this issue, of systemic identity, that the *Zohar* taught, *"on the third occasion, the stain spreads from one side to the other."* While it takes only one violation to contaminate a body part's independent identity, it takes three violations to fully contaminate the systemic identity, to the extent that all the other body parts "contained" within it also become affected.

That is why the intermediate position requires three rounds of fasting, to detoxify the systemic contamination that was completed through three violations (Based on *Likutei Sichos* volume 39, pp. 124-5).

SECTION TWO: WHEN NOT TO FAST

11TH TAMMUZ REGULAR | 15TH TAMMUZ LEAP

The *Tanya* has endorsed the "consensus" view that for multiple violations of the same sin, one should fast three times the number of fasts recommended by *Arizal.*

This would mean, for example, that a person who "emitted seed in vain" multiple times in his youth (which was apparently a common concern among the *Tanya's* readership), would have to carry out (3 times 84 which equals) 252 fasts at some point in his life, in order *"to be desirable to G-d, as pleasing and cherished to Him as he was before the sin."*

Clearly, this would be a punishing regime to follow. In this section the *Tanya* airs some concerns about the negative implications of excessive fasting.

אֲכֵן כָּל זֶה בְּאָדָם חָזָק וּבָרִיא — **However the above is for a person who is strong**

הצומות מזיק לו כלל לבריאות גופו וכמו בדורות
הראשונים. אבל מי שריבוי הצומות מזיק לו שאפשר
שיוכל לבא לידי חולי או מיחוש ח"ו כמו בדורותינו
אלה. אסור לו להרבות בתעניות אפי' על כריתות
ומיתות ב"ד ומכ"ש על מ"ע ומל"ת שאין בהן כרת.
אלא כפי אשר ישער בנפשו שבודאי לא יזיק לו כלל.
כי אפי' בדורות הראשונים בימי תנאים ואמוראים לא

שֶׁאֵין רִבּוּי הַצּוֹמוֹת מַזִּיק לוֹ כְּלָל לִבְרִיאוּת גּוּפוֹ — such that and in good health, וּכְמוֹ בַּדּוֹרוֹת — multiple fasts will not damage the health of his body at all, הָרִאשׁוֹנִים — as was the case in the early generations, when people were accustomed to fast more.

אֲבָל מִי שֶׁרִבּוּי הַצּוֹמוֹת מַזִּיק לוֹ — But for a person whose health would be injured by multiple fasts, שֶׁאֶפְשָׁר שֶׁיּוּכַל לָבוֹא לִידֵי חֹלִי אוֹ מֵיחוֹשׁ חַס וְשָׁלוֹם — because they might bring him sickness or pain, G-d forbid, כְּמוֹ בְּדוֹרוֹתֵינוּ אֵלֶּה — as is the case with most people in these generations, אָסוּר לוֹ לְהַרְבּוֹת בְּתַעֲנִיּוֹת — in such a case, Jewish law forbids a person to fast too much, אֲפִלּוּ עַל כְּרֵיתוֹת — (even for a transgression punishable by kareis or the death וּמִיתוֹת בֵּית דִּין penalty, וּמִכָּל שֶׁכֵּן עַל מִצְווֹת עֲשֵׂה וּמִצְווֹת לֹא תַעֲשֶׂה שֶׁאֵין בָּהֶן כָּרֵת — and certainly for positive commands or prohibitions that are not punishable by kareis).

אֶלָּא כְּפִי אֲשֶׁר יְשַׁעֵר בְּנַפְשׁוֹ שֶׁבְּוַדַּאי לֹא יַזִּיק לוֹ כְּלָל — Rather a person may only fast to the extent that he is absolutely sure he will not be injured by it.

כִּי אֲפִלּוּ בַּדּוֹרוֹת הָרִאשׁוֹנִים — For even in earlier generations, בִּימֵי תַּנָּאִים וַאֲמוֹרָאִים — the period of the earlier and later Talmudic sages, לֹא הָיוּ מִתְעַנִּין — were not accustomed to fast...

A CHASIDIC THOUGHT

"It is not advisable to take upon oneself extra fasts in addition to those which are already in the calendar, this is based on the words of the *Alter Rebbe*. One of the reasons which he mentions in this connection is that the generations have weakened, and are no longer fit to have extra fasts. Obviously, my suggestion to you, therefore, is valid even now. The would-be resolution to undertake a fast should be changed to a resolution to serve G-d with an extra measure of joy, and to endeavor to spread good influence in the environment in this direction."

(From a Letter of the Lubavitcher Rebbe, 15th of Iyar, 5724)

היו מתענין בכה"ג אלא הבריאים דמצו לצעורי נפשייהו
ודלא מצי לצעורי נפשיה ומתענה נקרא חוטא בגמ'
פ"ק דתענית. ואפי' מתענה על עבירות שבידו כדפרש"י
שם וכדאיתא בגמ' פ"ק דזבחים שאין לך אדם מישראל
שאינו מחוייב עשה וכו'. ומכ"ש מי שהוא בעל
תורה שחוטא ונענש בכפליים כי מחמת חלישות

בְּכְהַאי גַּוְונָא אֶלָּא הַבְּרִיאִים דְּמָצוּ לְצַעוֹרֵי נַפְשַׁיְהוּ — only healthy people who could withstand the strain would fast to such an extent.

We have learned that for *"a person whose health would be injured by multiple fasts.... Jewish law forbids a person to fast too much."* The *Tanya* now cites a source from the *Talmud* for this point.

וּדְלָא מָצֵי לְצַעוֹרֵי נַפְשֵׁיה וּמִתְעַנֶּה נִקְרָא חוֹטֵא בַּגְּמָרָא פֶּרֶק קַמָּא דְּתַעֲנִית — If a person cannot withstand the strain and fasts nonetheless, his act is called "sinful" by the *Talmud*, *Ta'anis* chapter 1.

"Shmuel said: Whoever sits in observance of a fast is called a sinner" (*Ta'anis* 11b).

Shmuel's words are directed even at an individual who has committed sins and wishes to fast for them, as the *Tanya* now proves from *Rashi*.

וַאֲפִלּוּ מִתְעַנֶּה עַל עֲבֵרוֹת שֶׁבְּיָדוֹ — Even if he fasts for his accumulated sins, כְּדְפֵרֵשׁ רַשִׁ"י שָׁם — as *Rashi* (ibid. 11a) states, that these fasts *"cleanse his sins."*

Nevertheless, if he fasts for these sins, when he is physically unable to do so, he is called a "sinner."

The *Tanya* offers another proof that Shmuel's teaching, *"whoever sits in observance of a fast is called a sinner,"* applies even to a person that has committed sins and wishes to fast for them.

וְכִדְאִיתָא בַּגְּמָרָא פֶּרֶק קַמָּא דִּזְבָחִים — And as the *Talmud* states, *Zevachim* chapter 1 (7a), שֶׁאֵין לְךָ אָדָם מִיִּשְׂרָאֵל שֶׁאֵינוֹ מְחָיָב עֲשֵׂה וְכוּ' — that there is no person in Israel who is not guilty of neglecting a positive command.

Everyone has at least one positive command that they have neglected. So Shmuel's instruction not to carry out fasts clearly applies even to a person who has sinned.

וּמִכֹּל שֶׁכֵּן מִי שֶׁהוּא בַּעַל תּוֹרָה — And this is true to a greater extent for a Torah scholar, שֶׁחוֹטֵא וְנֶעֱנָשׁ בִּכְפָלַיִם — who will be punished doubly for this sin of damaging his body through fasting, כִּי מֵחֲמַת חֲלִישׁוּת הַתַּעֲנִית לֹא יוּכַל לַעֲסֹק בָּהּ — כָּרָאוּי — when he is subsequently unable to study properly because his health has been weakened by fasting.

התענית לא יוכל לעסוק בה כראוי. אלא מאי תקנתי'
כדכתיב וחטאך בצדקה פרוק. וכמ"ש הפוסקים ליתן
בעד כל יום תענית של תשובה ערך ח"י ג"פ וכו'

Through excessive fasting, the Torah scholar commits two sins: 1.) The sin of damaging his body; 2.) The sin of lost Torah study from his subsequent weakness.

SECTION THREE: A PRACTICAL SOLUTION

In Section One the *Tanya* endorsed the "intermediate" view that for multiple violations of the same sin, one should fast three times the number of fasts recommended by *Arizal* for a single violation. In Section Two, the *Tanya* discouraged us from carrying out excessive fasting, since it is likely to damage the body.

PRACTICAL LESSONS

It is forbidden to hurt your body through fasting.

Nowadays, a penitential fast can be redeemed through donating around seven dollars to charity.

אֶלָּא מַאי תַּקַּנְתֵּיה — **So what is the solution?**

How are we to acquire the spiritual benefits of these fasts when our bodies are not capable of them?

The *Tanya* suggests an innovative solution.

כְּדִכְתִיב וַחֲטָאָךְ בְּצִדְקָה פְרָק — **By following the verse, "Redeem your sin through charity"** (*Daniel* 4:24).

In substitute for fasting, it is possible to offer a charitable donation.

The *Tanya* quantifies how much charity is to be given.

וּכְמוֹ שֶׁכָּתְבוּ הַפּוֹסְקִים — **And the legal codes recommend** twelve small coins (*peshitim*; Rema, Orach Chaim 334:26), לִתֵּן בְּעַד כָּל יוֹם תַּעֲנִית שֶׁל תְּשׁוּבָה עֶרֶךְ ח"י גְּדוֹלִים פּוֹלִישׁ וְכוּ' — **to be given for each *teshuvah* fast day**, which is equivalent to **eighteen large polish** coins (*gulden*; *Magen Avraham* ibid. sec. 34), or 12.82 grams of silver, nowadays.

Eighteen *peshitim* are equivalent to the Biblical measurement of one *sela* (*Shulchan Aruch Ha-Rav*, ibid.). Twelve *peshitim* (or eighteen Polish *gulden*) are therefore equivalent to two-thirds of a *sela*. The contemporary value of a *sela* can be easily calculated, since the sum through which we carry out the redemption of the firstborn is five *selaim* (*Igros Kodesh*, vol. 2, p. 61ff). Five *selaim* is 96.15 grams of silver (Rabbi Chaim Na'oh, *Shiurei Torah* 3:43), so two-thirds of a *sela* is 12.82 grams of silver (approximately $7, as of this writing).

וְהֶעָשִׁיר יוֹסִיף לְפִי עָשְׁרוֹ וְכוּ' כְּמ"ש הַמ"א הִלְכוֹת תַעֲנִית:

וּמִ"מ   כָּל בַּעַל נֶפֶשׁ הֶחָפֵץ קִרְבַת ה' לְתַקֵּן נַפְשׁוֹ
לְהָשִׁיבָה אֶל ה' בִּתְשׁוּבָה מְעוּלָה מִן הַמּוּבְחָר.
יַחֲמִיר עַל עַצְמוֹ לְהַשְׁלִים עכ"פ פַּעַם א' כָּל יְמֵי חַיָּיו
מִסְפַּר הַצוֹמוֹת לְכָל עָוֹן וְעָוֹן מֵעֲווֹנוֹת הַחֲמוּרִים שֶׁחַיָּיבִין   93A

'וְהֶעָשִׁיר יוֹסִיף לְפִי עָשְׁרוֹ וְכוּ — This figure of twelve *peshitim* represents the minimum, **but a wealthy person should increase according to his means, etc.,** כְּמוֹ שֶׁכָּתַב הַמָגֵן אַבְרָהָם הִלְכוֹת תַּעֲנִית — **as** *Magen Avraham* **writes in the** *Laws of Fasting* (*Orach Chaim* 568:12).

SECTION FOUR: A MORE STRINGENT APPROACH

12TH TAMMUZ REGULAR | 16TH TAMMUZ LEAP

In Section Three the *Tanya* proposed a solution to our earlier dilemma. According to the "consensus opinion," we should really fast three times the number of fasts recommended by *Arizal* for transgressing multiple violations. On the other hand, in Section Two the *Tanya* argued that we should refrain from fasting, since it is damaging to our health. The solution proposed in Section Three was to redeem the required fasts through charitable donation.

It turns out, however, that the proposal in Section Three was a minimalist solution.

וּמִכָּל מָקוֹם — **Nevertheless,** כָּל בַּעַל נֶפֶשׁ הֶחָפֵץ קִרְבַת ה' — **any person who val-ues his soul and desires to be close to G-d,** לְתַקֵּן נַפְשׁוֹ לַהֲשִׁיבָה אֶל ה' בִּתְשׁוּבָה — **to repair his soul and return it to G-d with the best** *teshu-vah* **possible,** מְעוּלָה מִן הַמּוּבְחָר — לְהַשְׁלִים עַל כָּל — **should be stringent on himself,** יַחֲמִיר עַל עַצְמוֹ — **to complete, at least** פְּנִים פַּעַם אַחַת כָּל יְמֵי חַיָּיו מִסְפַּר הַצוֹמוֹת לְכָל עָוֹן וְעָוֹן — **once in his life, the recommended number of fasts for each transgression** recommended by *Arizal*.

Here in Section Four, the *Tanya* suggests a more demanding path, to try to actually adhere to the "consensus opinion" of fasting three times the number recommended by *Arizal*. Of the three times, at least one should preferably be carried out in the form of full fasts (the other two rounds of fasting can be carried out with a further leniency, as will be discussed below).

The *Tanya* places a limit on this recommendation.

מֵעֲווֹנוֹת הַחֲמוּרִים שֶׁחַיָּיבִין עֲלֵיהֶם מִיתָה עַל כָּל פָּנִים — **You should do this at least**

עֲלֵיהֶם מִיתָה עכ"פ וַאֲפִי' בִּידֵי שָׁמַיִם בִּלְבָד כְּגוֹן
לְהוֹצָאוֹת ז"ל פ"ד צוֹמוֹת פ"א בִּימֵי חַיָּיו. וְיָכוֹל לִדְחוֹתָן
לְיָמִים הַקְּצָרִים בַּחֹרֶף וְיִתְעַנֶּה כְּעֶשֶׂר תַּעֲנִיּוֹת עַד"מ
בַּחֹרֶף א' אוֹ פָּחוֹת וְיִגְמוֹר מִסְפַּר הַפ"ד צוֹמוֹת בט'
שָׁנִים אוֹ יוֹתֵר כְּפִי כֹחוֹ (וְגַם יָכוֹל לֶאֱכוֹל מְעַט כג'
שָׁעוֹת לִפְנֵי נ"ה וַאעפ"כ נֶחְשָׁב לְתַעֲנִית אִם הִתְנָה

for the serious transgressions which carry the death penalty, וַאֲפִלּוּ בִּידֵי שָׁמַיִם בִּלְבָד — including **even** those sins which carry the death penalty **through the agency of heaven.**

כְּגוֹן לְהוֹצָאוֹת זֶרַע לְבַטָּלָה פ"ד צוֹמוֹת פַּעַם אַחַת בִּימֵי חַיָּיו — In our above **example** of **emitting seed in vain,** even multiple times, you should carry out **84** full **fasts at least once in your life.**

However, since our ability to fast is weak (as noted in Section Two), the *Tanya* proposes certain acceptable leniencies when fasting.

וְיָכוֹל לִדְחוֹתָן לַיָּמִים הַקְּצָרִים בַּחֹרֶף — These fasts **could be delayed until the short days in the winter, וְיִתְעַנֶּה כְּעֶשֶׂר תַּעֲנִיּוֹת עַל דֶּרֶךְ מָשָׁל בְּחֹרֶף אֶחָד אוֹ פָּחוֹת** — and you might carry out, for example, around ten (or less) fasts during one **winter, וְיִגְמוֹר מִסְפַּר הַפ"ד צוֹמוֹת בְּתֵשַׁע שָׁנִים** — so that the total of 84 fasts are **completed in nine years, אוֹ יוֹתֵר כְּפִי כֹחוֹ** — or in more** time, if necessary, **depending on your abilities.**

Since you have a lifetime to complete this one-time schedule of fasting, it can be spread over many years. The *Tanya* advises it to be carried out in the winter months since fasting is until nightfall and the days are short in winter.

The *Tanya* suggests another leniency.

(וְגַם יָכוֹל לֶאֱכוֹל מְעַט כְּשָׁלֹשׁ שָׁעוֹת לִפְנֵי נֵץ הַחַמָּה — **And you could also** ease the fast by **eating a little** up until **three hours before sunrise,** since eating before sunrise early in the morning will also ease the fast.

Here the author of *Tanya* recommends doing so only until three hours before sunrise, but in his *Shulchan Aruch* (ch. 564) and *Siddur* (*Seder Sefiras Ha-Omer*), he permits eating until the later time of *alos ha-shachar,* the crack of dawn (see *Notes on Tanya; Igros Kodesh,* vol. 3, p. 75ff.).

The *Tanya* notes a requirement for those who wish to follow this practice.

וְאַף עַל פִּי כֵן נֶחְשָׁב לְתַעֲנִית אִם הִתְנָה כֵּן) — **And it will still be considered a fast if you stipulated** the previous day that you were going to eat upon arising.

Shulchan Aruch teaches that a person may only eat before dawn on a fast day, *"if he did not go to sleep. But if he went to sleep, he cannot then eat or*

כן) ולתשלום רנ"ב צומות כנ"ל יתענה עוד ד' פעמים
פ"ד עד אחר חצות היום בלבד דמיחשב ג"כ תענית
בירושלמי. וב' חצאי יום נחשבים לו ליום א' לענין
זה. וכן לשאר עוונות כיוצא בהן אשר כל לב יודע
מרת נפשו וחפץ בהצדקה:

drink (even before dawn) unless he made a stipulation (before going to sleep)
that he was going to eat or drink (later on)" (Orach Chaim 564:1).

As we have learned, the "consensus opinion" requires three times the number of fasts recommended by *Arizal* (which, for spilling seed in vain is 3 x 84 =
252). The *Tanya's* schedule of nine years of winter fasting has accounted for
one of those three times (84 fasts), how are the other two times to be carried
out to complete the total number of 252?

וּלְתַשְׁלוּם רנ"ב צומות כַּנַּ"ל — **And to complete the recommended number of**
252 fasts mentioned above, — יִתְעַנֶּה עוֹד אַרְבַּע פְּעָמִים פ"ד — **one could carry out**
a further 84 half **fasts, four times over,** עַד אַחַר חֲצוֹת הַיּוֹם בִּלְבַד — a half-fast
meaning that one fasts **until just after midday.**

To complete the remaining fasts, the *Tanya* suggests a further leniency of
combining two half-fasts (which are relatively easy to perform), as one.

דְּמִיחֲשַׁב גַּם כֵּן תַּעֲנִית בִּירוּשַׁלְמִי — **This is acceptable according to the Jerusa-**
lem *Talmud* (Nedarim 8:1), — וּשְׁנֵי חֲצָאֵי יוֹם נֶחֱשָׁבִים לוֹ לְיוֹם אֶחָד לְעִנְיָן זֶה — since
two half-days are considered as one single day, in this context.

This has clarified how even an ordinary person can carry out the 252 fasts
required for spilling seed in vain.

וְכֵן לִשְׁאָר עֲווֹנוֹת כַּיּוֹצֵא בָּהֶן — **And the same approach can be applied to the**
fasts required **for other sins,** which do not carry a severe punishment.

אֲשֶׁר כָּל לֵב יוֹדֵעַ מָרַת נַפְשׁוֹ וְחָפֵץ בְּהַצְּדָקָה — **For each** *"heart knows its own bit-*
terness" (Proverbs 14:10), **and desires to be free of blame.**

Obviously, any person knows which sins he has committed. Why did the *Tan-*
ya need to cite Scripture to prove this point?

The *Tanya* refers to a situation where you are certain you have committed
an act, but you are doubtful if the act was sinful. For example, becoming angry
is a sin for which *Arizal* recommends multiple fasts, but there are instances
where anger is "kosher," as an act of righteous indignation (see, for example,
Shulchan Aruch, Yoreh De'ah 246:11).

When you have become angry, how do you know if you have sinned or not?
The *Tanya* answers: your *"heart knows"* (Based on *Likutei Sichos* volume 39,
p. 199).

אָכֵן מספר הצומות העודפי' על רנ"ב וכה"ג שהיה צריך להתענות לחוש לדעת המחמירי' להתענות מספר הצומות שעל כל חטא וחטא כפי מספר הפעמים שחטא כנ"ל. יפדה כולן בצדקה ערך ח"י ג"פ בעד כל יום. וכן שאר כל תעניות שצריך להתענות על עבירות שאין בהן מיתה ואפי' על ביטול מ"ע דאוריי' ודרבנן ות"ת כנגד כולם כפי המספר המפורש בתיקוני התשובה מהאר"י ז"ל (ורובם נזכרים במשנת חסידים

17TH TAMMUZ LEAP

As we have learned, the "consensus opinion" requires just three times the number of fasts recommended by *Arizal* for multiple violations.

But what if a person desired to follow the stringent opinion (mentioned in Section One) and carry out the number of fasts recommended by *Arizal* for *every* violation?

The *Tanya* discourages such an approach.

אָכֵן מִסְפַּר הַצּוֹמוֹת הָעוֹדְפִים עַל רנ"ב — **But fasting beyond the** "consensus opinion" of three times *Arizal's* recommended **number**, which in the above case of spilling seed in vain was 3 x 84 =**252**, וּכְהַאי גַּוְונָא — **or whatever that** number **might be,** in the case of other fasts, שֶׁהָיָה צָרִיךְ לְהִתְעַנּוֹת לָחֹשׁ לְדַעַת הַמַּחֲמִירִים **in** — לְהִתְעַנּוֹת מִסְפַּר הַצּוֹמוֹת שֶׁעַל כָּל חֵטְא וְחֵטְא כְּפִי מִסְפַּר הַפְּעָמִים שֶׁחָטָא כַּנַּ"ל **order to follow the stringent position and fast the recommended number of fasts for each type of transgression, taking into account the number of times the sin was committed,** is not recommended.

יִפְדֶה כֻּלָּן בִּצְדָקָה עֵרֶךְ ח"י גְּדוֹלִים פּוֹלִישׁ בְּעַד כָּל יוֹם — **One should not actually fast** this excess amount, but **redeem all such** additional fasts **through charity, to the amount of 18 polish** *gulden* **for each** fast **day.**

The *Tanya* recommends the consensus opinion as the *maximum limit* for actual fasting. If one wishes to take the stringent position into account, the additional fasts should be redeemed through charity (as explained in Section Three).

וְכֵן שְׁאָר כָּל תַּעֲנִיּוֹת שֶׁצָּרִיךְ לְהִתְעַנּוֹת עַל עֲבֵרוֹת שֶׁאֵין בָּהֶן מִיתָה — **Likewise,** one should redeem through charity **any fasts required for sins which do not carry the death penalty,** וַאֲפִלּוּ עַל בִּטּוּל מִצְווֹת עֲשֵׂה דְּאוֹרָיְיתָא וּדְרַבָּנָן — **even for failing to observe positive commands, Biblical or Rabbinic,** וְתַלְמוּד תּוֹרָה כְּנֶגֶד **Torah study equaling them all** *(Peah* 1:1), כָּלָם — כְּפִי הַמִּסְפָּר הַמְפֹרָשׁ בְּתִקּוּנֵי **giving to charity according to the amount** of fasts stated in the *teshuvah* recommendations of *Arizal,* הַתְּשׁוּבָה מֵהָאֲרִ"י ז"ל — וְרֻבָּם נִזְכָּרִים בְּמִשְׁנַת חֲסִידִים

במס' התשובה) הכל כאשר לכל יפדה בצדקה כנ"ל
אי לא מצי לצעורי נפשי' כנ"ל. ואף שיעלה לסך
מסויים אין לחוש משום אל יבזבז יותר מחומש.
דלא מקרי בזבוז בכה"ג מאחר שעושה לפדות נפשו

בְּמַסֶּכֶת הַתְּשׁוּבָה) — most of which are stated in *Mishnas Chasidim, Maseches Teshuvah.*

Actual fasting is the preferable way to observe the "consensus opinion" (following the leniencies mentioned above), only in the case of severe sins (which carry the death penalty). All other fasts ought to be redeemed through charity alone.

הַכֹּל כַּאֲשֶׁר לַכֹּל יִפָּדֶה בִּצְדָקָה כַּנַּ"ל — *"It is the same for all"* (*Ecclesiastes* 9:2), all fasts should **be redeemed with charity, as above,** and not through actual fasting, אִי לָא מָצֵי לְצַעוּרֵי נַפְשֵׁיהּ כַּנַּ"ל — **if a person cannot withstand** fasting, **as above.**

If a person is unable to fast without injuring himself, all fasts must be redeemed through charitable donation.

SECTION FIVE: IS THERE A LIMIT TO CHARITY?

Following the above advice may result in huge sums being owed to charity. This may pose a problem, since the *Talmud* warns a person not to give more than a fifth of his income to charity. The *Tanya* now addresses this concern.

וְאַף שֶׁיַּעֲלֶה לְסַךְ מְסָיָם — **Even if** the above redemption of multiple fasts through charity **will add up to a considerable sum,** totaling more than a fifth of your income, אֵין לָחוּשׁ מִשּׁוּם אַל יְבַזְבֵּז יוֹתֵר מֵחֹמֶשׁ — **you need not be concerned about the warning, "Do not overspend more than a fifth** (of your income on charity)" (*Talmud, Kesubos* 50a).

The *Talmud* placed an upper limit on charitable donations of one-fifth of income, to ensure that a person would retain enough money for himself, and not become dependent on others.

However the *Tanya* will argue that the *Talmud's* ruling does not apply to this case.

דְּלָא מִקְרֵי בִּזְבּוּז בִּכְהַאי גַּוְונָא — **Because, in this instance,** the redemption of fasts **is not called** charitable **"overspending,"** מֵאַחַר שֶׁעוֹשֶׂה לִפְדוֹת נַפְשׁוֹ מִתַּעֲנִיּוֹת וְסָגּוּפִים — **because** "charity" means giving away money *to help another,* but this money is being given for *your own sake,* **to redeem your own soul, from fasting and affliction.**

מתעניות וסיגופים. ולא גרעא מרפואת הגוף ושאר
צרכיו. ולפי שמספר הצומות המוזכרי' בתקוני תשובה
הנ"ל רבו במאד מאד לכן נהגו עכשיו כל החרדים
לדבר ה' להרבות מאד מאד בצדקה. מחמת חלישות
הדור דלא מצו לצעורי נפשם כולי האי (וכמ"ש במ"א
ע"פ חסדי ה' כי לא תמנו):

938

The *Talmud's* warning not to give more than a fifth of your income refers to funds given to help others. The *Talmud's* warning is: Don't help others so much that in the end you'll need help from others.

But in this case, you are redeeming the fasts with charitable donations *to help yourself,* so that you will *"be desirable to G-d, as pleasing and cherished to Him as you were before the sin."* And, when it comes to self-care, there is no limit to how much money you can spend.

וְלָא גְרָעָא מֵרְפוּאַת הַגּוּף וּשְׁאָר צְרָכָיו — Redeeming the fasts is therefore **no less important than healing the body, or any other** personal **need,** in which case there is no restriction to how much you may spend.

Redeeming the fasts for your spiritual wellbeing, is, legally speaking, no different to paying a medical bill for your physical wellbeing. There is no upper limit.

PRACTICAL LESSONS

There is no limit to the charity you can give to redeem penitential fasts.

Practically speaking this means:

וּלְפִי שֶׁמִּסְפַּר הַצוֹמוֹת הַמֻּזְכָּרִים בְּתִקּוּנֵי תְּשׁוּבָה הַנַּ"ל רַבּוּ בְּמְאֹד מְאֹד — **Since the number of** *teshuvah* related **fasts described above is very large in number,** most people need to give huge sums to charity to redeem these fasts, לָכֵן נָהֲגוּ עַכְשָׁו כָּל הַחֲרֵדִים לִדְבַר ה' לְהַרְבּוֹת מְאֹד מְאֹד בִּצְדָקָה — **therefore, nowadays all those** who *"fear the word of G-d"* (Isaiah 66:5), **are accustomed to give a lot of money to charity.**

מֵחֲמַת חֲלִישׁוּת הַדּוֹר — This is **due to the weakness of** the people of our **generation,** דְּלָא מָצוּ לְצַעוּרֵי נַפְשָׁם כּוּלֵי הַאי — **who are unable to strain themselves so much** with excessive fasting.

(וּכְמוֹ שֶׁנִּתְבָּאֵר בְּמָקוֹם אַחֵר עַל פָּסוּק חַסְדֵי ה' כִּי לֹא תָמְנוּ) — **As is explained elsewhere** in the *Tanya's* commentary **on the verse,** *"The kindnesses of G-d, for they are not concluded"* (Eichah 3:22; see Tanya, Igeres Ha-Kodesh sec. 10).

פרק ד ואולם כל הנ"ל הוא לגמר הכפרה ומירוק
הנפש לה' אחר התשובה כמ"ש
לעיל מהגמ' פ"ק דזבחים דעולה דורון היא לאחר
שריצה הפרקליט וכו'. אמנם התחלת מצות התשובה
ועיקרה לשוב עד ה' באמת ובלב שלם. ההכרח
לבאר היטב בהרחבת הביאור. בהקדים מ"ש בזוה"ק
בביאור מלת תשובה ע"ד הסוד. תשוב ה'. ה'

CHAPTER 4

G-D'S NAME IN YOUR SOUL
SECTION ONE: SOME QUESTIONS ON TESHUVAH

13TH TAMMUZ REGULAR | 18TH TAMMUZ LEAP

In Chapters Two and Three the *Tanya* has digressed to discuss the atonement (and post-atonement) role of fasting. In this chapter we will return to our central theme: *teshuvah.*

Before probing deeper into the spiritual dynamic of *teshuvah*, the *Tanya* will first pose some questions, from key texts on our subject.

וְאוּלָם כָּל הַנַּ"ל הוּא לִגְמֹר הַכַּפָּרָה וּמֵרוּק הַנֶּפֶשׁ לַה' אַחַר הַתְּשׁוּבָה — **However, all the above** we have learned in Chapters Two and Three about fasting and charity **is to complete atonement and cleanse the soul to G-d *after teshuvah,*** כְּמוֹ שֶׁנִּתְבָּאֵר לְעֵיל מֵהַגְּמָרָא פֶּרֶק קַמָּא דִּזְבָחִים — **as has been explained above from the *Talmud,*** Tractate *Zevachim,* Chapter One, דְּעוֹלָה דּוֹרוֹן הִיא לְאַחַר שֶׁרָצָה הַפְּרַקְלִיט וְכוּ' — **that the Burnt Offering is a "gift" after the "mediator" has made his plea.**

אָמְנָם הַתְחָלַת מִצְוַת הַתְּשׁוּבָה וְעִקָּרָה לָשׁוּב עַד ה' בֶּאֱמֶת וּבְלֵב שָׁלֵם — **However, the beginning of the *mitzvah* of *teshuvah* and its main thrust, is to return to G-d authentically, with a whole heart,** as we have explained in Chapter One.

הַהֶכְרֵחַ לְבָאֵר הֵיטֵב בְּהַרְחָבַת הַבֵּאוּר — **This** now **requires more extensive clarification** from Jewish mystical sources.

בְּהַקְדִּים מַה שֶּׁכָּתוּב בַּזֹּהַר הַקָּדוֹשׁ — **Let us begin with a teaching from the holy** *Zohar* (3, 122b, *Raya Mehemna*), בְּבֵאוּר מִלַּת תְּשׁוּבָה עַל דֶּרֶךְ הַסּוֹד תָּשׁוּב הֵ"א — **which explains the word *teshuvah* mystically, as *tashuv-hei*, "return** the letter *hei."*

תתאה תשובה תתאה. ה' עילאה תשובה עילאה.
וגם מ"ש בזוה"ק בקצת מקומות שאין תשובה מועלת
לפוגם בריתו ומוציא ז"ל. והוא דבר תמוה מאד שאין

Teshuvah has restorative powers. It heals the soul of the penitent and it recti-
fies spiritual energies in the Divine realm that were "damaged" by the sin.

G-d's most sacred name, the Tetragrammaton (spelled *yud-hei* followed by
vav-hei), as we will see later in the chapter, can be read as a code depicting
the energies in the Divine realm. The "damage" to these worlds is described
metaphorically as a "fragmentation" of the Tetragrammaton, as its component
letters become disconnected from each other.

Specifically, it is the letter *hei* which becomes dislocated through sin. *Teshuvah* is the process by which the *hei* is restored to the Tetragrammaton and in-
corporated back in it. This is hinted to by the word *teshuvah* itself, which is the
combination of two words: *tashuv-hei* meaning, *"return (the letter) hei."*

The letter *hei* appears twice in the Tetragrammaton, hinting to two levels of
teshuvah.

הֵ"א תַּתָּאָה תְּשׁוּבָה תַּתָּאָה — Restoring the last, **"lower" *hei*** of the Tetragrammaton is **"lower *teshuvah*,"** הֵ"א עִילָאָה תְּשׁוּבָה עִילָאָה — Restoring the first, **"upper" *hei*** of the Tetragrammaton is **"upper *teshuvah*"** (Rabbi Chaim Vital, *Sha'ar
Tikunei Avonos*, chapter 1; *Sha'ar Hagilgulim,* chapter 21).

While we have touched upon these two levels of *teshuvah* in Part One
(p. 208), they will be more central to the discussion in *Igeres Ha-Teshuvah.*
Later we will explain them in detail, as well as the meaning of each of the four
letters of the Tetragrammaton. First the *Tanya* will ask another question on one
of the *Zohar's* teachings, which seems to limit the power of *teshuvah.*

וְגַם מַה שֶׁכָּתוּב בַּזֹּהַר הַקָּדוֹשׁ בְּקצָת מְקוֹמוֹת — We also need to clarify the *Zohar's*
statement in a few places (1, 62a; 219b), שֶׁאֵין תְּשׁוּבָה מוֹעֶלֶת לְפוֹגֵם בְּרִיתוֹ וּמוֹצִיא
זֶרַע לְבַטָּלָה — that *teshuvah* is not effective for sexual sins ("blemishing the
covenant"), or for the sin of emitting semen in vain, וְהוּא דָבָר תָּמוּהַּ מְאֹד —

A CHASIDIC THOUGHT

"There can be no question that *teshuvah* is effective in every case and whatever the transgression, for *teshuvah* is one of G-d's commandments, and G-d does not require of us the
impossible.

(From a Letter of the Rebbe, Erev Shavu'os 5716)

לְךָ דָבָר עוֹמֵד בִּפְנֵי הַתְּשׁוּבָה וַאֲפִילוּ ע"ז וג"ע וכו'.
וּפִי' בר"ח שְׁכַּוָּנַת הַזֹּהַר שֶׁאֵין מוֹעֶלֶת תְּשׁוּבָה תַּתָּאָה
כ"א תְּשׁוּבָה עִילָּאָה וכו'. הִנֵּה לְהָבִין זֹאת מְעַט מִזְּעֵיר
צָרִיךְ לְהַקְדִּים מַה שֶּׁמְּבֹאָר מֵהַכָּתוּב וּמִדִּבְרֵי רַז"ל עִנְיַן
הַכָּרֵת וּמִיתָה בִּידֵי שָׁמַיִם כְּשֶׁעָבַר עֲבֵרָה שֶׁחַיָּיבִי' עָלֶי'
כָּרֵת הָיָ' מֵת מַמָּשׁ קוֹדֶם חֲמִשִּׁים שָׁנָה. וּבְמִיתָה בִּידֵי

for we — שֶׁאֵין לְךָ דָבָר עוֹמֵד בִּפְנֵי הַתְּשׁוּבָה **which is a very shocking statement,** have been taught that *"nothing stands in the way of teshuvah"* (*Jerusalem Talmud, Pe'ah* 1:1; *Rambam, Laws of Teshuvah* end of chap. 3), וַאֲפִילוּ עֲבוֹדָה זָרָה — **even** the most serious violations of **idol worship, and forbidden relations** and murder. — וְגִלּוּי עֲרָיוֹת וְכוּ'

How can the *Zohar* claim *teshuvah* to be ineffective in *any* scenario?

וּפֵרֵשׁ בְּרֵאשִׁית חָכְמָה **Reishis Chochmah answers,** שֶׁכַּוָּנַת הַזֹּהַר שֶׁאֵין מוֹעֶלֶת — **that what the** *Zohar* **means to say is that "lower** *teshuvah*" is תְּשׁוּבָה תַּתָּאָה **ineffective** for sexual sins and for emitting seed in vain, כִּי אִם תְּשׁוּבָה עִילָּאָה וְכוּ' — **and "higher** *teshuvah*" is required in this case (*Reishis Chochmah, Sha'ar Ha-Kedushah* chapter 17). But this requires further explanation.

This matter will not be fully clarified until Chapter Nine. First we will probe the meaning of *teshuvah* more deeply.

הִנֵּה לְהָבִין זֹאת מְעַט מִזְּעֵיר — **In order to understand** *teshuvah* **a little** more, צָרִיךְ לְהַקְדִּים מַה שֶּׁמְּבֹאָר מֵהַכָּתוּב וּמִדִּבְרֵי רַז"ל עִנְיַן הַכָּרֵת וּמִיתָה בִּידֵי שָׁמַיִם — **let us first turn to some comments from Scripture and our Sages about** *kareis* **and "death through the agency of heaven."**

As we learned in Chapter One, the violation of a Torah prohibition carries a stated penalty. Two of the most severe of these are a (Divinely imposed) "cutting" (*kareis*) of the soul, and "death through the agency of heaven."

The *Tanya* now explores the physical consequences of receiving these punishments in more detail.

כְּשֶׁעָבַר עֲבֵרָה שֶׁחַיָּיבִים עָלֶיהָ כָּרֵת — **For a transgression whose punishment is** *kareis,* הָיָה מֵת מַמָּשׁ קֹדֶם חֲמִשִּׁים שָׁנָה — **in earlier times the transgressor would actually die** physically **before reaching the age of fifty,** וּבְמִיתָה בִּידֵי שָׁמַיִם מֵת מַמָּשׁ קֹדֶם שִׁשִּׁים שָׁנָה — and for a transgression whose punishment is **"death through the agency of heaven," he would literally die** physically **before reaching the age of sixty** (see *Genesis* 17:14; *Leviticus* 22:3; *Talmud, Mo'ed Katan* 28a; *Jerusalem Talmud, Bikurim* 2:1).

While *kareis* and "death through the agency of heaven" may seem to be spiritual punishments, since they are not administered by the earthly court, the

שמים מת ממש קודם ששים שנה כחנניה בן עזור
הנביא בירמי' (ולפעמי' גם במיתה בידי שמים נפרעין

Tanya notes that in earlier times these punishments would have very physical consequences of premature death.

כַּחֲנַנְיָה בֶּן עַזּוּר הַנָּבִיא בִּיִרְמְיָה — An example of this is **the case of Chananya ben Azur the** false **prophet,** mentioned **in** *Jeremiah.*

Chananya ben Azur was initially an authentic prophet (*Jerusalem Talmud, Sanhedrin* 11:5). He later became guilty of false prophecy, saying, *"Thus speaks the G-d of hosts, the G-d of Israel, saying, 'I have broken the yoke of the king of Babylon. Within two full years will I bring again into this place all the vessels of G-d's house, that Nebuchadnezzar king of Babylon took away from this place, and carried them to Babylon"* (*Jeremiah* 28:2-3).

This contradicted Jeremiah's correct prophecy that the Temple was to be destroyed.

Jeremiah subsequently informed Chananya ben Azur of a message he had received from G-d, conveying a punishment: *"Therefore this is what G-d says, 'Behold, I will cast you from off the face of the earth: this year you shall die'"* (*ibid.* 16).

The verse stresses that it was *G-d* who said, "I will cast you off *etc.,*" indicating that this was "death through *the agency of heaven.*"

Indeed, we find that the punishment materialized physically, *"and Chananya the prophet died the same year"* (*ibid.* 17).

We learned above that for a transgression whose punishment is "death through the agency of heaven," a person *"would literally die physically before reaching the age of sixty."* Why, then, did Chananya ben Azur die "the same year"? The *Tanya* explains:

(וְלִפְעָמִים גַּם בְּמִיתָה בִּידֵי שָׁמַיִם נִפְרָעִין לְאַלְתַּר כְּמוֹ שֶׁמָּצִינוּ בְּעֵר וְאוֹנָן) — **And occasionally "death through the agency of heaven" is even administered immediately, as in the case of Er and Onan.**

A CHASIDIC THOUGHT

"Whoever transgresses the commandments of Torah, it is as if he damages above and damages below; he damages himself, and damages all worlds. This may be compared to sailors sitting side by side on a ship, when one fool among them stands up and decides to drill a hole."

(*Zohar* 3, 122a)

לאלתר כמו שמצינו בער ואונן) והרי נמצאו בכל דור
כמה וכמה חייבי כריתות ומיתות והאריכו ימיהם
(ושניהם) [ושנותיהם] בנעימים. אך הענין יובן עפ"י
מ"ש כי חלק ה' עמו וכו' חלק משם הוי' ב"ה כדכתיב

Er and Onan were *"evil in the eyes of G-d"* for wasting their seed (punishable by "death through the agency of heaven") and were put to death immediately by G-d (*Genesis* 38:7-10).

This was, however, in Biblical times. The *Tanya* now questions why we do not find these punishments administered from heaven in later generations.

וַהֲרֵי נִמְצְאוּ בְּכָל דּוֹר כַּמָּה וְכַמָּה חַיָּבֵי כָּרֵתוֹת וּמִיתוֹת וְהֶאֱרִיכוּ יְמֵיהֶם וּשְׁנוֹתֵיהֶם בַּנְּעִימִים — This is problematic **since there are countless individuals through-out history who** performed acts **punishable by *kareis* or death** by the agency of heaven **and yet have lived long, happy lives?**

If the lives of these individuals had been miserable, one might argue that they had received a punishment somehow equivalent to "death." But how do we understand that, in place of "death through the agency of heaven," a person would live a *"long, happy"* life?

SECTION TWO: THE SOUL'S ROOT

14TH TAMMUZ REGULAR | 19TH TAMMUZ LEAP

To answer these questions we need to understand the *teshuvah* process more deeply. The *Tanya* will begin with a discussion of the soul and its unique origins.

The *Tanya* has already taught in Part One, Chapter Two, that the *"soul in the Israelite, is 'a piece of G-d above' (Job* 31:2), *literally."* We return to this theme.

אַךְ הָעִנְיָן יוּבַן עַל פִּי מַה שֶּׁכָּתוּב כִּי חֵלֶק ה' עַמּוֹ וְכוּ' — **We can explain** all **this by** first **examining the verse, *"For G-d's (Havayah's) portion are His people etc.,"*** (*Deuteronomy* 32:9), חֵלֶק מִשֵּׁם הֲוָיָ"ה בָּרוּךְ הוּא — **which implies that** G-d's peo-ple are **a "portion" of the blessed** Divine name *Havayah,* the Tetragrammaton (see Rabbi Yosef Karo, *Magid Meisharim, Parshas Acharei*).

The Divine origins of the soul are hinted to in *Deuteronomy* 32:9. "*Havayah's* portion" is read hyperliterally: G-d's "people," the verse tells us, contain a soul which is actually a "portion of *Havayah.*"

(As we have noted previously, *Havayah* is a term used to denote the Tetra-grammaton, G-d's four-lettered name, spelled *yud-hei* followed by *vav-hei.*

ויפח באפיו נשמת חיים ומאן דנפח מתוכו נפח וכו'.
ואף שאין לו דמות הגוף וכו' ח"ו. אך דברה תורה
כלשון בנ"א. כי כמו שיש הפרש והבדל גדול באדם   94A
התחתון עד"מ בין ההבל שיוצא מפיו בדיבורו להבל
היוצא ע"י נפיחה. שביוצא בדיבורו מלובש בו כח

Since this name is too sacred to pronounce, it is denoted by saying the word in inverse: *Havayah*).

The description of the soul as "literally" Divine and a "portion" of G-d is striking, since Jewish teachings are usually careful to emphasize a sharp distinction between the Creator and His creations. Rabbi Chaim Vital explains: *"The soul's light arises and flows from the light of the ten sefiros (Divine powers) themselves, without any intermediary; which is why the verse states, 'You are children of G-d your G-d' (Deuteronomy 14:1); for (the soul) is like a child who is completely attached to his father, from whom his being flows"* (Sha'arei Ha-Kedushah 3:2).

The *Tanya* reiterates the sources for this idea, stated in Part One.

כְּדִכְתִיב וַיִּפַּח בְּאַפָּיו נִשְׁמַת חַיִּים — **As the verse states,** *"And (G-d) blew into his nostrils the breath of life"* (Genesis 2:7), וּמַאן דְּנָפַח מִתּוֹכוֹ נָפַח וְכוּ' — **and "One who blows, blows from his innards,"** (cited in Part One, p. 45 in the name of the *Zohar*).

As the *Tanya* (ibid.) explains, G-d blew: *"from the innermost depths of His being for when a person blows forcibly, he exhales with a deep-rooted, inner energy."*

The Biblical metaphor of "blowing" man's soul suggests that G-d has a deep, inward attachment to the soul, as opposed to the rest of creation, which arose through the more superficial "speech" of G-d, ("G-d *said*, let there be...").

וְאַף שֶׁאֵין לוֹ דְּמוּת הַגּוּף וְכוּ' חַס וְשָׁלוֹם — **And while G-d** *"has no semblance of a body"* (Liturgy, Yigdal; Rambam, Third Principle of Faith), **G-d forbid, so G-d's** "blowing" is clearly not meant in a physical sense, אַךְ דִּבְּרָה תּוֹרָה כִּלְשׁוֹן בְּנֵי אָדָם — **nevertheless, *"The Torah speaks of G-d in human terms"*** (Talmud, Brachos 31b; see Part One, p. 248), employing the metaphor of "blowing" to imply a deep spiritual attachment.

The *Tanya* elaborates:

כִּי כְּמוֹ שֶׁיֵּשׁ הֶפְרֵשׁ וְהֶבְדֵּל גָּדוֹל בָּאָדָם הַתַּחְתּוֹן עַל דֶּרֶךְ מָשָׁל בֵּין הַהֶבֶל שֶׁיּוֹצֵא מִפִּיו בְּדִבּוּרוֹ לַהֶבֶל הַיּוֹצֵא עַל יְדֵי נְפִיחָה — **For just as, for example, the** intensity of breath coming from the mouth of a mortal human differs greatly between speaking and blowing, שֶׁבְּיוֹצֵא בְּדִבּוּרוֹ מְלֻבָּשׁ בּוֹ כֹּחַ וְחַיּוּת מְעַט מִזְעֵיר — for

 וחיות מעט מזעיר והוא בחי׳ חיצוניות מנפש החיה
שבקרבו. אבל ביוצא בכח הנופח דמתוכו נפח מלובש
בו כח וחיות פנימי׳ מבחי׳ הנפש החיה וכו׳. ככה
ממש עד"מ המבדיל הבדלות לאין קץ. יש הפרש
עצום מאד למעלה בין כל צבא השמים ואפי׳ המלאכי׳
שנבראו מאין ליש וחיים וקיימי׳ מבחי׳ חיצוניות החיות
והשפע שמשפיע א"ס ב"ה להחיות העולמות ובחי׳
זו נקראת בשם רוח פיו עד"מ כמ"ש וברוח פיו כל

when he speaks only a minuscule amount of power/energy is invested, וְהוּא
בְּחִינַת חִיצוֹנִיּוֹת מִנֶּפֶשׁ הַחַיָּה שֶׁבְּקִרְבּוֹ — meaning that speaking is a superficial
expression of the living soul within him, אֲבָל בַּיּוֹצֵא בְּכֹחַ הַנּוֹפֵחַ דְּמִתּוֹכוֹ נָפַח —
whereas when he blows powerfully it comes from inside himself, מְלֻבָּשׁ בּוֹ כֹּחַ
וְחַיּוּת פְּנִימִית מִבְּחִינַת הַנֶּפֶשׁ הַחַיָּה וְכוּ׳ — expressing a deep power/energy of his
living soul, etc.

PRACTICAL LESSONS

There is a radical
difference between
the Divine energy
invested in your soul
and the Divine energy
invested in the rest
of the universe.

The energy in
your soul is from
deep within G-d,
His "breath." The
energy in the rest
of the universe is
relatively superficial,
like "speech."

כָּכָה מַמָּשׁ עַל דֶּרֶךְ מָשָׁל — The same is true (figuratively
speaking) with G-d, הַמַּבְדִּיל הַבְדָּלוֹת לְאֵין קֵץ — (although the comparison is obviously an utterly inadequate one, since a human being is infinitely removed
from G-d).

The Tanya explains the difference between the energetic content of G-d's "speaking" and His "blowing."

יֵשׁ הֶפְרֵשׁ עָצוּם מְאֹד לְמַעְלָה בֵּין כָּל צְבָא הַשָּׁמַיִם וַאֲפִלּוּ
הַמַּלְאָכִים — Above, in the spiritual realms, there is a
radical difference between the Divine energy invested in the "hosts of the heavens," (even the angels),
and the Divine energy invested in the soul.

שֶׁנִּבְרְאוּ מֵאַיִן לְיֵשׁ — The angels were created something-from-nothing by G-d's speech, וְחַיִּים וְקַיָּמִים
מִבְּחִינַת חִיצוֹנִיּוּת הַחַיּוּת וְהַשֶּׁפַע — meaning that they
are energized and sustained from an external flow
of energy, similar to the superficial energy invested in
"speech," שֶׁמַּשְׁפִּיעַ אֵין סוֹף בָּרוּךְ הוּא לְהַחֲיוֹת הָעוֹלָמוֹת
— which G-d, the Blessed Infinite One, produces in
order to energize the universe.

וּבְחִינָה זוֹ נִקְרֵאת בְּשֵׁם רוּחַ פִּיו עַל דֶּרֶךְ מָשָׁל — This external flow is referred to

צבאם והיא בחי' חיות המלובשת באותיות שבעשרה
מאמרות (שהן בחי' כלים והמשכות וכו' כמ"ש בלק"א
ח"ב פי"א). ובין נשמת האדם שנמשכה תחלה מבחי'
פנימי' החיות והשפע שמשפיע א"ס ב"ה כמ"ש ויפח
וכו' ואח"כ ירדה בסתר המדרגה ג"כ ע"י בחי' האותיות

by scripture with the metaphor, "breath of His mouth," כְּמוֹ שֶׁכָּתוּב וּבְרוּחַ פִּיו כָּל
צְבָאָם — as in the verse, *"and (from) the breath of His mouth, all (the world's)
contents (come to be)"* (Psalms 33:6; see Part One, p. 553; Part Two, p. 36).

וְהִיא בְּחִינַת חַיּוּת הַמִּלְבֶּשֶׁת בָּאוֹתִיּוֹת שֶׁבַּעֲשָׂרָה מַאֲמָרוֹת — This "breath" refers
to the Divine energy which is embodied in the spoken letters of the "ten
statements" in *Genesis* through which the world was created, (שֶׁהֵן בְּחִינַת כֵּלִים)
שֶׁהֵן בְּחִינַת כֵּלִים (וְהַמְשָׁכוֹת וְכוּ' כְּמוֹ שֶׁנִּתְבָּאֵר בְּלִקּוּטֵי אֲמָרִים חֵלֶק ב' פֶּרֶק י"א — for the letters are,
in fact, **packages of** Divine energy, *etc.,* as has been explained in *Tanya,* **Part
Two, Chapter Eleven).**

G-d created the world through "ten statements" of Divine "speech" recorded in *Genesis* 1. As we have explained in Part Two of *Tanya,* this speech represents creative energy; in fact, even the component letters of the speech are
really "packets" of Divine energy.

The Torah describes this energy as "speech," (which is effortless and detached), to indicate less of an energetic "investment" on G-d's part, when compared to the soul which was produced by a deep "blowing."

וּבֵין נִשְׁמַת הָאָדָם — Compare this external, superficial flow of Divine energy
which powers the universe **to the deep flow in the human soul,** שֶׁנִּמְשְׁכָה תְּחִלָּה
מִבְּחִינַת פְּנִימִיּוּת הַחַיּוּת וְהַשֶּׁפַע שֶׁמַּשְׁפִּיעַ אֵין סוֹף בָּרוּךְ הוּא — the energetic flow to
the soul is **the first emergence of a** *deep flow* **of Divine energy, produced by
the Blessed Infinite One,** כְּמוֹ שֶׁכָּתוּב וַיִּפַּח וְכוּ' — **which is the meaning of the
verse, "And (G-d) blew."**

In contrast to the Divine energy which powers the universe, the soul's energy
is "the *first emergence* and *deep flow* of Divine energy."

If G-d's connection with our souls is so profound, why do we not always
feel it?

The *Tanya* explains:

וְאַחַר כָּךְ יָרְדָה בְּסֵתֶר הַמַּדְרֵגָה — Afterwards, the soul **journeys downwards
through** *"the hidden places in the steps"* (Song 2:14), it passes down through
the spiritual worlds, a process which masks its inner energy.

The soul never loses its deep attachment with G-d, but the relationship does
become veiled as the soul descends down from the heavens.

שבמאמר נעשה אדם וכו' כדי להתלבש בגוף עוה"ז
התחתון. ולכן נקראו המלאכי' בשם אלקים בכתוב
וכמ"ש כי ה' אלקיכם אלקי האלקי' כו' הודו לאלקי

גַּם כֵּן עַל יְדֵי בְּחִינַת הָאוֹתִיּוֹת שֶׁבְּמַאֲמַר נַעֲשֶׂה אָדָם וְכוּ' — And the soul **is also** channeled **through the letters of the verbal statement,** *"Let us make man"* (Genesis 1:26), **כְּדֵי לְהִתְלַבֵּשׁ בְּגוּף עוֹלָם הַזֶּה הַתַּחְתּוֹן** — to enter a body, in this physical world.

While the soul is rooted in the deep energy of G-d's "blowing," it nevertheless has to pass through the filter of the more superficial energy of G-d's "speech," because *everything* in the universe is created through Divine speech. This is the meaning of the Divine statement, *"Let us make man":* G-d took the high-energy "breath" of the soul and filtered it through His lower-energy "speech."

We have explained how the soul is rooted in G-d's most sacred name, the Tetragrammaton, based on the verse, *"For G-d's (Havayah's) portion are His people."* This is in contrast to the rest of creation that is associated with the Divine name *Elokim,* referring to G-d's power of restraint and diminishment (see Part Two, Chapter 4).

וְלָכֵן נִקְרְאוּ הַמַּלְאָכִים בְּשֵׁם אֱלֹקִים בַּכָּתוּב — And that is why Scripture will sometimes **refer to the angels with the name** *elokim,* a name which usually refers to G-d.

Elokim literally means "judges." While it is a term which usually refers to G-d, scripture occasionally uses *elokim* to refer to angels, as the *Tanya* now demonstrates.

וּכְמוֹ שֶׁכָּתוּב כִּי ה' אֱלֹקֵיכֶם [הוּא] אֱלֹקֵי הָאֱלֹקִים כו' — As the verse states, *"For G-d your G-d is the G-d of elokim etc.,"* (Deuteronomy 10:17), **הוֹדוּ לֵאלֹקֵי הָאֱלֹקִים כו'** — and the verse states, *"Give thanks to the G-d of elokim etc.,"* (Psalms 136:2),

A CHASIDIC THOUGHT

"Our Sages said that 'each and every soul was in the presence of His Divine Majesty before coming down to this earth,' and that 'the souls are hewn from under the Seat of Glory.' These sayings emphasize the essential nature of the soul, its holiness and purity, and its being completely divorced from anything material and physical; the soul itself, by its very nature, is not subject to any material desires or temptations."

(From a Letter of the Rebbe, 10th Kislev 5714)

האלקי' כו' ויבאו בני האלקי' להתייצב כו'. לפי שיניקת
חיותם היא מבחי' חיצוניות שהיא בחי' האותיות לבד
ושם אלקים הוא בחי' חיצוניות לגבי שם הוי' ב"ה.
אבל נשמת האדם שהיא מבחי' פנימי' החיות היא
חלק שם הוי' ב"ה. כי שם הוי' מורה על פנימי' החיות
שהיא למעלה מעלה מבחי' האותיות. וביאור הענין
כנודע ממאמר אליהו אנת הוא דאפיקת עשר תיקונין

וַיָּבֹאוּ בְּנֵי הָאֱלֹקִים לְהִתְיַצֵּב כו' — and the verse states, ***"The children of elokim
came to stand etc.,"*** (Job 1:6).

(The *Tanya* cites three verses corresponding to angels in the three spiritual
worlds of *Beriah, Yetzirah* and *Asiyah—Likutei Levi Yitzchak.*)

Why are the angels called "*elokim*"?

לְפִי שֶׁיְּנִיקַת חַיּוּתָם הִיא מִבְּחִינַת חִיצוֹנִיּוּת — **Because** angels **receive their energy from an external** energetic flow from G-d, **שֶׁהִיא בְּחִינַת הָאוֹתִיּוֹת לְבַד** —
the mere "letters" of Divine "speech," **וְשֵׁם אֱלֹקִים הוּא בְּחִינַת חִיצוֹנִיּוּת לְגַבֵּי שֵׁם
הֲוָיָ"ה בָּרוּךְ הוּא** — **and the** Divine name *Elokim* is "**external**" **compared with the
blessed Divine name** *Havayah*.

The angels are derived from the diminished energy of G-d's "speech." As a
hint to this, they are sometimes referred to as "*elokim*," a name indicating the
diminishment of Divine energy.

אֲבָל נִשְׁמַת הָאָדָם — **Man's soul, on the other hand,** **שֶׁהִיא מִבְּחִינַת פְּנִימִיּוּת הַחַיּוּת** —
is from a deep Divine **energy,** **הִיא חֵלֶק שֵׁם הֲוָיָ"ה בָּרוּךְ הוּא** — **it is a "portion" of the Divine name** *Havayah,* **כִּי שֵׁם הֲוָיָ"ה מוֹרֶה עַל פְּנִימִיּוּת הַחַיּוּת** — **and
*Havayah*** is a name that **refers to a deep energy,** **שֶׁהִיא לְמַעְלָה מַעְלָה מִבְּחִינַת
הָאוֹתִיּוֹת** — **which vastly transcends the level of** Divine "**letters**" of "speech."

SECTION THREE: THE TETRAGRAMMATON

15TH TAMMUZ REGULAR | 21ST TAMMUZ LEAP

In Section Three the *Tanya* explained how the soul, in its root, is connected
with the sacred Tetragrammaton. In this section we will decode the meaning of
the four letters of the Tetragrammaton.

וּבֵאוּר הָעִנְיָן — **Let's explore the matter further.**

כַּנּוֹדָע מִמַּאֲמָר אֵלִיָּהוּ — **We are familiar with Elijah's teaching** in *Tikunei Zohar*
(17a).

וקרינן להון עשר ספירן לאנהגא בהון עלמין סתימין
וכו'. אנת חכים ולא בחכמה ידיעא אנת מבין ולא
בבינה ידיעא וכו'. וכל הי' ספירות נכללות ונרמזות

94B

אַנְתְּ הוּא דְאַפֵּיקַת עֲשַׂר תִּקּוּנִין וְקָרֵינַן לְהוֹן עֲשַׂר סְפִירָן לְאַנְהָגָא בְּהוֹן עָלְמִין סְתִימִין
וְכוּ' — **"It is You who produced ten 'adornments,' we call them the ten sefiros,
to conduct hidden worlds...."** אַנְתְּ חַכִּים וְלָא בְּחָכְמָה
יְדִיעָא — **"You are wise, but not with a known wisdom
(chochmah),"** אַנְתְּ מֵבִין וְלָא בְּבִינָה יְדִיעָא וְכוּ' — **"You
understand, but not with a known understanding
(binah) etc."**

PRACTICAL LESSONS

The ten fundamental
Divine energies
(*sefiros*) are:

chochmah (inquiry);

binah (cognition);

da'as (recognition);

chesed, (love;
kindness; giving);

gevurah (power;
judgment;
discipline, fear);

tiferes (beauty;
compassion;
harmony; truth);

netzach (endurance);

hod (splendor;
gratitude);

yesod (connection);

malchus (control;
manifestation).

This is a primary source text for the ten *sefiros* (energies) which constitute the Divine realm. The ten *sefiros* are: *chochmah* (inquiry), *binah* (cognition), *da'as* (recognition), *chesed*, (love; kindness; giving), *gevurah* (power; judgment; discipline; fear), *tiferes* (beauty; compassion; harmony; truth), *netzach* (endurance), and *hod* (splendor; gratitude), *yesod* (connection), and *malchus* (control; manifestation).

(Sometimes the list of ten *sefiros* also includes the transcendent energy of *keser* (crown; will), in which case *da'as* is excluded from the list; see *Etz Chaim* 23:8.)

The *sefiros* are not *creations*, separate from G-d, but rather, *emanations* or *energies* that remain bound with His absolute oneness, *"like a flame in a burning coal"* (*Sefer Yetzirah* 1:7; see Translator's Introduction to Part Two, pp. xi-xvii).

וְכָל הָעֲשַׂר סְפִירוֹת נִכְלָלוֹת וְנִרְמָזוֹת בְּשֵׁם הֲוָיָ"ה בָּרוּךְ הוּא
— **All the ten *sefiros* are represented in the** letters of the name *Havayah* and they are also **hinted to by the** shapes of the letters.

The four-lettered Tetragrammaton contains the ten *sefiros* in code. As we shall see, the *sefiros* are even encoded in the *shape* of the letters.

How are *ten* energies represented by just *four* letters? The *Tanya* will devote the rest of this section to explaining the "code" in detail.

בשם הוי' ב"ה. כי היו"ד שהיא בחי' נקודה לבד
מרמזת לחכמתו ית' שהיא בבחי' העלם והסתר קודם
שבאה לבחי' התפשטות וגילוי ההשגה וההבנה (והקוץ
שעל היו"ד רומז לבחי' רצון העליון ב"ה שלמעלה

(The *sefiros* are found both in the Divine realm and in the human soul. Through identifying the human experience associated with each of the *sefiros* we can begin to imagine how that energy manifests in the Divine realm.)

כִּי הַיּוֹ"ד שֶׁהִיא בְּחִינַת נְקֻדָּה לְבַד — **The first letter** of the Tetragrammaton, *yud,* which typographically **is just a small point,** מְרַמֶּזֶת לְחָכְמָתוֹ יִתְבָּרֵךְ — **hints to G-d's** *chochmah,* שֶׁהִיא בְּבְחִינַת הָעֶלֶם וְהֶסְתֵּר קֹדֶם שֶׁבָּאָה לִבְחִינַת הִתְפַּשְּׁטוּת וְגִלּוּי הַהַשָּׂגָה וְהַהֲבָנָה — **which begins in a totally concealed state and then diffuses outwards to power the intellectual process.**

As we discussed in Part One (Chapter Three), *chochmah* is the beginning of the intellectual process, the moment when an inspirational idea or concept pops into your head. It is the *initial experience* of thought which is *undeveloped*. In the Divine realm it corresponds to the first emergence of energy which powers everything that follows, and is represented by the *first* letter of the Tetragrammaton. The form of that letter, the *yud*, is a relatively shapeless point ('), hinting to the undeveloped nature of *chochmah*.

Chochmah is a bridge between formlessness and form. The energies below *chochmah* have distinct forms, far more than a simple "point." The energies above *chochmah* have no form at all, and cannot be represented typographically. *Chochmah* sits in the middle: it is the initial emergence of form, but undeveloped. It is just a dot.

(וְהַקּוֹץ שֶׁעַל הַיּוֹ"ד רוֹמֵז לִבְחִינַת רָצוֹן הָעֶלְיוֹן בָּרוּךְ הוּא שֶׁלְמַעְלָה מַעְלָה מִמַּדְרֵגַת בְּחִינַת חָכְמָה עִילָּאָה כַּנּוֹדָע) — **And the "thorn" above the *yud* hints to the Divine will,** *keser,* **which utterly transcends supernal** *chochmah,* **as is known** from *Zohar* (3, 2a).

← THORN

When drawn scribally, the *yud* is not a completely shapeless dot; it contains a thorn-like protrusion. Unlike the main body of the *yud*, which, while small, does manage to spread itself across a certain space, the thorn is tiny and thin, and merely points to something else. It is as if the thorn is saying, "What I represent is too subtle to be depicted visually by a letter, so I am just pointing to something outside and beyond." The thorn of the *yud*, which points upwards, alludes to the transcendent quality of *will* which drives all of our activities—mental, emotional and practical—and yet cannot be associated with a certain organ or "place" in our bodies. In the Divine realm, the thorn of the *yud* represents the formless energies which transcend *chochmah*.

מעלה ממדרגת בחי' חכמה עילאה כנודע). ואחר
שבאה לבחי' התפשטות וגילוי ההשגה וההבנה לעלמין
סתימין נכללת ונרמזת באות ה"א שיש לה בחי'
התפשטות לרוחב המורה ומרמז על הרחבת הביאור
וההבנה וגם לאורך המורה על בחי' ההמשכה וההשפעה
מלמעלה למטה לעלמין סתימין. ואח"כ כשנמשכת
המשכה וההשפעה זו יותר למטה לעלמין דאתגליין.
וכמו האדם שרוצה לגלות חכמתו לאחרים ע"י דיבורו
עד"מ. נכללת ונרמזת המשכה זו באותיות ו"ה. כי

וְאַחַר שֶׁבָּאָה לִבְחִינַת הִתְפַּשְּׁטוּת וְגִלּוּי הַהַשָּׂגָה וְהַהֲבָנָה לְעָלְמִין סְתִימִין — **Afterwards, when** *chochmah* **diffuses further and is disclosed within the mental process of** *binah* **in the hidden worlds,** נִכְלֶלֶת וְנִרְמֶזֶת בְּאוֹת הֵ"א — **it is represented by the** second **letter** of the Tetragrammaton, *hei,* **and hinted to by** its shape.

שֶׁיֵּשׁ לָהּ בְּחִינַת הִתְפַּשְּׁטוּת לָרֹחַב הַמּוֹרָה וּמְרַמֵּז עַל הַרְחָבַת הַבֵּאוּר וְהַהֲבָנָה — *Hei* hints to *binah* **since** typographically the letter **fills the full width** of the font, **representing and hinting to the outward expression** of a concept, as it becomes clarified and understood.

וְגַם לָאֹרֶךְ הַמּוֹרֶה עַל בְּחִינַת — **The** *hei* also fills the full letter **height** of the font, הַהַמְשָׁכָה וְהַהַשְׁפָּעָה מִלְמַעְלָה לְמַטָּה לְעָלְמִין סְתִימִין — **hinting to the downward flow of energy,** filling **the "hidden worlds"** of *chochmah* and *binah.*

Since *chochmah* is a mere point or flash of intellect, it seeks articulation, which requires assistance from a completely different energy. The faculty of *binah* (cognition) is represented by the second letter of the Tetragrammaton, *hei* (ה). Spatially, the *hei* has everything the *yud* lacks: it is fully formed in both dimensions of width and height, indicative of the cognitive ability to flesh out a raw idea and explore all its possible ramifications, rationally and objectively. In the Divine realm, the height and width of the *hei* represents the full development of forms within *binah.*

Binah absorbs the spark of *chochmah*, shapes it and refines it. It systematizes, organizes and characterizes, focusing entirely on the parts rather than the whole.

כְּשֶׁנִּמְשֶׁכֶת הַמְשָׁכָה וְהַשְׁפָּעָה זוֹ יוֹתֵר לְמַטָּה לְעָלְמִין — **Subsequently,** וְאַחַר כָּךְ דְּאִתְגַּלְיָין — **when this flow reaches further downwards, to the "revealed worlds,"** וּכְמוֹ הָאָדָם שֶׁרוֹצֶה לְגַלּוֹת חָכְמָתוֹ לַאֲחֵרִים עַל יְדֵי דִּבּוּרוֹ עַל דֶּרֶךְ מָשָׁל — **like the stage, for example, where a person wants to disclose his idea verbally to somebody else,** נִכְלֶלֶת וְנִרְמֶזֶת הַמְשָׁכָה זוֹ בְּאוֹתִיּוֹת ו"ה — this stage **is represented by the** last **two letters** of the Tetragrammaton, *vav* and *hei,* **and hinted by** their shape.

הוי"ו מורה על ההמשכה מלמעלה למטה. וגם
המשכה זו היא ע"י מדת חסדו וטובו ושאר מדותיו
הקדושות הנכללות בדרך כלל במספר שש שבפסוק
לך ה' הגדולה וכו' עד לך ה' הממלכה וכו' ולא עד

The four letters of the Tetragrammaton are divided into two groups. The first two letters, *yud* and *hei*, have a mental energy, and are described as "hidden worlds," like your thoughts that are hidden from other people. The last two letters, *vav* and *hei* have an emotional energy, which is "revealed," like your emotions which express you feelings.

In the "hidden worlds" Divine energies are nurtured and formed *in potential*. That is why *binah* is compared to a Divine "womb," in which energies grow and gestate before they are disclosed. Once they emerge from *binah* the energies shift to the second two letters of the Tetragrammaton, which represent "revealed worlds."

(All this is of course, *relatively speaking*. These are still energies *within* the Divine realm before they are disclosed to the universe.)

The *Tanya* decodes the significance of the last two letters.

כִּי הַוָּי"ו מוֹרֶה עַל הַהַמְשָׁכָה מִלְמַעְלָה לְמַטָּה — **Since the *vav*,** a vertical line which resembles a downward arrow, **represents the flow downwards** from the "hidden worlds" (*yud* and *hei*) into the "revealed worlds," וְגַם הַמְשָׁכָה זוֹ הִיא עַל יְדֵי — **and this flow is also powered by G-d's** emotional **attribute** מִדַּת חַסְדּוֹ וְטוּבוֹ of *chesed* **(benevolence) and goodness,** וּשְׁאָר מִדּוֹתָיו הַקְּדוֹשׁוֹת — **and His** other five holy emotional **attributes,** הַנִּכְלָלוֹת בְּדֶרֶךְ כְּלָל בְּמִסְפַּר שֵׁשׁ — **which are all included in the general category** of the *vav*, **whose numerical value is six.**

The significance of the *vav*, the third letter of the Tetragrammaton, is twofold. The *vav* is a vertical line visually depicting the journey of communication, taking the energy of *chochmah* through *binah*, and processing it through the emotions. In the Divine realm this represents the emergence of potential energies from the "womb" of *binah* and their outward manifestation into "revealed worlds."

A further significance of the *vav* is its numerical value, six. This hints to the fact that the "emotional" energies represented by this letter are six in number.

שֶׁבַּפָּסוּק לְךָ ה' הַגְּדֻלָּה וְכו' — These are the six Divine emotional attributes **mentioned in the verse, "Yours, G-d are gedulah,** *gevurah, tiferes, netzach, and hod, for all (ba-kol) that is in heaven and earth"* (1 Chronicles 29:11).

The energies which G-d possesses (they are "Yours") are: *gedulah* (another name for *chesed*), *gevurah*, *tiferes*, *netzach*, and *hod*. *"For all"* (*ba-kol*) is *yesod*

בכלל. כי מדת מלכותו ית' נק' בשם דבר ה' כמ"ש
באשר דבר מלך שלטון ונכללת ונרמזת באות ה"א

(connection), the sixth energy, which gathers "all" of the energies above it and channels them below.

The verse continues: *"Yours, G-d is the kingdom."* The *Tanya* now clarifies that this refers to a different energy, not included with the previous six.

עַד לְךָ ה' הַמַּמְלָכָה וְכוּ' וְלֹא עַד בִּכְלָל — The six energies of the *vav* are represented by the words in the verse **until *"Yours, G-d is the kingdom etc.,"* up to but not including** this phrase.

"Yours, G-d is the kingdom" refers to *malchus* (control; manifestation), which, as we shall see, is represented by the last letter of the Tetragrammaton, the second *hei*.

PRACTICAL LESSONS

The four letters of the Tetragrammaton represent the flow of energy in the Divine realm which is mirrored by the flow of intellect and emotions in your soul.

The *Tanya* explains why *malchus* is different from the six energies above it (represented by the *vav*), therefore requiring a different letter.

כִּי מִדַּת מַלְכוּתוֹ יִתְבָּרַךְ נִקְרֵאת בְּשֵׁם דְּבַר ה' — *"Yours, G-d is the kingdom"* refers to G-d's **attribute of *malchus* which is** not considered one of the six emotional attributes of G-d, rather **it is called G-d's *"word,"*** כְּמוֹ שֶׁכָּתוּב בַּאֲשֶׁר דְּבַר מֶלֶךְ שִׁלְטוֹן — **as the verse states,** *"For a king's word is power"* (*Ecclesiastes* 8:4).

The six emotional energies represented by the *vav* remain inwardly experienced feelings. They are outwardly directed: they are feelings about something or somebody else; but they are not yet actually expressed.

Malchus, on the other hand, is the power of *actual* manifestation; it is the only Divine energy which has a *direct influence* on the universe. That is why it is compared to sovereign power, which directly controls a country. *Malchus* is also symbolized by speech, a *tool of influence,* that follows after internal processing through intellect and emotion.

וְנִכְלֶלֶת וְנִרְמֶזֶת בְּאוֹת ה"א אַחֲרוֹנָה שֶׁל שֵׁם הֲוָיָ"ה — *Malchus* **is represented by the final *hei* of the Tetragrammaton, and hinted to** by the shape of the *hei,* as follows.

In order to explain the metaphor of *malchus* as Divine speech, the *Tanya* will first review the physiology of human speech, as described in Jewish mystical sources.

אחרונה של שם הוי'. כי פנימי' ומקור הדיבור הוא ההבל
העולה מן הלב ומתחלק לה' מוצאות הפה אחה"ע
מהגרון וכו'. וגם הברת הה"א היא בחי' הבל לבד
כמ"ש אתא קלילא דלית בה מששא. ואף שאין לו

כִּי פְּנִימִיּוּת וּמְקוֹר הַדִּבּוּר הוּא הַהֶבֶל הָעוֹלֶה מִן הַלֵּב — **The source of speech** inside **the body is the breath that rises from** the thoracic cavity around **the heart,** וּמִתְחַלֵּק לַחֲמֵשׁ מוֹצָאוֹת הַפֶּה — and that breath **is then divided by the five organs of speech,** the throat, palate, tongue, teeth and lips, into various letters (*Sefer Yetzirah* 2:3; see *Tanya,* Part Two, p. 35).

אחה"ע מֵהַגָּרוֹן וְכוּ' — The letters *alef, ches, hei* and *ayin* are formed **by the throat, etc.**

The letters *beis, vav, mem* and *pei* are formed by the lips.

The letters *zayin, samech, tzadik* and *shin* are formed by the teeth.

The letters *daled, tes, lamed, nun* and *taf* are formed by the tongue.

The letters *gimmel, yud, kaf* and *kuf* are formed by the palette (*Zohar* 3, 227b).

The letter *hei,* whose numerical value is five, therefore hints to "speech," since speech is produced by five "organs."

וְגַם הֲבָרַת הַהֵ"א הִיא בְּחִינַת הֶבֶל לְבַד — The letter *hei* has a **further** connection with speech since it is a letter **produced from pure breath,** without any organ of speech, כְּמוֹ שֶׁכָּתוּב אָתָא קַלִּילָא דְּלֵית בַּהּ מַשָּׁשָׁא — as **stated** in the liturgical poem *Akdamus* that the *hei* is, *"a light letter that has no substance."*

Hei (like the letter 'h' in English) is produced from breath alone. It therefore is a direct expression of *"the source of speech inside the body... the breath that rises from the thoracic cavity around the heart."*

For these reasons, the last letter of the Tetragrammaton, *hei,* hints to Divine "speech," *i.e., malchus.* As a number, *hei* hints to the five organs of speech; and as a letter it hints to the breath which powers that speech.

Obviously, G-d does not have a physical body, so how are we to understand this very physical analogy of "breath," "thoracic cavity" and "speech organs" in reference to G-d?

PRACTICAL LESSONS

When the Torah uses the metaphor of "speech" in reference to G-d, it means His power of manifestation (*malchus*).

The "letters" of G-d's speech are packets of energy which power the universe.

דְּמוּת הַגּוּף ח"ו. אַךְ דִּבְּרָה תוֹרָה כִּלְשׁוֹן בְּנֵי אָדָם.
בְּשֶׁגַּם שֶׁגַּם דְּבַר ה' כ"ב אוֹתִיּוֹת הַמִּתְחַלְּקוֹת לְה'
חֶלְקֵי הַמּוֹצָאוֹת וּבָהֶן נִבְרָא כָּל הַיְצוּר (וּכְמ"ש בְּלִקּ"א

95A

וְאַף שֶׁאֵין לוֹ דְּמוּת הַגּוּף חַס וְשָׁלוֹם — **And while G-d "has no semblance of a body"** (*Liturgy, Yigdal; Rambam, Third Principle of Faith*), **G-d forbid,** אַךְ דִּבְּרָה תוֹרָה כִּלְשׁוֹן בְּנֵי אָדָם — **nevertheless, "the Torah speaks** (of G-d) **in human terms"** (*Talmud, Brachos* 31b), employing these metaphors to teach us about spiritual energies that resemble, in some subtle way, the role of these physical forms.

בְּשֶׁגַּם שֶׁגַּם דְּבַר ה' כ"ב אוֹתִיּוֹת הַמִּתְחַלְּקוֹת לַחֲמֵשׁ חֶלְקֵי הַמּוֹצָאוֹת — Metaphorical-ly, **even G-d's "word,"** *malchus,* **also has twenty-two "letters" that are divided by five** Divine **"organs" of articulation,** וּבָהֶן נִבְרָא כָּל הַיְצוּר — **through which every form was created.**

In Kabbalah and Chasidus, the physical descriptions of G-d refer to *real spiritual phenomena.* G-d's "speech" and even "speech organs" describe the energy of *malchus* which has a similar role to human speech, that of *outward manifestation.*

(וּכְמוֹ שֶׁנִּתְבָּאֵר בְּלִקּוּטֵי אֲמָרִים חֵלֶק ב פֶּרֶק י"א בְּאוֹר עִנְיָן אוֹתִיּוֹת אֵלּוּ) — **As was ex-plained in** *Tanya,* **Part Two, Chapter Eleven, in the discussion of these** Divine **letters.**

"All forms of energy and power which flow from the Divine attributes to the lower worlds to create them something-from-nothing, to energize them and sustain them, are called "sacred (Divine) letters," the channels of energy which flow from G-d's will/intellect/emotions to create the worlds and energize them" (Part Two, page 159).

"Now the (Divine letters) are twenty-two different channels of energy flow, powers that differ from one another and through them all the worlds were created, upper and lower, as well as all the creatures within them, for it arose in G-d's will and wisdom to create the world with exactly twenty-two types of energetic flow, no more, and no less" (ibid., page 163).

SECTION THREE: THE TETRAGRAMMATON IN THE SOUL

16TH TAMMUZ LEAP

In Section Two we discussed the Tetragrammaton primarily as it applies to the energies *of the Divine realm.* The *Tanya* will teach us here how the same energies are present, albeit in an "infinitely removed" way, *in the human soul,* since the soul is derived from G-d's inner self.

ח"ב פי"א ביאור ענין אותיות אלו). וככה ממש עד"מ
המבדיל הבדלות לאין קץ בנשמת האדם שהיא בחי'
נפש האלקי' דמתוכיה נפח יש בה בחי' שכל הנעלם
המרומז באות יו"ד שבכחו לצאת אל הגילוי להבין
ולהשכיל באמתתו ית' ובגדולתו וכו' כל חד וחד לפום
שיעורא דילי' לפי רוחב שכלו ובינתו. וכפי אשר
מעמיק שכלו ומרחיב דעתו ובינתו להתבונן בגדולתו
ית' אזי מרומזת בינתו באות ה"א שיש לה רוחב וגם
אורך המורה ההמשכה מלמעלה למטה להוליד מבינתו

וְכָכָה מַמָּשׁ עַל דֶּרֶךְ מָשָׁל — **And the same** Tetragrammaton is present **precise-**
ly (though **figuratively speaking**), in the human soul, **הַמַּבְדִּיל הַבְדָּלוֹת לְאֵין קֵץ**
— (since the comparison is obviously an utterly inadequate one, as a human
being is **infinitely removed** from G-d).

בְּנִשְׁמַת הָאָדָם — The Tetragrammaton is present in **the human soul, שֶׁהִיא**
בְּחִינַת נֶפֶשׁ הָאֱלֹקִית דְּמִתּוֹכֵיהּ נָפַח — meaning to say, it is present in **the Divine**
soul, which G-d **blew from within Himself,** as we discussed in Section One.

We learned in Part One (Chapter One), that a person possesses two souls, a
Divine Soul and an Animal Soul. The *Tanya* makes clear that we are speaking
here of the former.

The *Tanya* will now take each of the four letters of the Tetragrammaton and
explain their expression in human worship.

יֵשׁ בָּהּ בְּחִינַת שֵׂכֶל הַנֶּעֱלָם הַמְרֻמָּז בְּאוֹת יוֹ"ד — The Divine soul **contains** *choch-*
mah, an undeveloped and therefore **elusive intellect, hinted by the letter** *yud,*
שֶׁבְּכֹחוֹ לָצֵאת אֶל הַגִּלּוּי לְהָבִין וּלְהַשְׂכִּיל בַּאֲמִתָּתוֹ יִתְבָּרֵךְ וּבִגְדֻלָּתוֹ וְכוּ' — **which then**
powers the tangible intellectual processing of *binah,* which in terms of prac-
tical worship means **understanding the truth of G-d and His greatness, etc.,**
כָּל חַד וְחַד לְפוּם שִׁעוּרָא דִּילֵיהּ לְפִי רֹחַב שִׂכְלוֹ וּבִינָתוֹ — *"each individual accord-*
ing to his own capabilities" (*Zohar* 1:103a), **according to his** or her **intellectual/**
cognitive capacity.

The *Tanya* explains how this is hinted to in the shape of the *hei.*

וּכְפִי אֲשֶׁר מַעֲמִיק שִׂכְלוֹ וּמַרְחִיב דַּעְתּוֹ וּבִינָתוֹ לְהִתְבּוֹנֵן בִּגְדֻלָּתוֹ יִתְבָּרֵךְ — **When a**
person thinks deeply, expanding his or her **mind and cognitive powers, to**
contemplate the greatness of G-d, אֲזַי מְרֻמֶּזֶת בִּינָתוֹ בְּאוֹת ה"א — **that process**
of *binah* **is hinted to by the** shape of the **letter** *hei,* **שֶׁיֵּשׁ לָהּ רֹחַב** — **which is a**
wide letter, representing the expansion of cognitive powers.

וְהִתְבּוֹנְנוּתוֹ בִּגְדוּלַת ה' אַהֲבָה וְיִרְאָה וְתוֹלְדוֹתֵיהֶן
בְּמוֹחוֹ וְתַעֲלוּמוֹת לִבּוֹ וְאַחַ"כ בִּבְחִי' הִתְגַּלּוּת לִבּוֹ.
וּמִזֶּה נִמְשְׁכָה עֲבוֹדָה הָאֲמִיתִית בְּעֵסֶק הַתּוֹרָה וְהַמִּצְוֹת
בְּקוֹל וְדִבּוּר אוֹ מַעֲשֶׂה הֵן אוֹתִיּוֹת וָא"ו ה"א וְכוּ'. וְגַם
הַהִתְבּוֹנְנוּת לְהָבִין וּלְהַשְׂכִּיל בַּאֲמִתַּתוֹ וּגְדוּלָתוֹ יִת'
נִמְשְׁכָה גַּ"כ מֵהַתּוֹרָה דְּאוֹרַיְיתָא מֵחָכְמָה נָפְקָא הִיא
בְּחִי' יוּ"ד שֶׁל שֵׁם הֲוָי' וְכוּ':

וְגַם אֹרֶךְ הַמּוֹרֶה הַהַמְשָׁכָה מִלְמַעְלָה לְמַטָּה — **And the** vertical **height of the** *hei* signifies **the application** of the idea, לְהוֹלִיד מִבְּינָתוֹ וְהִתְבּוֹנְנוּתוֹ בִּגְדֻלַּת ה' אַהֲבָה, **to produce love and reverence** of G-d **from the** *binah* **process and contemplation of G-d's greatness,** וְתוֹלְדוֹתֵיהֶן — **and** to produce **the derivative** emotions which arise from love and reverence.

We turn to the "experience" of the last two letters of the Tetragrammaton, *vav* and *hei*.

בְּמוֹחוֹ וְתַעֲלוּמוֹת לִבּוֹ — **The emotions generated by** *binah* initially arise **in the brain and in the "hidden places in the heart"** (*Psalms* 44:22; see Part One, p. 191), וְאַחַר כָּךְ בִּבְחִינַת הִתְגַּלּוּת לִבּוֹ — **and subsequently they become palpable in the heart,** which is the "experience" of *vav,* emotional expression.

וּמִזֶּה נִמְשְׁכָה עֲבוֹדָה הָאֲמִתִּית — **Love and reverence of G-d** (*vav*) then **lead to genuine worship** which is the "experience" of *hei,* actual manifestation, בְּעֵסֶק הַתּוֹרָה וְהַמִּצְוֹת — **through Torah study and** *mitzvah* **observance,** בְּקוֹל וְדִבּוּר אוֹ מַעֲשֶׂה — **verbally, using the voice, or through action.**

הֵן אוֹתִיּוֹת וָא"ו ה"א וְכוּ' — **These two processes** of: a.) emotional expression; followed by, b.) practical worship, **are represented by the** last two **letters** of the Tetragrammaton *vav* **and** *hei,* respectively.

In a concluding thought, the *Tanya* notes a further allusion in the letter *yud*.

וְגַם הַהִתְבּוֹנְנוּת לְהָבִין וּלְהַשְׂכִּיל בַּאֲמִתָּתוֹ וּגְדֻלָּתוֹ יִתְבָּרַךְ נִמְשָׁכָה גַּם כֵּן מֵהַתּוֹרָה — **The contemplative process** of *binah,* **the cognition and comprehension of the truth of G-d's existence and His greatness, is also powered by the Torah,** דְּאוֹרַיְיתָא מֵחָכְמָה נָפְקָא — **for** *"Torah emerged from chochmah"* (*Zohar* 2, 85a), הִיא בְּחִינַת יוּ"ד שֶׁל שֵׁם הֲוָי"ה וְכוּ' — **and** *chochmah* **is the** *yud* **of the Tetragrammaton.**

In the Tetragrammaton, *yud* is followed by *hei* to indicate that contemplation (*binah; hei*) is powered by *chochmah* (*yud*). Practically speaking we use Torah sources to provide the raw materials for our contemplation process. This is a further hint in the *yud,* which also alludes to the Torah which *"emerged from chochmah."*

פרק ה והנה   המשכת וירידת הנפש האלקי׳
לעוה״ז להתלבש בגוף האדם
נמשכה מבחי׳ פנימי׳ ומקור הדיבור הוא הבל העליון

CHAPTER 5

HOW SINS AFFECT YOUR SOUL

SECTION ONE: THE SOUL'S CONNECTION IN THIS WORLD

17TH TAMMUZ REGULAR | 22ND TAMMUZ LEAP

In Chapter Four the *Tanya* explained how, in its heavenly source, your soul is rooted in G-d's sacred name, the Tetragrammaton. Now we will learn how even when your soul descends into this world, it retains that connection.

וְהִנֵּה הַמְשָׁכַת וִירִידַת הַנֶּפֶשׁ הָאֱלֹקִית לָעוֹלָם הַזֶּה — **Now** as for **the process of bringing down the Divine soul** from its heavenly source **into this world,** לְהִתְלַבֵּשׁ **and placing it in a person's body,** בְּגוּף הָאָדָם — נִמְשָׁכָה מִבְּחִינַת פְּנִימִיּוּת וּמְקוֹר הַדִּבּוּר — this process **is powered by** Divine **speech,** or, to be precise, **the deep source** of Divine speech, הוּא הֶבֶל הָעֶלְיוֹן — **which is the Divine "breath."**

In Chapter Four we learned that speech contains two components. *Letters* are the "superficial" expression of speech, formed when breath hits one of the five organs of speech. *Breath* is the "inner" aspect of speech, which rises from deep inside the thoracic cavity.

This is also true of Divine "speech," (a metaphor for G-d's power of manifestation, *malchus*). The "superficial" expression of Divine "speech" is its constituent "letters," which are "packets" of creative energy. Within those letters is the "deep source" of Divine speech, namely, the Divine "breath."

The *Tanya* teaches us here that the soul, *even as it is found below in this world,* retains a connection with "the deep source" of Divine speech, the Divine "breath."

הַמְרֻמָּז בְּאוֹת הֵ"א תַּתָּאָה כַּנַּ"ל — **This is hinted to by the second letter** *hei* of the Tetragrammaton, **mentioned above.**

As we learned in Chapter Four, the letter *hei* (comparable to 'h' in English) is produced from breath alone. It therefore is a direct expression of, *"the source of speech inside the body... the breath that rises from the thoracic cavity around the heart."*

המרומז באות ה"א תתאה כנ"ל וכמ"ש ויפח באפיו
נשמת חיים ויהי האדם לנפש חיה ומאן דנפח וכו'.
וז"ש כי חלק ה' עמו יעקב חבל נחלתו פי' כמו חבל
עד"מ שראשו א' קשור למעלה וקצהו למטה. כי הנה

The Divine "breath" with which the soul retains a connection in this world is represented by the last *hei* of the Tetragrammaton.

The *Tanya* cites proof from scripture.

וּכְמוֹ שֶׁכָּתוּב וַיִּפַּח בְּאַפָּיו נִשְׁמַת חַיִּים וַיְהִי הָאָדָם לְנֶפֶשׁ חַיָה — **As the verse states, "And (G-d) blew into his nostrils the breath of life, and the man had a living soul"** (*Genesis* 2:7), וּמַאן דְּנָפַח וְכוּ' — **And "one who blows,** blows from his innards," (cited in Part One, p. 45 in the name of the *Zohar*).

This verse describes the soul's shifting identity as it passes from its heavenly source into a body. In heaven, G-d "blew" the soul *"from His innards."*

PRACTICAL LESSONS

Even after descending into this world, the soul retains a connection with the Tetragrammaton, specifically its last letter *hei*.

However, the fact that the soul's passage down to earth (*"and the man had a living soul"*) is mentioned in the *same verse* as G-d's initial blowing, suggests that even on earth the soul doesn't totally forget its connection with the innermost depths of G-d.

The *Tanya* offers us another proof for this idea.

וְזֶהוּ שֶׁכָּתוּב כִּי חֵלֶק ה' עַמּוֹ יַעֲקֹב חֶבֶל נַחֲלָתוֹ — **And this is the meaning of the verse, "For G-d's portion is His people, Ya'akov His allotted (chevel) inheritance"** (*Deuteronomy* 32:9; see Part One, p. 584).

The unusual use of the term *chevel* here, which usually refers to a "rope," invites interpretation.

The soul remains connected to the deeper level of Divine "breath" in contrast to the rest of the universe which only has a connection to the more superficial Divine "speech."

פֵּרוּשׁ כְּמוֹ חֶבֶל עַל דֶּרֶךְ מָשָׁל — **This means that** the soul below remains connected above, **like a rope, for example,** שֶׁרֹאשׁוֹ אֶחָד קָשׁוּר לְמַעְלָה וְקָצֵהוּ לְמַטָּה — **that is tied on one end above, and the other end below.**

The "rope" analogy hints to the soul's ongoing connection with its source, despite its formidable journey into this world.

פשט הכתוב מ"ש ויפח הוא להורות לנו כמו שעד"מ
כשהאדם נופח לאיזה מקום אם יש איזה דבר חוצץ
ומפסיק בינתיים אין הבל הנופח עולה ומגיע כלל
לאותו מקום ממש אם יש דבר חוצץ ומפסיק

95B

SECTION TWO: THE SPIRITUAL MEANING OF KAREIS

The remainder of Chapter Five is aimed at clarifying a question posed in Chapter Four: What is the *spiritual mechanism* of *kareis* and "death through the agency of heaven"? To answer this question, we need to examine what happens to the soul when a person sins.

מַה שֶּׁכָּתוּב וַיִּפַּח כִּי הִנֵּה פְּשַׁט הַכָּתוּב — **Now the simple meaning of the verse,** הוּא לְהוֹרוֹת לָנוּ כְּמוֹ שֶׁעַל — **of what is written, "***And (G-d) blew,***" is to teach us,** דֶּרֶךְ מָשָׁל כְּשֶׁהָאָדָם נוֹפֵחַ לְאֵיזֶה מָקוֹם — **that, for example, when a person blows toward a certain destination,** אִם יֵשׁ אֵיזֶה דָּבָר חוֹצֵץ וּמַפְסִיק בֵּינְתַיִם — **and there is some sort of blockage or obstruction between the** person and that destination, אֵין הֶבֶל הַנּוֹפֵחַ עוֹלֶה וּמַגִּיעַ כְּלָל לְאוֹתוֹ מָקוֹם — **the air which has been blown will not travel toward or reach its destination at all.**

Above we explained G-d's "blowing" of the soul as a hint to the soul's deep root in Divine energy. Here the *Tanya* offers us a different interpretation of the metaphor. The success of blowing air depends on the absence of any blockage between the blower and the chosen destination.

כָּכָה מַמָּשׁ אִם יֵשׁ דָּבָר חוֹצֵץ וּמַפְסִיק בֵּין הָאָדָם וּבֵין גּוּף לִבְחִינַת הֶבֶל הָעֶלְיוֹן — **In the exact same way, if there is something blocking or obstructing a person's body from Divine "breath,"** that "breath" will not reach the body.

Speech, on the other hand, *can* pass through a physical obstruction and be heard.

The "obstruction" here refers to a sin which carries the penalty of *kareis* or "death through the agency of heaven." Such an obstruction blocks the person's connection to deep Divine energy, compared to "breath"; but it will not block the connection to Divine "speech," the general energy which powers the universe.

This explains why *"in earlier times the transgressor would actually die physically"* (above, Chapter Four). Premature death was an inevitable, *natural consequence* of the sin. Once a Divine Soul (from Divine "breath") becomes disconnected from its source, a person's core energy has been lost, and he will die prematurely.

בֵּין גּוּף הָאָדָם לַבְּחִי' הַבֶל הָעֶלְיוֹן. אַךְ בֶּאֱמֶת אֵין
שׁוּם דָּבָר גַשְׁמִי וְרוּחָנִי חוֹצֵץ לְפָנָיו ית' כִּי הֲלֹא אֶת
הַשָּׁמַיִם וְאֶת הָאָרֶץ אֲנִי מָלֵא וּמְלֹא כָּל הָאָרֶץ כְּבוֹדוֹ
וְלֵית אֲתָר פָּנוּי מִינֵי' בַּשָּׁמַיִם מִמַּעַל וְעַל הָאָרֶץ מִתָּחַת
אֵין עוֹד וְאִיהוּ מְמַלֵּא כָל עָלְמִין וְכוּ' אֶלָּא כמ"ש בִּישַׁעְיָ'
כִּי אִם עֲווֹנוֹתֵיכֶם הָיוּ מַבְדִּילִים בֵּינֵיכֶם לְבֵין אֱלֹקֵיכֶם.

But that is only the case for one who possesses a Divine Soul. That is why other creations who do not have this soul, do not experience *kareis* (Based on *Likutei Sichos* vol. 39, p. 68).

The *Tanya* presents a problem with the above analysis:

אַךְ בֶּאֱמֶת אֵין שׁוּם דָּבָר גַּשְׁמִי וְרוּחָנִי חוֹצֵץ לְפָנָיו יִתְבָּרַךְ — **However, in reality, there is no physical or spiritual thing that can obstruct G-d's presence,** כִּי הֲלֹא אֶת הַשָּׁמַיִם וְאֶת הָאָרֶץ אֲנִי מָלֵא — **for "'Do I not fill heaven and earth?' says G-d"** (*Jeremiah* 23:24), וּמְלֹא כָל הָאָרֶץ כְּבוֹדוֹ — **and "All the earth is filled with His glory"** (*Isaiah* 6:3), וְלֵית אֲתָר פָּנוּי מִינֵיהּ — **and "there is no place empty of Him"** (*Tikunei Zohar* 91b), בַּשָּׁמַיִם מִמַּעַל וְעַל הָאָרֶץ מִתָּחַת אֵין עוֹד — **"G-d is G-d in the heavens above and on the earth below, there is none else"** (*Deuteronomy* 4:39), וְאִיהוּ מְמַלֵּא כָּל עָלְמִין וְכוּ' — **and G-d, "fills all worlds"** (see *Zohar* 3, 225a).

What does it mean, then, for the soul to be "disconnected" from G-d? Isn't G-d found everywhere?

The *Tanya* answers:

אֶלָּא כְּמוֹ שֶׁכָּתוּב בִּישַׁעְיָהוּ כִּי אִם עֲוֹנֹתֵיכֶם הָיוּ מַבְדִּלִים בֵּינֵכֶם לְבֵין אֱלֹקֵיכֶם — **Rather** the meaning of this "disconnection" is, **as written in *Isaiah*, "But your sins have separated between you and your G-d"** (*Isaiah* 59:2).

G-d is indeed found everywhere. The disconnection which occurs through sin does not mean that G-d's presence has departed; rather, it means that *the person is unable to receive it.*

A CHASIDIC THOUGHT

"When a person follows the paths of Torah, he draws upon himself a holy supernal spirit, as the verse states, *'Until a spirit from on high is poured upon us'* (*Isaiah* 32:15). But when a person perverts his ways, he draws upon himself another spirit from the *Sitra Achra*, which is the side of impurity."

(*Zohar* 3, 122a)

וְהַטַּעַם לְפִי שֶׁהֵם נֶגֶד רָצוֹן הָעֶלְיוֹן ב"ה המחי' את
הכל כמ"ש כל אשר חפץ ה' עשה בשמים ובארץ
(וכמש"ל שהוא מקור השפעת שם הוי' ונרמז בקוצו
של יו"ד). וזהו ענין הכרת. שנכרת ונפסק חבל
ההמשכה משם הוי' ב"ה שנמשכה מה"א תתאה

This is the meaning of the verse, "Your sins have separated *between you* and your G-d." The separation is from your perspective, not from G-d's.

וְהַטַּעַם לְפִי שֶׁהֵם נֶגֶד רָצוֹן הָעֶלְיוֹן בָּרוּךְ הוּא הַמְחַיֶּה אֶת הַכֹּל — **And the reason for this is because** sins **are a violation of the Divine will, which is the energetic** source **of everything,** כְּמוֹ שֶׁכָּתוּב כֹּל אֲשֶׁר חָפֵץ ה' עָשָׂה בַּשָּׁמַיִם וּבָאָרֶץ — **as the verse states,** *"Whatever G-d desired, He did in the heavens and in the earth"* (*Psalms* 135:6).

Nothing in the universe can, of its own accord, disconnect from its Maker. But *if G-d wills so* there can be a disconnection. G-d's will is the energetic source of everything, and a sin represents a violation of that will (or "desire"). Once G-d's will is no longer present, *"the energetic source of everything"* is lacking, and we have a disconnect.

(וּכְמוֹ שֶׁנִּתְבָּאֵר לְעֵיל שֶׁהוּא מְקוֹר הַשֶּׁפַע שֵׁם הֲוָיָ"ה וְנִרְמָז בְּקוֹצוֹ שֶׁל יוּ"ד) — **As ex-plained above** in Chapter Four, **that the Divine will is the source of energetic flow to the universe through the Tetragrammaton, hinted to by the "thorn" of the** *yud.*

As we learned in Chapter Four, the most elevated portion of the Tetragram-maton is the "thorn" of the *yud,* which represents the Divine will.

The "thorn" is the *source* of the energy of the Tetragrammaton's four letters. If the "thorn" is damaged, through violating the Divine will, the flow of energy to the remaining four letters will be compromised.

וְזֶהוּ עִנְיַן הַכָּרֵת — **And this explains the** spiritual dynamic **of** *kareis* and "death through the agency of heaven," שֶׁנִּכְרֵת וְנִפְסַק חֶבֶל הַהַמְשָׁכָה מִשֵּׁם הֲוָיָ"ה בָּרוּךְ הוּא — **that the "rope" channeling** energy **from the Tetragrammaton** to the person **is "cut" and interrupted.**

Kareis is therefore not an imposed punishment, that follows after a sin. Rath-er, it is an inevitable, natural consequence of the sin. The "apparatus" carrying the flow is damaged, so the flow stops.

The *Tanya* reminds us of the "location" in the Tetragrammaton where the soul is connected.

שֶׁנִּמְשְׁכָה מֵהֵ"א תַּתָּאָה כַּנַּ"ל — **As stated above,** at the beginning of this chapter, **that** the Divine soul is connected to G-d's deep **flow** of energy **through the second** *hei* of the Tetragrammaton.

כנ"ל. וכמ"ש בפ' אמור ונכרתה הנפש ההיא מלפני
אני ה'. מלפני דייקא. ובשאר עבירות שאין בהן כרת
עכ"פ הן פוגמין הנפש כנודע. ופגם הוא מלשון
פגימת הסכין והוא עד"מ מחבל עב שזור מתרי"ג חבלים
דקים ככה חבל ההמשכה הנ"ל כלול מתרי"ג מצות
וכשעובר ח"ו על אחת מהנה נפסק חבל הדק וכו'.

The *Tanya* cites a verse that illustrates this point:

וּכְמוֹ שֶׁכָּתוּב בְּפָרָשַׁת אֱמוֹר וְנִכְרְתָה הַנֶּפֶשׁ הַהִיא מִלְפָנַי אֲנִי ה' — **As stated in the Torah portion of** *Emor*, *"And that soul will be cut off from before Me, I am G-d"* (*Leviticus* 22:3), מִלְפָנַי דַּיְיקָא — **the verse stresses** *"from before Me."*

Being *"cut off… from before Me,"* implies that the soul is disconnected from the Tetragrammaton ("Me").

SECTION THREE: THE SPIRITUAL MEANING OF OTHER SINS

In Section Two we learned that through a sin which carries the penalty of *kareis* or "death through the agency of heaven" the Divine Soul becomes completely "cut off" from its source in the Tetragrammaton.

Now we turn to the issue of lesser sins that do not have this severe penalty. What happens to the soul when they are violated?

וּבִשְׁאָר עֲבֵרוֹת שֶׁאֵין בָּהֶן כָּרֵת — **And in the case of other sins that are not punishable by** *kareis* **or "death through the agency of heaven,"** עַל כָּל פָּנִים הֵן פּוֹגְמִין הַנֶּפֶשׁ כַּנּוֹדָע — **they do at least inflict some damage (***pegam***) to the soul,** even though they do not cut it off completely, **as is known** (*Zohar* 1, 73b).

What, exactly, is this "damage"? Is it something undesirable that is *added* to the soul, or something that is *taken away*?

וּפְגָם הוּא מִלְשׁוֹן פְּגִימַת הַסַּכִּין — **The term** *pegam* **here has the connotation of the "defect" in a knife** (*Talmud*, *Chulin* 17b).

A knife used for ritual slaughter becomes defective when part of the blade *is lacking*. The *Tanya* therefore informs us: the *pegam* of the soul means that part of its connection is taken away.

מֵחֶבֶל עָב שָׁזוּר מִתַּרְיַ"ג חֲבָלִים — **A good illustration of this,** וְהוּא עַל דֶּרֶךְ מָשָׁל — **is a thick rope woven of 613 fine strands,** כָּכָה חֶבֶל הַהַמְשָׁכָה הַנַּ"ל כָּלוּל — **since the above-mentioned energetic flow** from the Tetragrammaton to the soul **is through the 613** *mitzvos,* מִתַּרְיַ"ג מִצְוֹת — **and when a person, G-d forbid, transgresses one** וּכְשֶׁעוֹבֵר חַס וְשָׁלוֹם עַל אַחַת **of them, a fine strand** of the rope is cut. מֵהֶנָה נִפְסַק חֶבֶל הַדַּק וְכוּ'

אַךְ גַּם בְּחַיָּיב כָּרֵת וּמִיתָה נִשְׁאַר עֲדַיִין בּוֹ הָרְשִׁימוּ
מִנַּפְשׁוֹ הָאֱלֹקִי' וְעִי"ז יָכוֹל לִחְיוֹת עַד נ' אוֹ ס' שָׁנָה
וְלֹא יוֹתֵר (וּמַ"שׁ בְּשֵׁם הָאֲרִיזַ"ל שֶׁנִּכְנְסָה בּוֹ בְּחִי'

The violation of *any* of the 613 *mitzvos* compromises, to some extent, the connection between the soul and its root in the Tetragrammaton.

Multiple transgressions of different sins are also *cumulative,* they each sever one strand of the "rope" (as we will discuss below, in Chapter Seven).

But this does not compare to *kareis* which causes a disconnect of the *entire soul* from its root in the Tetragrammaton.

SECTION FOUR: THE DELAYED EFFECTS OF KAREIS

In Chapter Four we learned: *"In earlier times the transgressor would actually die physically before reaching the age of fifty, and for a transgression whose punishment is 'death through the agency of heaven,' he would literally die physically before reaching the age of sixty."*

But if, as we have learned in this chapter, *kareis* causes the soul to be disconnected *immediately,* how is it possible for the person to continue living at all?

אַךְ גַּם בְּחַיָּיב כָּרֵת וּמִיתָה — However, even a person who is punishable by *kareis* or death, נִשְׁאַר עֲדַיִין בּוֹ הָרְשִׁימוּ מִנַּפְשׁוֹ הָאֱלֹקִית — still retains an "impression" of his Divine Soul, וְעַל יְדֵי זֶה יָכוֹל לִחְיוֹת עַד חֲמִשִּׁים אוֹ שִׁשִּׁים שָׁנָה — through which he can live until the age of fifty or sixty years, וְלֹא יוֹתֵר — but no more than that.

While the soul remains disconnected from its source after *kareis,* nevertheless, an "impression" of the soul's energy remains in the body — not unlike the impression made by a pen on the sheet of paper underneath the sheet you have written on.

Since this "impression" has a reduced energy, in earlier times it would bring about a reduced lifespan.

(וּמַה שֶּׁאָמְרוּ בְּשֵׁם הָאֲרִיזַ"ל שֶׁנִּכְנְסָה בּוֹ בְּחִינַת הַמַּקִּיף וְכוּ' — And as for the teaching attributed to *Arizal,* that one who is liable for *kareis* receives a *makif* soul (*Likutei Torah, Isaiah* 57).

Arizal speaks of two elements to the soul: an inner energy and a "surrounding" (*makif*) one. One who is liable for *kareis* still has the latter, so why would the *makif* not enable him to live more than fifty years?

The *Tanya* answers:

הַמַּקִּיף וכו' אינו ענין לחיי גשמיות הגוף ומיירי עד נ'
שנה או בזמן הזה כדלקמן):

אֵינוֹ עִנְיָן לְחַיֵּי גַּשְׁמִיּוּת הַגּוּף — The *makif* is a "surrounding," *non-interactive* energy that **does not relate to the physical life of the body** and therefore cannot
sustain it.

Arizal's teaching about the presence of a *makif* is therefore relevant to somebody that is *already* alive. That person will not be kept alive by the *makif*.

וּמַיְירֵי עַד חֲמִשִּׁים שָׁנָה — **Namely,** someone **before the age of fifty** in earlier
times, (**אוֹ בַּזְּמַן הַזֶּה כְּדִלְקַמָּן**) — **or** someone in **the current era,** when the limit of
fifty years no longer applies, **as we shall explain** in Chapter 6.

פרק ו אמנם זהו בזמן שהיו ישראל במדרגה
עליונה כשהיתה השכינה שורה
בישראל בבהמ"ק. ואז לא היו מקבלים חיות לגופם
רק ע"י נפש האלקי' לבדה מבחי' פנימי' השפע
שמשפיע א"ס ב"ה ע"י שם הוי' ב"ה כנ"ל. אך לאחר

96A

CHAPTER 6

THE MEANING OF "EXILE"

SECTION ONE: THE (NON)EFFECT OF KAREIS DURING EXILE

18TH TAMMUZ REGULAR | 23RD TAMMUZ LEAP

In Chapter Four the *Tanya* noted that, *"In earlier times the transgressor would actually die physically before reaching the age of fifty, and for a transgression whose punishment is 'death through the agency of heaven,' he would literally die physically before reaching the age of sixty."*

Why did this only occur "in earlier times" and not nowadays?

The *Tanya* will now address this point.

אָמְנָם זֶהוּ בִּזְמַן שֶׁהָיוּ יִשְׂרָאֵל בְּמַדְרֵגָה עֶלְיוֹנָה — **However, this** physical death resulting from *kareis* only occurred in earlier generations **when the Jewish people were at a high** spiritual level, **כְּשֶׁהָיְתָה הַשְּׁכִינָה שׁוֹרָה בְּיִשְׂרָאֵל בְּבֵית הַמִּקְדָּשׁ — and when the *Shechinah*** (Divine Presence) **rested in Israel, in the holy Temple.**

This "high spiritual level" resulted in a different relationship between the Divine soul and its body.

וְאָז לֹא הָיוּ מְקַבְּלִים חַיּוּת לְגוּפָם — **And then,** being at a high spiritual level the people of Israel **only received energy to their bodies,** רַק עַל יְדֵי נֶפֶשׁ הָאֱלֹקִית מִבְּחִינַת פְּנִימִיּוּת הַשֶּׁפַע שֶׁמַּשְׁפִּיעַ אֵין סוֹף לְבַדָּהּ — **through the Divine Soul alone,** בָּרוּךְ הוּא עַל יְדֵי שֵׁם הֲוָיָ"ה בָּרוּךְ הוּא — *i.e.,* **from a deep flow coming from the Blessed Infinite One through the Tetragrammaton,** כַּנַּ"ל — **as above,** Chapter Four.

In Temple times, the body was *directly* powered by the Divine Soul (which, as we learned earlier, delivers the energy of the Tetragrammaton).

שירדו ממדרגתם וגרמו במעשיהם סוד גלות השכינה כמ"ש ובפשעיכם שולחה אמכם דהיינו שירדה השפעת בחי' ה"א תתאה הנ"ל ונשתלשלה ממדרגה למדרגה למטה מטה עד שנתלבשה השפעתה בי"ס דנוגה

אַךְ לְאַחַר שֶׁיָּרְדוּ מִמַּדְרֵגָתָם — **However,** this changed **after their** spiritual **level declined,** with the Temple's destruction, וְגָרְמוּ בְּמַעֲשֵׂיהֶם סוֹד גָּלוּת הַשְּׁכִינָה — **and they caused through their** negative **actions, the mystical "exile of the *Shechinah,"*** כְּמוֹ שֶׁכָּתוּב וּבְפִשְׁעֵיכֶם שֻׁלְּחָה אִמְּכֶם — **as the verse states, *"Through your transgressions is your mother sent away"*** (*Isaiah* 50:1; *Zohar* 1, 22b; *Eimek Ha-Melech, Sha'ar Tikunei Avonos* chapter 9).

The destruction of the Temple was not only a physical displacement from our most holy site, it also caused an alienation of the Divine Presence (*Shechinah*) from the world. This is called the mystical "exile of the *Shechinah*." (Since *Shechinah* is feminine Divine energy, its exile is referred to by the verse "your mother (is) sent away.")

How does the departure of *Shechinah* affect the energetic flow to our world?

דְּהַיְינוּ שֶׁיָּרְדָה הַשְׁפָּעַת בְּחִינַת הֵ"א תַּתָּאָה הַנַּ"ל וְנִשְׁתַּלְשְׁלָה מִמַּדְרֵגָה לְמַדְרֵגָה לְמַטָּה מַטָּה — **This means to say that the** energetic **flow from the** second, **"lower" *hei* of the Tetragrammaton, mentioned above** (Chapters 4-5), **was downgraded multiple times, in a descending chain of events,** עַד שֶׁנִּתְלַבְּשָׁה הַשְׁפָּעָתָהּ בְּעֶשֶׂר סְפִירוֹת דְּנֹגַהּ — **to the point where the energy** of the second *hei* of the Tetragrammaton **became filtered through the ten *sefiros*** **(energies) of *nogah.***

As we learned at length in Part One of *Tanya, nogah* is a type of *kelipah* (negative energy) that conceals the presence of G-d. *Nogah,* too, has "ten (negative) *sefiros"* mirroring the ten positive energies. This is because *"G-d has made one opposite the other"* (*Ecclesiastes* 7:14), so that the architecture of the negative realm mirrors the positive (see Part One, Chapter 6).

A CHASIDIC THOUGHT

"We recognize the exile as a punishment and rectification for failure to live up to our obligations in the past as, indeed, we acknowledge in our prayers, 'For our sins we were banished from our land.' But punishment, according to our Torah, called *Toras Chesed* (a Torah of kindness), must also essentially be *Chesed.*"

(From a Letter of the Rebbe)

המשפיעות שפע וחיות ע"י המזלות וכל צבא השמים
והשרים שעליהם לכל החי הגשמי שבעוה"ז וגם לכל
הצומח כמארז"ל אין לך כל עשב מלמטה שאין לו
מזל וכו'. ואזי יכול גם החוטא ופושעי ישראל לקבל
חיות לגופם ונפשם הבהמיות כמו שאר בע"ח ממש

The *Tanya* teaches us here that while in Temple times the soul had direct access to the energy of the Tetragrammaton, once the *Shechinah* was exiled that access stopped. Now the entire universe is sustained through the filter of *kelipah,* which hides G-d's presence.

הַמַּשְׁפִּיעוֹת שֶׁפַע וְחַיּוּת עַל יְדֵי הַמַּזָּלוֹת וְכָל צְבָא הַשָּׁמַיִם וְהַשָּׂרִים שֶׁעֲלֵיהֶם — Prior to that, the ten *sefiros* of *nogah* already **provided the energetic flow of energy to the constellations and all the heavenly bodies, and the angels appointed over them,** לְכָל הַחַי הַגַּשְׁמִי שֶׁבָּעוֹלָם הַזֶּה—which provide the energetic flow **to every living thing in this physical world,** וְגַם לְכָל הַצּוֹמֵחַ — **even to vegetation,** כְּמַאֲמַר רַזַ"ל אֵין לְךָ כָּל עֵשֶׂב מִלְּמַטָּה שֶׁאֵין לוֹ מַזָּל וְכוּ' — **as in the teaching of our Sages, *"There is no blade of grass below that does not have a mazal (spiritual energy) that strikes it and says, 'Grow!'"* (*Genesis Rabah* 10:6)**

The physical world had always been powered by *nogah.* In Temple times *an exception was made,* and the bodies of Israel were able to be powered directly through the energy of the Tetragrammaton in their souls. With the destruction of the Temple and the departure of the *Shechinah,* this stopped, and the bodies of Israel became powered by *nogah,* like the rest of the physical world.

וַאֲזַי יָכוֹל גַּם הַחוֹטֵא וּפוֹשְׁעֵי יִשְׂרָאֵל — **So then,** during exile, **even people who transgress** and join *"the sinners of Israel"* (see *Talmud, Rosh Hashanah* 17a), לְקַבֵּל חַיּוּת לְגוּפָם וְנַפְשָׁם הַבַּהֲמִיּוֹת כְּמוֹ שְׁאָר בַּעֲלֵי חַיִּים מַמָּשׁ — **receive energy for their bodies and Animal Souls in exactly the same way as other living creatures,** כְּמוֹ שֶׁכָּתוּב נִמְשַׁל כַּבְּהֵמוֹת נִדְמוּ — **as the verse states, *"He is likened to beasts that are doomed"* (*Psalms* 39:13).**

G-d energizes the powers of *nogah* regardless of their behavior. So, during exile, even if a person receives *kareis* and is cut off from the Tetragrammaton, he can continue to live, since his body is in any case not energized by the Tetragrammaton but from *nogah,* whose energetic flow is unconditional.

SECTION TWO: WHY THE WICKED PROSPER

We have clarified why *"in earlier times the transgressor would actually die physically before reaching the age of fifty,"* but not in exile times.

כמ"ש נמשל כבהמות נדמו. ואדרבה ביתר שאת
ויתר עז עפ"י המבואר מזוה"ק פ' פקודי שכל שפע
וחיות הנשפעת לאדם התחתון בשעה ורגע שעושה
הרע בעיני ה' במעשה או בדיבור או בהרהורי עבירה
וכו' הכל נשפע לו מהיכלות הסט"א המבוארים שם

Now we will turn to another question posed in Chapter Four: How could those who are liable for *kareis* live "long, happy lives"?

וְאַדְרַבָּה בְּיֶתֶר שְׂאֵת וְיֶתֶר עֹז — **On the contrary** those who are liable for *kareis* can receive their energetic flow more powerfully, *"with more strength and more power"* (*Genesis* 49:3), and therefore they live "long, happy lives."

The *Tanya* explains this irony based on a teaching of the *Zohar*.

עַל פִּי הַמְבֹאָר מִזֹּהַר הַקָּדוֹשׁ פָּרָשַׁת פְּקוּדֵי — **As is explained by the holy Zohar in** its commentary **on the Torah portion of** *Pekudei* (2, 236b; 247a), שֶׁכָּל שֶׁפַע וְחַיּוּת, הַנִּשְׁפַּעַת לְאָדָם הַתַּחְתּוֹן בְּשָׁעָה וְרֶגַע שֶׁעוֹשֶׂה הָרַע בְּעֵינֵי ה' — **that all of the ener-getic flow which a person receives** in this world **below, at the very moment he** sins and does *"evil in the eyes of G-d"* (*ibid.*, 38:7), בְּמַעֲשֶׂה אוֹ בְּדִבּוּר אוֹ בְּהִרְהוּרֵי — by transgressing **in action, in speech or in** thought, (through con-templating a sin, etc.), עֲבֵרָה וְכוּ' — הַכֹּל נִשְׁפָּע לוֹ מֵהֵיכְלוֹת הַסִּטְרָא אַחֲרָא — at that moment energy **flows to him exclusively from the chambers of** *Sitra Achra,* הַמְבֹאָרִים שָׁם בַּזֹּהַר הַקָּדוֹשׁ — as explained in the *Zohar* (*ibid.*, 242b. 244b, 263a).

As we have seen in the previous section, during exile times the body is en-ergized by the negative forces of *nogah*. However, if a person chooses to sin, at that moment his body is energized by a far more negative energy: the *Sitra Achra* which is *completely* negative.

(*Nogah*, on the other hand, has a positive side, and can become a vehicle for the positive and the holy, through the appropriate actions and consciousness.)

A CHASIDIC THOUGHT

"The extraordinary quality of *teshuvah*, which transcends all limitations, including the limita-tions of time, is that 'in one moment' it trans-forms the whole past, to the degree of absolute perfection in quality and spirituality."

(From a Letter of the Rebbe, 6th Tishrei 5739)

96B

בזוה"ק. והאדם הוא בעל בחירה אם לקבל השפעתו
מהיכלות הסט"א או מהיכלות הקדושה שמהם נשפעות
כל מחשבות טובות וקדושות וכו'. כי זה לעו"ז עשה
האלקי' וכו'. והיכלות הסט"א מקבלים ויונקים חיותם
מהתלבשות והשתלשלות השפע די"ס דנוגה הכלולה
מבחי' טו"ר היא בחי' עה"ד וכו' כנודע לי"ח. והנה
יעקב חבל נחלתו כתיב. עד"מ כמו החבל שראשו

וְהָאָדָם הוּא בַּעַל בְּחִירָה אִם לְקַבֵּל הַשְׁפָעָתוֹ — **And a person has free choice,** מֵהֵיכְלוֹת הַסִּטְרָא אַחֲרָא — **whether to accept the** completely negative **flow from the chambers of** *Sitra Achra,* אוֹ מֵהֵיכְלוֹת הַקְּדָשָׁה שֶׁמֵּהֶם נִשְׁפָּעוֹת כָּל מַחֲשָׁבוֹת טוֹבוֹת וּקְדוֹשׁוֹת וְכוּ' — **or** to receive flow **from the chambers of holiness, which power all good thoughts etc.,** כִּי זֶה לְעֻמַּת זֶה עָשָׂה הָאֱלֹקִים וְכוּ' — **for** *"G-d has made one opposite the other,"* (*Ecclesiastes* 7:14; see Part One, p. 83), and we have the choice.

As we discussed at length in Part One, everything we do, say or think can either strengthen the forces of good or the *Sitra Achra,* depending on the choice of activity and the consciousness with which we direct it.

The *Tanya* further explains the damage caused by a sin.

וְהֵיכְלוֹת הַסִּטְרָא אַחֲרָא מְקַבְּלִים וְיוֹנְקִים חַיּוּתָם מֵהִתְלַבְּשׁוּת וְהִשְׁתַּלְשְׁלוּת הַשֶּׁפַע דְּעֶשֶׂר סְפִירוֹת דְּנֹגַהּ — **Without sinful activity, the chambers of** *Sitra Achra* usually **receive and suck their energetic flow from what has been downgraded and filtered into the ten** *sefiros* **of** *nogah,* הַכְּלוּלָה מִבְּחִינַת טוֹב וָרַע — and *nogah* **is not completely evil, and contains both good and evil,** הִיא בְּחִינַת עֵץ הַדַּעַת וְכוּ' — **having the energy of the "Tree of Knowledge of good and evil," as is known to Kabbalists** (*Etz Chaim* 49:2; see Part One, Chapter One). כַּנּוֹדָע לְיוֹדְעֵי חֵ"ן

In the absence of sinful activity, the *Sitra Achra* receives its energy from *nogah,* which contains a mixture of good and evil.

Through a sin, however, the *Sitra Achra* is granted an independent source of energy from the soul of the sinner (powered by the Tetragrammaton!) and this inflates the *Sitra Achra* with a power it should never have.

19TH TAMMUZ REGULAR | 24TH TAMMUZ LEAP

The *Tanya* will illustrate this point with our earlier "rope" (*chevel*) analogy, used in a different context above, in Chapter Five. (For its application here see *Shaloh, Beis Hashem Beis David.*)

וְהִנֵּה יַעֲקֹב חֶבֶל נַחֲלָתוֹ כְּתִיב — **Now the verse states,** *"Ya'akov His allotted*

א' למעלה וראשו השני למטה אם ימשוך אדם בראשו
השני ינענע וימשך אחריו גם ראשו הראשון כמה
שאפשר לו להמשך. וככה ממש בשרש נשמת האדם
ומקורה מבחי' ה"א תתאה הנ"ל הוא ממשיך ומוריד
השפעתה ע"י מעשיו הרעים ומחשבותיו עד תוך
היכלות הסט"א כביכול שמשם מקבל מחשבותיו
ומעשיו. ומפני שהוא הוא הממשיך להם ההשפעה
לכן הוא נוטל חלק בראש וד"ל. וזהו שאמרו רז"ל

(chevel) inheritance" (Deuteronomy 32:9), עַל דֶּרֶךְ מָשָׁל — which offers us a practical illustration of how a sin channels negative energy, as follows.

כְּמוֹ הַחֶבֶל שֶׁרֹאשׁוֹ אֶחָד לְמַעְלָה וְרֹאשׁוֹ הַשֵּׁנִי לְמַטָּה — Just as with a rope, which has one end above and the other below, אִם יִמְשֹׁךְ אָדָם בְּרֹאשׁוֹ הַשֵּׁנִי — if a person will pull at the second, bottom end, יְנַעְנֵעַ וְיִמָּשֵׁךְ אַחֲרָיו גַּם רֹאשׁוֹ הָרִאשׁוֹן — the top end will move and be drawn towards him, to the extent that he is able to pull it, וְכָכָה מַמָּשׁ בְּשֹׁרֶשׁ נִשְׁמַת הָאָדָם וּמְקוֹרָהּ מִבְּחִינַת ה"א תַּתָּאָה הַנַּ"ל — so too, precisely, is the case with a human soul, rooted in the energy of the second, "lower hei" of the Tetragrammaton, as above, הוּא מַמְשִׁיךְ וּמוֹרִיד הַשְׁפָּעָתָהּ עַל יְדֵי מַעֲשָׂיו הָרָעִים וּמַחְשְׁבוֹתָיו עַד תּוֹךְ הֵיכְלוֹת הַסִּטְרָא אַחֲרָא כְּבְיָכוֹל — a person's bad actions/thoughts cause the energy of the lower hei to, so to speak, be drawn and pulled down into the chambers of Sitra Achra!

And this explains why those liable for kareis live "long, happy lives," since they draw from the Sitra Achra more powerfully.

שֶׁמִּשָּׁם מְקַבֵּל מַחְשְׁבוֹתָיו וּמַעֲשָׂיו — For the Sitra Achra is where the evil thoughts and deeds are received, וּמִפְּנֵי שֶׁהוּא הוּא הַמַּמְשִׁיךְ לָהֶם הַהַשְׁפָּעָה — and since this person is the one who is directing the flow there, giving the power of the Tetragrammaton to the Sitra Achra, לָכֵן הוּא נוֹטֵל חֵלֶק בְּרֹאשׁ — therefore this person is the one that receives "the first portion" (Talmud, Yoma 14a), of flow from the Sitra Achra.

The sinner has provided the Sitra Achra with a far greater energy supply than it could otherwise have obtained, so the Sitra Achra rewards the sinner with "the first portion," a bountiful flow of energy. That is why sinners can live "long, happy lives."

PRACTICAL LESSONS

If you sin, it drags the energy of the Tetragrammaton from your soul down into the negative forces.

אֵין בְּיָדֵינוּ לֹא מִשַּׁלְוַת הָרְשָׁעִים וְכוּ' בְּיָדֵינוּ דּוּקָא
כְּלוֹמַר בִּזְמַן הַגָּלוּת אַחַר הַחוּרְבָּן. וְזוֹהִי בְּחִי' גָלוּת
הַשְּׁכִינָה כִּבְיָכוֹל לְהַשְׁפִּיעַ לְהֵיכְלוֹת הַסְטְ"א אֲשֶׁר
שָׂנֵא נַפְשׁוֹ יִתְ'. וּכְשֶׁהָאָדָם עוֹשֶׂה תְשׁוּבָה נְכוֹנָה אֲזַי
מְסַלֵּק מֵהֶם הַהַשְׁפָּעָה שֶׁהִמְשִׁיךְ בְּמַעֲשָׂיו וּמַחְשְׁבוֹתָיו.

וְדַי לַמֵּבִין — **And this** explanation **should suffice for the intelligent** reader.

The *Tanya* offers a further support for the above explanation from the *Mishnah.*

וְזֶהוּ שֶׁאָמְרוּ רַזַ"ל אֵין בְּיָדֵינוּ לֹא מִשַּׁלְוַת הָרְשָׁעִים וְכוּ' — **And this is the meaning of** what our Sages taught, *"It is not in our hands to fathom the peace of the wicked or the suffering of the righteous"* (Mishnah, Avos 4:15), בְּיָדֵינוּ דּוּקָא — **the key emphasis here being,** *"our hands,"* כְּלוֹמַר בִּזְמַן הַגָּלוּת אַחַר הַחוּרְבָּן — **mean- ing** our **post Temple, exilic times.**

A close reading of the *Mishnah* supports our above insight into the "long happy lives" of the wicked. The *Mishnah,* which was authored during exile, states, *"It is not in our hands to fathom the peace of the wicked,"* suggesting that the happy lives of the wicked is a phenomenon of "our hands," *i.e.,* exile times.

The above explanation will also help us to explain more profoundly "the exile of the *Shechinah*" in metaphysical terms.

וְזוֹהִי בְּחִינַת גָּלוּת הַשְּׁכִינָה כִּבְיָכוֹל — **And this is "the exile of the *Shechinah*,"** so to speak, לְהַשְׁפִּיעַ לְהֵיכְלוֹת הַסְטְרָא אַחֲרָא אֲשֶׁר שָׂנֵא נַפְשׁוֹ יִתְבָּרֵךְ — that she is forced **to provide** energetic **flow to the chambers of the *Sitra Achra*, which G-d deeply detests.**

Above we learned that during exile, the lower *hei* of the Tetragrammaton is "exiled" within the *partially* negative energy of *nogah.* Through sinful activity, however, an even deeper exile occurs as the energy of the lower *hei* of the Tetragrammaton is directed by the sinner (from his soul) into the *totally* nega- tive forces of *Sitra Achra.* This is a true "exile of the *Shechinah.*"

The chapter concludes on a positive note, how this damage can be rectified though *teshuvah.*

וּכְשֶׁהָאָדָם עוֹשֶׂה תְשׁוּבָה נְכוֹנָה — **And when the person will repent in an acceptable fashion,** אֲזַי מְסַלֵּק מֵהֶם הַהַשְׁפָּעָה שֶׁהִמְשִׁיךְ בְּמַעֲשָׂיו וּמַחְשְׁבוֹתָיו — he or she **removes the flow which he** or she **brought** to the chambers of the *Sitra Achra,* **through his** or her **deeds and thoughts,** כִּי בִּתְשׁוּבָתוֹ מַחֲזִיר הַשְׁפָּעַת הַשְּׁכִינָה לִמְקוֹמָהּ — **because his** or her **repentance restores the flow of** *Shechinah* **to its** appropriate **place.**

כי בתשובתו מחזיר השפעת השכינה למקומה. וזהו
תשוב ה"א תתאה מבחי' גלות וכמ"ש ושב ה' אלקיך
את שבותך כלומר עם שבותך וכמאמר רז"ל והשיב
לא נאמר וכו':

וְזֶהוּ תָּשׁוּב הֵ"א תַּתָּאָה מִבְּחִינַת גָּלוּת — **And this is the meaning of** *teshuvah* **spelling** *"tashuv (return) hei,"* (above, Chapter Four), **since it returns the lower** *hei*
(which is the *Shechinah*) **from a state of exile.**

וּכְמוֹ שֶׁכָּתוּב וְשָׁב ה' אֱלֹקֶיךָ אֶת שְׁבוּתְךָ — **As the verse states,** *"G-d, your G-d, will
return you from your captivity,"* (Deuteronomy 30:3), כְּלוֹמַר עִם שְׁבוּתֶךָ — **as if
to say:** *Shechinah* **will herself return** *with* **your captivity.**

The *Tanya* cites a teaching of the *Talmud* which illustrates this idea.

וּכְמַאֲמַר רַזַ"ל וְהֵשִׁיב לֹא נֶאֱמַר וְכוּ' — **As in the saying of our Sages,** *"The verse
does not say, 'He will bring back,' but that He Himself will return"* (Talmud,
Megillah 29a, cited in *Rashi* ibid.).

In the following chapter we will discuss this concept, and its practical implementation, in more detail.

פרק ז ואולם   דרך האמת והישר לבחי' תשובה
תתאה ה"א תתאה הנ"ל הם ב'

CHAPTER 7

KEEPING IT AUTHENTIC

SECTION ONE: TWO SUGGESTIONS FOR AUTHENTIC TESHUVAH

20TH TAMMUZ REGULAR | 25TH TAMMUZ LEAP

We learned in Chapter Six that unlike the rest of creation, which is formed through the more superficial power of G-d's "speech," your soul is rooted in a deeper Divine energy, compared to Divine "breath." Another way the *Tanya* phrased this idea was: your soul is connected with the Tetragrammaton, the actual "name" (deep energy) of G-d.

In its heavenly setting, your soul is intimately connected with all four letters of the Tetragrammaton. Remarkably, even after your soul has descended into your body, it still retains a connection with the Tetragrammaton, with the final letter, *hei.*

This gives you tremendous power and if you sin, that power (of *hei*) is handed over to the negative forces of the *Sitra Achra!* But your subsequent *teshuvah* has the power to retrieve the energy of *hei* which was temporarily handed to the negative forces, and return it to G-d.

This is the meaning of *teshuvah* spelled as *"tashuv (return) hei."* You restore the *hei*, the power of the Tetragrammaton which was misdirected to the negative forces, back to its source.

וְאוּלָם דֶּרֶךְ הָאֱמֶת וְהַיָּשָׁר לִבְחִינַת תְּשׁוּבָה תַּתָּאָה הֵ"א תַּתָּאָה הַנַּ"ל — **Now** the following is the **true and authentic path to returning the lower** *hei*, **mentioned above, which is "lower** *teshuvah.*"

As the *Tanya* taught in Chapter Four, the letter *hei* appears twice in the Tetragrammaton, hinting to two levels of *teshuvah.* "*Restoring the last, 'lower' hei of the Tetragrammaton is 'lower teshuvah.' Restoring the first, 'upper' hei of the Tetragrammaton is 'upper teshuvah.'*"

The discussions in Chapters Four-Six have clarified the spiritual dynamic of "lower *teshuvah*," explaining what it means to "*restore the last, 'lower' hei of the Tetragrammaton.*" In this chapter we will learn some practical techniques to enhance the "lower *teshuvah*" process.

דברים דרך כלל. הא' הוא לעורר רחמים העליונים
ממקור הרחמים על נשמתו ונפשו האלקי' שנפלה

הֵם שְׁנֵי דְבָרִים דֶּרֶךְ כְּלָל — The "true and authentic path" to "lower *teshuvah"* **is based, generally speaking, on two activities.**

We have not yet been taught how to carry out "upper *teshuvah"*; that will be our focus in the coming chapters. But the method of basic, "lower *teshuvah"* has already been clarified in Chapter One: *"1.) A person resolves with a full heart that he will not 'return to foolishness,' (and do the sin again), and 2.) that he will not rebel against G-d's authority."*

This seems perfectly clear and sufficient. Why does the *Tanya* need to add further activities in this chapter, to achieve a *teshuvah* which is "true and authentic"?

The *Tanya's* concern here is the second element of *teshuvah,* that the decision "not to rebel against G-d's authority" should be "true and authentic." It should be "true" in that *it emanates from an inner conviction;* and "authentic" in that *it is not motivated by any ulterior motive* or influence. In that way the *teshuvah* will be both sustainable and "real," stemming directly from the soul's connection with G-d, and not out of fear of repercussions.

To achieve this goal of "true and authentic" *teshuvah,* the *Tanya* now offers us two pieces of practical advice (Based on *Likutei Sichos* vol. 39, pp. 79-82).

SECTION TWO: FEELING G-D'S PRESENCE MORE

Why does the *Tanya* offer us *two* suggestions in this chapter?

As we have seen, "true and authentic" *teshuvah* means that the acceptance of G-d's authority is sincere. To achieve that, two meditations are required:

1.) *You need to feel the presence of G-d more,* because your sin resulted from not feeling His presence enough.

2.) *You need to be more loyal to G-d,* even when you don't feel His presence.

The two suggestions of this chapter are aimed at these two goals (ibid. pp. 82-83).

Our first meditation focuses on feeling G-d's tangible presence more, particularly, the presence of G-d *in your soul.*

הָאֶחָד הוּא לְעוֹרֵר רַחֲמִים הָעֶלְיוֹנִים מִמְּקוֹר הָרַחֲמִים עַל נִשְׁמָתוֹ — **One** practical **suggestion to achieve "true and authentic"** *teshuvah* **is to awaken from the source of compassion, great compassion for your soul, וְנַפְשׁוֹ הָאֱלֹקִית,** — both

מאיגרא רמה חיי החיים ב"ה לבירא עמיקתא הן
היכלות הטומאה והסט"א. ועל מקורה במקור החיים
הוא שם הוי' ב"ה וכמ"ש וישוב אל הוי' וירחמהו.
פי' לעורר רחמים על השפעת שם הוי' ב"ה שנשתלשלה

as **your soul** exists in its heavenly source **and as your Divine Soul** exists, embodied down here.

שֶׁנָּפְלָה מֵאִיגְרָא רָמָה — Meditate on the thought that your soul **has fallen**
*"a plunge from **a high roof** to a deep pit"* (*Talmud, Chagigah* 5b).

חַיֵּי הַחַיִּים בָּרוּךְ הוּא — The "high roof," being **the Blessed Source of Life,** לְבֵירָא
עֲמִיקְתָא — *"to a deep pit,"* הֵן הֵיכְלוֹת הַטֻּמְאָה וְהַסִּטְרָא אַחֲרָא — **namely, the**
chambers of impurity and *Sitra Achra,* which were energized by your sin (as
we learned in the previous chapter).

PRACTICAL LESSONS

Your sin has "trapped" G-d so to speak, causing the "exile of the *Shechinah* (Divine Presence)." Have compassion on your Divine soul for having been forced into such an act!

The contrast could not be more sharp. Your sin took the most elevated and sacred energy in the universe, the very name of G-d, and plunged it into the darkest and corrupt of places, the *Sitra Achra.*

וְעַל מְקוֹרָהּ בִּמְקוֹר הַחַיִּים — Awaken compassion **for the source of** your soul **in the Source of Life,** הוּא שֵׁם הֲוָי"ה בָּרוּךְ הוּא — **which is the blessed Tetragramma-ton!**

The *Tanya* cites a verse which illustrates this point.

וּכְמוֹ שֶׁכָּתוּב וְיָשֹׁב אֶל הֲוָי"ה וִירַחֲמֵהוּ — **As the verse states, *"Let him return to Havayah, and He will have compassion for him"*** (Isaiah 55:7; see Part One, p. 585).

Literally, this verse describes a mirroring of Divine compassion in response to human *teshuvah.* When the person will *"return to G-d,"* as a result, G-d *"will have compassion for him,"* i.e., on the person who did *teshuvah.*

The *Tanya* reads the second part of the verse differently, translating it: *"he will have compassion on it."* The verse is interpreted to mean: *"Let him return to Havayah, and he (the person) will have compassion for it (for Havayah)."* The way to do *teshuvah,* the verse tells us, is to have compassion for the energy of *Havayah* in your soul which has been misused and handed over to the nega-tive forces.

פֵּרוּשׁ — **Meaning to say,** לְעוֹרֵר רַחֲמִים עַל הַשְׁפָּעַת שֵׁם הֲוָי"ה בָּרוּךְ הוּא — awak-en compassion **on the flow from the Blessed Tetragrammaton** in your soul,

וירדה תוך היכלות הסט"א הטמאים להחיותם ע"י
מעשה אנוש ותחבולותיו ומחשבותיו הרעות וכמ"ש
מלך אסור ברהטים ברהיטי מוחא וכו' היא בחי'
גלות השכינה כנ"ל. וזמן המסוגל לזה הוא בתיקון

שֶׁנִּשְׁתַּלְשְׁלָה וְיָרְדָה תּוֹךְ הֵיכְלוֹת הַסִּטְרָא אַחֲרָא הַטְּמֵאִים לְהַחֲיוֹתָם — which has
been progressively downgraded into the chambers of *Sitra Achra* and im-
purity, energizing them, עַל יְדֵי מַעֲשֵׂה אֱנוֹשׁ וְתַחְבּוּלוֹתָיו וּמַחְשְׁבוֹתָיו הָרָעוֹת —
through *"the deeds of men and their tactics"* (Liturgy, High Holy Days), and
their bad thoughts.

The *Tanya* cites another verse which illustrates this idea (which we learned
in Part One, p. 584).

וּכְמוֹ שֶׁכָּתוּב מֶלֶךְ אָסוּר בָּרְהָטִים — As the verse states, *"(Even) a king is captivated by (your) flowing hair (rehatim)"* (Song 7:6), בְּרְהִיטֵי מוֹחָא וְכוּ' — and *Tikunei
Zohar* (144b) interprets *rehatim* as **"flow of the mind."**

The *Tanya* combines the literal and *Zoharic* interpretations together to suggest that "the King" (G-d) is "captivated" (*i.e.,* trapped, so to speak), by *the inappropriate thoughts* of your mind, in which your holy soul is enmeshed.

Contemplating how you have "trapped" G-d in such a way, causing the "exile
of the *Shechinah* (Divine Presence)," ought to evoke more compassion.

הִיא בְּחִינַת גָּלוּת הַשְּׁכִינָה כַּנַּ"ל — And this is the **"exile of the *Shechinah*"** mentioned above, Chapter Six, which we interpreted to mean the misdirection of
the *hei* of the Tetragrammaton (*Shechinah*) toward the negative forces.

The *Tanya* suggests a time for the above meditation.

וּזְמַן הַמְסֻגָּל לָזֶה הוּא בְּתִקּוּן חֲצוֹת — An effective time for this meditation is at
Tikun Chatzos (Midnight Prayer), when the mood is somber, כְּמוֹ שֶׁכָּתוּב בַּסִּדּוּר
בְּהֶעָרָה — as stated in *Siddur Admor Hazaken* in the note to *Seder Tikun Chatzos,* עַיֵּן שָׁם בֵּאוּרוֹ — see the explanation there.

Tikun Chatzos is a service mourning the destruction of the Temple consisting
of selected Psalms, *vidui* (confession) and *kinos* (dirges), to be recited at midnight by individuals or small groups, sitting on the ground. It was instituted in
the Sixteenth Century C.E. in the Kabbalistic circles of Safed.

Nowadays, *Tikun Chatzos* is barely practiced and an appropriate time to carry out these meditations is during the prayers before retiring at night (see Rabbi
Shalom Dovber Schneersohn, *Toras Shalom,* p. 6).

The *Tanya* quotes a passage from *Tikun Chatzos* which is evocative of the
above theme.

חצות כמ"ש בסידור בהערה עש"ב. וז"ש שם נפלה
עטרת ראשינו אוי נא לנו כי חטאנו. ולכן נקרא
הקדב"ה מלך עלוב בפרקי היכלות כמ"ש הרמ"ק ז"ל
כי אין לך עלבון גדול מזה. ובפרט כאשר יתבונן
המשכיל בגדולת א"ס ב"ה ממכ"ע וסכ"ע כל א' וא'
לפי שיעור שכלו והבנתו יתמרמר ע"ז מאד מאד:

97A

וְזֶהוּ שֶׁכָּתוּב שָׁם נָפְלָה עֲטֶרֶת רֹאשֵׁנוּ אוֹי נָא לָנוּ כִּי חָטָאנוּ — **And this is the meaning of the verse cited** in *Tikun Chatzos, "The crown of our head has fallen, woe to us, for we have sinned"* (*Eichah* 5:16).

The "crown of our head" refers to the soul's sacred root in the Tetragrammaton. Since "we have sinned," this energy has "fallen" into the *Sitra Achra*.

וְלָכֵן נִקְרָא הַקָּדוֹשׁ בָּרוּךְ הוּא מֶלֶךְ עָלוּב בְּפִרְקֵי הֵיכָלוֹת — **That is why in** *Pirkei Heichalos* (ch. 18), **G-d is called the "humiliated King,"** כְּמוֹ שֶׁכָּתַב הָרְמַ"ק זַ"ל — **as Rabbi Moshe Cordovero, of blessed memory, writes,** כִּי אֵין לְךָ עֶלְבּוֹן גָּדוֹל מִזֶּה — *"There is no humiliation greater than this one"* (cited in *Reishis Chochmah, Sha'ar Ha-Yirah* chapter 10).

PRACTICAL LESSONS

Sins trap Divine energy in a negative place. *Teshuvah* releases it.

G-d is "humiliated" since we use His name, the sacred Tetragrammaton to damage His own creation. He grants us the power of His name in order for us to worship Him, and we use it for negative purposes!

Reishis Chochmah (ibid.) offers the following analogy.

"This is like a king who gives his servant money to buy bread and support himself, but the servant uses the money to buy a rod to hit his master! Is there a worse servant than that?"

"Nevertheless, even though G-d is so humiliated, He overlooks transgression and is slow to anger."

As we have seen, this first meditation focuses on feeling G-d's tangible presence. Up to this point we have focused on the presence of G-d *in your soul*. We conclude with a meditation on G-d's presence *in general*.

וּבִפְרָט כַּאֲשֶׁר יִתְבּוֹנֵן הַמַּשְׂכִּיל בִּגְדֻלַּת אֵין סוֹף בָּרוּךְ הוּא מְמַלֵּא כָּל עָלְמִין וְסוֹבֵב כָּל עָלְמִין — **And particularly when an intelligent person will meditate on the greatness of the Blessed Infinite Light,** *"who fills all worlds"* **and** *"transcends all worlds"* (see *Zohar* 3, 225a), כָּל אֶחָד וְאֶחָד לְפִי שִׁעוּר שִׂכְלוֹ וַהֲבָנָתוֹ — **each individual according to the capacity of his mind and understanding,** יִתְמַרְמֵר

וְהב' לבטש ולהכניע הקליפה וסט"א אשר כל חיותה
היא רק בחי' גסות והגבהה כמ"ש אם תגביה כנשר
וכו'. והביטוש וההכנעה עד עפר ממש זוהי מיתתה
וביטולה. והיינו ע"י לב נשבר ונדכה ולהיות נבזה

עַל זֶה מְאֹד מְאֹד — he will become profoundly aware of the presence of G-d and
be deeply embittered about his actions.

SECTION THREE: A MEDITATION TO HUMILIATE THE EGO

In the previous section, the *Tanya* offered us a meditation to ensure that the acceptance of G-d's authority during *teshuvah* is sincere, by sensitizing ourselves
to His presence.

In this section we will be offered a second meditation, to help us to be loyal to
G-d even when we don't feel his presence. The key to achieving this self-con-
trol will be through *humiliating the ego*. (Many of these meditations already
appeared in Part One of *Tanya*, as cited below.)

וְהַשֵּׁנִי — **And the second** approach to ensure *teshuvah* is sincere, לְבַטֵּשׁ
וּלְהַכְנִיעַ הַקְלִפָּה וְסִטְרָא אַחֲרָא — **is to crush and subdue the** *Sitra Achra* **(see
Part One, p. 531),** אֲשֶׁר כָּל חַיּוּתָהּ הִיא רַק בְּחִינַת גַּסּוּת וְהַגְבָּהָה — **whose entire life
force is just "inflated ego"** (see *Talmud, Sotah* 4b), **and arrogance.**

Your desire to sin comes from the *Sitra Achra*. In order to reduce that desire,
the *Sitra Achra* needs to be "crushed," or at least "subdued." The secret to
doing this is the realization that *Sitra Achra* lacks real substance (see Part One,
p. 253).

כְּמוֹ שֶׁכָּתוּב אִם תַּגְבִּיהַ כַּנֶּשֶׁר וְכו' — **As the verse states,** *"If you lift yourself high
like an eagle... from there I will bring you down,' says G-d"* (*Ovadiah* 1:4; see
Part One, p. 310).

The *Sitra Achra* is arrogant and must be humiliated, put in its place.

וְהַבִּטּוּשׁ וְהַהַכְנָעָה עַד עָפָר מַמָּשׁ זוֹהִי מִיתָתָהּ וּבְטוּלָהּ — **The crushing and sub-
jugation** of the *Sitra Achra,* **literally razing it to the ground, is its "death" and
neutralization.**

Practically this is done:

וְהַיְנוּ עַל יְדֵי לֵב נִשְׁבָּר וְנִדְכֶּה וְלִהְיוֹת נִבְזֶה בְּעֵינָיו נִמְאָס וְכו' — **Through** *"a broken,
crushed heart"* (*Psalms* 51:19), contemplating that your body's sensuality and
vulgarity are, *"disgusting in your eyes, and repulsive"* (ibid. 15:4; see Part One
p. 326).

בְּעֵינָיו נִמְאָס וכו'. וכמ"ש בזוה"ק ע"פ זִבְחֵי אֱלֹקִי'
רוּחַ נִשְׁבָּרָה לֵב נִשְׁבָּר וְנִדְכֶּה וכו'. כִּי כָּל קָרְבָּן מִן
הַבְּהֵמָה הוּא לְשֵׁם הֲוָי' הִיא מִדַּת הָרַחֲמִים. אֲבָל
לְשֵׁם אֱלֹקִים הִיא מִדַּת הַדִּין אֵין מַקְרִיבִין קָרְבָּן בְּהֵמָה
כ"א לְשַׁבֵּר וּלְהַעֲבִיר רוּחַ הַטּוּמְאָה וְהַסִּטְרָא אָחֳרָא וְזֶהוּ רוּחַ
נִשְׁבָּרָה. וְהָאֵיךְ נִשְׁבָּרָה רוּחַ הַסִּטְרָא אָחֳרָא. כְּשֶׁהַלֵּב נִשְׁבָּר

וּכְמוֹ שֶׁכָּתוּב בַּזֹּהַר הַקָּדוֹשׁ עַל פָּסוּק זִבְחֵי אֱלֹקִים רוּחַ נִשְׁבָּרָה לֵב נִשְׁבָּר וְנִדְכֶּה וְכוּ' —
As the holy *Zohar* comments on the verse, *"A broken spirit is a sacrifice to Elokim, a broken, crushed heart You do not reject, O G-d"* (Psalms 51:19).

The Zohar states: *"When a man contaminates himself with his sins, he draws upon himself an impure spirit, which imposes itself on him, ruling over his desires...."*

"At the time when the Temple stood, a man would offer his sacrifice... and feel remorse, thereby breaking down that (impure) spirit.... But if that (impure) spirit is not broken, then his sacrifice is worth nothing and is given to the dogs...."

"And this is why Scripture says that the proper sacrifices of G-d are a 'broken spirit,' for that impure spirit has to be broken so that it will not be in control" (*Zohar* 3, 240a-b; see Part One, p. 207).

The verse in *Psalms* states *"A broken spirit is a sacrifice to Elokim,"* Elokim being associated with judgment. The *Tanya* comments on this point.

כִּי כָּל קָרְבָּן מִן הַבְּהֵמָה הוּא לְשֵׁם הֲוָי"ה — For all the animal sacrifices are "for G-d (*Havayah*)," הִיא מִדַּת הָרַחֲמִים — namely G-d's attribute of compassion, אֲבָל לְשֵׁם אֱלֹקִים — whereas to *Elokim*, הִיא מִדַּת הַדִּין — which is G-d's attribute of judgment, אֵין מַקְרִיבִין קָרְבָּן בְּהֵמָה — we do not offer animal sacrifices, כִּי אִם לְשַׁבֵּר וּלְהַעֲבִיר רוּחַ הַטּוּמְאָה וְהַסִּטְרָא אָחֳרָא — rather the "offering" to *Elokim* is to destroy and remove the spirit of impurity and *Sitra Achra*, וְזֶהוּ רוּחַ נִשְׁבָּרָה — and that is "a broken spirit."

וְהָאֵיךְ נִשְׁבָּרָה רוּחַ הַסִּטְרָא אָחֳרָא — And how is *Sitra Achra* destroyed?

A CHASIDIC THOUGHT

"Repentance must be carried out so thoroughly and sincerely as to make it possible for the repenter to shape the future without blemish, not only in deed, but also in word and thought."

(From a Letter of the Rebbe, Days of Selichos 5720)

ונדכה וכו'. .והאיך נשבר הלב ונדכה. הנה מעט
מזעיר הוא ע"י סיגופים ותעניות בדורותינו אלה שאין
לנו כח להתענות הרבה כדוד המלך כמאמר רז"ל
ע"פ ולבי חלל בקרבי שהרגו בתענית. אך עיקר
הכנעת הלב להיות נשבר ונדכה והעברת רוח הטומאה
וסט"א הוא להיות ממארי דחושבנא בעומק הדעת
להעמיק דעתו ובינתו שעה אחת בכל יום או לילה

כְּשֶׁהַלֵּב נִשְׁבָּר וְנִדְכֶּה וְכוּ' — **When the heart is** *"broken and crushed, etc."*

The *Tanya* offers a practical suggestion to achieve this goal.

וְהָאֵיךְ נִשְׁבָּר הַלֵּב וְנִדְכֶּה — **And,** practically speaking, **how is the heart** *"broken and crushed"*?

הִנֵּה מְעַט מִזְעֵיר הוּא עַל יְדֵי סִגּוּפִים וְתַעֲנִיּוֹת בְּדוֹרוֹתֵינוּ אֵלֶּה — **In our generations, the role of self imposed suffering and fasting is very minimal,** שֶׁאֵין לָנוּ כֹחַ לְהִתְעַנּוֹת הַרְבֵּה — **because we do not have the strength for extensive fasting,** כְּדָוִד הַמֶּלֶךְ כְּמַאֲמַר רַז"ל עַל פָּסוּק וְלִבִּי חָלָל בְּקִרְבִּי — **in the fashion of King David, as the Sages taught on the verse,** *"My heart is empty within me,"* (*Psalms* 109:22), שֶׁהֲרָגוֹ בְּתַעֲנִית — **that he annihilated** his "impulse to evil," **through fasting** (*Jerusalem Talmud, Sotah* 5:5; see Part One, p. 35).

We do not have the strength to "annihilate" the impulse to evil through fasting. What, then, is the solution for us?

אַךְ עִקַּר הַכְנָעַת הַלֵּב — **Rather, the main way in which the heart is humbled** nowadays, לִהְיוֹת נִשְׁבָּר וְנִדְכֶּה וְהַעֲבָרַת רוּחַ הַטֻמְאָה וְסִטְרָא אָחֳרָא — **to be** *"broken and crushed"* **so as to** *"remove the spirit of impurity"* (see *Zechariah* 13:2) **and** *Sitra Achra,* הוּא לִהְיוֹת מִמָּאֲרֵי דְחוּשְׁבָּנָא — **is to be an** *"expert accountant"* (*Zohar* 3, 178a; see Part One, p. 332).

The *Zohar* (ibid) states: *"A person must take account of the actions he did that day, repent for them, and ask for compassion for them…. And people who do this are called 'expert accountants.'"*

Having demonstrated the need and appropriateness of this "accounting" the *Tanya* now advises us regarding the *content* of the meditation.

לְהַעֲמִיק דַּעְתּוֹ וּבִינָתוֹ שָׁעָה בְּעֹמֶק הַדַּעַת — **To do this you must ponder deeply,** אַחַת בְּכָל יוֹם אוֹ לַיְלָה לִפְנֵי תִּקּוּן חֲצוֹת — **delving and thinking profoundly for a period of time every day, or at night before** *Tikun Chatzos,* לְהִתְבּוֹנֵן בְּמַה שֶּׁפָּעַל

לפני תיקון חצות להתבונן במה שפעל ועשה בחטאיו
בחי' גלות השכינה כנ"ל וגם [גרם] לעקור נשמתו
ונפשו האלקי' מחיי החיים ב"ה והורידה למקום הטומאה
והמות הן היכלות הסט"א ונעשית בבחי' מרכבה
אליהם לקבל מהם שפע וחיות להשפיע לגופו כנ"ל.
וזהו שאמרו רז"ל רשעים בחייהם קרויים מתים כלומר
שחייהם נמשכים ממקום המות והטומאה (וכן מ"ש
לא המתים יהללו כו' אינו כלועג לרש ח"ו אלא

97B

וְעָשָׂה בַּחֲטָאָיו בְּחִינַת גָּלוּת הַשְּׁכִינָה כַּנַּ"ל — contemplating what your sins have caused and contributed towards the "exile of the *Shechinah*," mentioned above, וְגָרַם לַעֲקוֹר נִשְׁמָתוֹ וְנַפְשׁוֹ הָאֱלֹקִית מֵחַיֵּי הַחַיִּים בָּרוּךְ הוּא — and how you have caused both the root of **your soul and your** embodied **Divine Soul to be disconnected from the Blessed Source of life,** וְהוֹרִידָהּ לִמְקוֹם הַטֻּמְאָה וְהַמָּוֶת — downgrading it to a zone of impurity and "death," הֵן הֵיכְלוֹת הַסִּטְרָא אַחֲרָא — namely the chambers of *Sitra Achra,* וְנַעֲשֵׂית בִּבְחִינַת מֶרְכָּבָה אֲלֵיהֶם לְקַבֵּל — and how you became a vehicle for the chambers of the *Sitra Achra,* receiving energetic flow from them into your body, as mentioned above.

This concludes the meditation.

The *Tanya* has referred to the *Sitra Achra* as *"a zone of death."* We will now elaborate briefly on this idea.

וְזֶהוּ שֶׁאָמְרוּ רַזַ"ל רְשָׁעִים בְּחַיֵּיהֶם קְרוּיִים מֵתִים — **And this is the meaning of our Sages teaching, that** *"the wicked are called 'dead' in their lifetime"* (*Talmud, Brachos* 18b; see Part One, p. 206), כְּלוֹמַר שֶׁחַיֵּיהֶם נִמְשָׁכִים מִמְּקוֹם הַמָּוֶת וְהַטֻּמְאָה — **meaning that their lives are powered from** the *Sitra Achra* which is **a zone of "death" and impurity.**

The energy which the *Sitra Achra* receives from G-d does not become properly absorbed by it. The *Sitra Achra's* life-energy is largely trapped and has split off. It has become anti-life, since "life" is really the presence of life-energy within something, and is therefore compared to "death" (see Part One, p. 252).

The *Tanya* offers a further support for this idea.

(וְכֵן מַה שֶּׁכָּתוּב לֹא הַמֵּתִים יְהַלְלוּ כוּ' — **As the verse states,** *"The dead will not praise G-d"* (*Psalms* 115:17), אֵינוּ כְּלוֹעֵג לָרָשׁ חַס וְשָׁלוֹם — **which clearly does not** refer to the actual dead, in which case it would fall under the prohibition of, *"mocking the unfortunate"* (*Proverbs* 17:5; *Talmud, Brachos* 18a), **G-d forbid.**

הכוונה על הרשעים שבחייהם קרויים מתים שמבלבלים
אותם במחשבות זרות בעודם ברשעם ואינם חפיצים
בתשובה כנודע). ואף מי שלא עבר על עון כרת וגם
לא על עון מיתה בידי שמים שהוא הוצאת ז"ל וכה"ג
אלא שאר עבירות קלות. אעפ"כ מאחר שהן פוגמים
בנשמה ונפש האלקית וכמשל פגימת ופסיקת חבלים
דקים כנ"ל. הרי ברבוי החטאים יכול להיות פגם

אֶלָּא הַכַּוָּנָה עַל הָרְשָׁעִים שֶׁבְּחַיֵּיהֶם קְרוּיִים מֵתִים — **Rather, the verse refers to the wicked who are called "dead" in their lifetime,** שֶׁמְבַלְבְּלִים אוֹתָם בְּמַחֲשָׁבוֹת זָרוֹת — **in that they are confused with inappropriate thoughts while still wicked, and so do not desire repentance,** (כַּנּוֹדָע) — **as is known** from *Sefer Chasidim.*

"You can't learn to connect your heart constantly to G-d unless you abandon sin, because sin separates you (from G-d) and causes you to forget your reverence (of Him)" (Sefer Chasidim, Chapter 35; see Part One, p. 533).

SECTION FOUR: THE CUMULATIVE EFFECT OF SMALLER SINS

22ND TAMMUZ REGULAR | 27TH TAMMUZ LEAP

The meditation described in Section Two advised contemplating, "how you have caused both the root of your soul and your embodied Divine Soul *to be disconnected* from the Blessed Source of life."

This would seem to be appropriate only for sins carrying the penalty of *kareis* or "death by the agency of heaven," which bring about a complete disconnect of the soul.

However, in this section the *Tanya* will explain that even lesser sins, which are not punishable by *kareis,* can eventually cause a complete disconnect of the soul, if they are violated in sufficient quantity.

וְאַף מִי שֶׁלֹּא עָבַר עַל עֲוֹן כָּרֵת — **And even if you have transgressed neither a sin punishable by** *kareis,* וְגַם לֹא עַל עֲוֹן מִיתָה בִּידֵי שָׁמַיִם — **nor a sin punishable by "death through the agency of heaven,"** שֶׁהוּא הוֹצָאַת זֶרַע לְבַטָּלָה וּכְהָאי — **(such as emitting seed in vain, etc.),** גַּוְונָא — **but only** אֶלָּא שְׁאָר עֲבֵרוֹת קַלּוֹת — **other, less serious sins,** אַף עַל פִּי כֵן מֵאַחַר שֶׁהֵן פּוֹגְמִים בַּנְּשָׁמָה וְנֶפֶשׁ הָאֱלֹקִית — **nevertheless, since** these less serious sins **have** caused at least some **damage** to your **soul's** heavenly root and your embodied **Divine Soul,** וְכִמְשַׁל פְּגִימַת — **as in the above illustration** from the rope whose threads have been diminished and severed, וּפְסִיקַת חֲבָלִים דַּקִּים כַּנַּ"ל — הֲרֵי בְּרִבּוּי הַחֲטָאִים יָכוֹל לִהְיוֹת פְּגָם

כְּמוֹ בְלָאו אֶחָד שֶׁיֵּשׁ בּוֹ כָּרֵת אוֹ מִיתָה. וַאֲפִי' בִּכְפִילַת
חֵטְא אֶחָד פְּעָמִים רַבּוֹת מְאֹד. כְּמוֹ שֶׁהִמְשִׁיל הַנָּבִיא
הַחֲטָאִים לֶעָנָן הַמַּאֲפִיל אוֹר הַשֶּׁמֶשׁ כְּמ"שׁ מָחִיתִי כָעָב
פְּשָׁעֶיךָ הֵם עֲבֵרוֹת חֲמוּרוֹת [הַמַּבְדִּילִים] בֵּין פְּנִימִית
הַשְׁפָּעַת שֵׁם הוי' ב"ה לַנֶּפֶשׁ הָאֱלֹקִית. כְּהַבְדָּלַת עָנָן
עָב וְחָשׁוּךְ הַמַּבְדִּיל בֵּין הַשֶּׁמֶשׁ לָאָרֶץ וְלַדָּרִים עָלֶיהָ
עָד"מ. וְכֶעָנָן חַטֹּאתֶיךָ הֵן עֲבֵרוֹת קַלּוֹת שֶׁאָדָם דָּשׁ
בַּעֲקֵבָיו הַמַּבְדִּילִים כְּהַבְדָּלַת עָנָן קַל וְקָלוּשׁ עָד"מ.

כְּמוֹ בְלָאו אֶחָד שֶׁיֵּשׁ בּוֹ כָּרֵת אוֹ מִיתָה — as a result many such sins could render the same level of damage as a single prohibition that is punishable by *kareis* or death.

PRACTICAL LESSONS

Your soul's connection is like a rope of many strands. This could be disconnected in one go through a severe violation. But many smaller sins, each of which severs just one strand, will add up to the same effect.

Your soul's connection is like a rope of many strands. This could be disconnected *in one go* through a violation that incurs *kareis*. But many smaller violations, each of which severs just one strand, will add up to the same effect.

וַאֲפִלוּ בִּכְפִילַת חֵטְא אֶחָד פְּעָמִים רַבּוֹת מְאֹד — Or even carrying out the same sin on very many occasions, would have a similar, cumulative effect.

The *Tanya* offers an illustration of this idea.

כְּמוֹ שֶׁהִמְשִׁיל הַנָּבִיא — As in the analogy of the prophet Isaiah, הַחֲטָאִים לֶעָנָן הַמַּאֲפִיל אוֹר הַשֶּׁמֶשׁ — comparing sins to a "cloud" masking the sunlight, כְּמוֹ שֶׁכָּתוּב מָחִיתִי כָעָב פְּשָׁעֶיךָ — as the verse states, *"I have blotted out, like a thick cloud, your transgressions, and, like a cloud, your sins"* (Isaiah 44:22).

הֵם עֲבֵרוֹת חֲמוּרוֹת [הַמַּבְדִּילִים] בֵּין פְּנִימִית הַשְׁפָּעַת שֵׁם הֲוָיָ"ה בָּרוּךְ הוּא לַנֶּפֶשׁ הָאֱלֹקִית — *"A thick cloud"* refers to serious transgressions, which completely block the inner flow from the Tetragrammaton to the Divine Soul, כְּהַבְדָּלַת עָנָן עָב וְחָשׁוּךְ הַמַּבְדִּיל בֵּין הַשֶּׁמֶשׁ לָאָרֶץ וְלַדָּרִים עָלֶיהָ עַל דֶּרֶךְ מָשָׁל — resembling a *thick* cloud which blocks the light from the sun to the earth and its inhabitants.

וְכֶעָנָן חַטֹּאתֶיךָ הֵן עֲבֵרוֹת קַלּוֹת שֶׁאָדָם דָּשׁ בַּעֲקֵבָיו — *"And, as a cloud, your sins"* refers to the less serious transgression which *"a person tramples under his feet"* (*Talmud, Avodah Zarah* 18b), and fails to take seriously, הַמַּבְדִּילִים כְּהַבְדָּלַת עָנָן קַל וְקָלוּשׁ עַל דֶּרֶךְ מָשָׁל — which resemble the disconnection caused by a lighter, thinner cloud.

וְהִנֵּה כְּמוֹ שֶׁבַּמָּשָׁל הַזֶּה אִם מְשִׂים אָדָם נֶגֶד אוֹר
הַשֶּׁמֶשׁ בַּחַלוֹן מְחִיצוֹת קַלוֹת וּקְלוּשׁוֹת לָרוֹב מְאֹד הֵן
מַאֲפִילוֹת כְּמוֹ מְחִיצָה אַחַת עָבָה וְיוֹתֵר. וְכָכָה מַמָּשׁ
הוּא בַּנִּמְשָׁל בְּכָל עֲווֹנוֹת שֶׁאָדָם דָּשׁ בַּעֲקֵבָיו וּמִכ"שׁ
הַמְפוּרְסָמוֹת מִדִּבְרֵי רַז"ל שֶׁהֵן מַמָּשׁ כַּע"ז וְג"ע וש"ד.

The *Tanya* explains how this verse proves the above point, about the cumulative effect of lesser sins.

וְהִנֵּה כְּמוֹ שֶׁבַּמָּשָׁל הַזֶּה — Now, just as in this analogy, אִם מְשִׂים אָדָם נֶגֶד אוֹר הַשֶּׁמֶשׁ בַּחַלוֹן מְחִיצוֹת קַלוֹת וּקְלוּשׁוֹת לָרוֹב מְאֹד — if a person places a very large number of thin curtains in his window, הֵן מַאֲפִילוֹת כְּמוֹ מְחִיצָה אַחַת עָבָה וְיוֹתֵר — they will block light as much, if not more, than one thick curtain, וְכָכָה מַמָּשׁ הוּא — so too, literally, בַּנִּמְשָׁל בְּכָל עֲווֹנוֹת דָּשׁ שֶׁאָדָם בַּעֲקֵבָיו — the large number of thin curtains **is comparable to** multiple **transgressions which "a person tramples under his feet,"** which will add up cumulatively to create a complete blockage and disconnect.

The *Tanya* notes that among "lesser sins" there are some which, while not carrying a severe punishment, are nevertheless described by the Sages as being particularly grave.

וּמִכָּל שֶׁכֵּן הַמְפוּרְסָמוֹת מִדִּבְרֵי רַז"ל שֶׁהֵן מַמָּשׁ כַּעֲבוֹדָה זָרָה וְגִלּוּי עֲרָיוֹת וּשְׁפִיכוּת דָּמִים — **And certainly** there is an especially strong damage caused to the soul by **those** transgressions **which our Sages have famously equated to idol worship, forbidden relations or murder, literally.**

The *Tanya* offers a number of examples.

A CHASIDIC THOUGHT

"*Teshuvah* has the power of *retroactivity*. For although the past is no longer under a man's prerogative, nevertheless, G-d, Who is beyond any category of time and therefore transcends the categories of time and limitation — has endowed Teshuvah with a special and wonderful quality, by means of which man can regain mastery over his past. Moreover, by means of this special power of *teshuvah*, man is able not only to render the past neutral and ineffective, but he can even reverse it and turn it into something positive, as our Sages of blessed memory expressed it: '*Willful wrongs become, in his case, as though they were merits (Talmud, Yoma* 86b)."

(From a letter of the Rebbe, Days of Selichos 5720)

כמו העלמת עין מן הצדקה כמ"ש השמר לך פן יהי'
דבר עם לבבך בליעל כו' ובליעל היא עע"א וכו'.
והמספר בגנות חבירו היא לה"ר השקולה כע"ז וג"ע
וש"ד וכל הכועס כאלו עע"ז וכן מי שיש בו גסות
הרוח. וכהנה רבות בגמרא. ות"ת כנגד כולן כמארז"ל
ויתר הקב"ה על ע"ז וכו'. ולכן סידרו בק"ש שעל
98A   המטה לקבל עליו ד' מיתות ב"ד וכו'. מלבד שעפ"י

כְּמוֹ הַעֲלָמַת עַיִן מִן הַצְּדָקָה — **Such as: 1.) Ignoring** pleas for **charity** (*Kesubos* 68a), כְּמוֹ שֶׁכָּתוּב הִשָּׁמֶר לְךָ פֶּן יִהְיֶה דָבָר עִם לְבָבְךָ בְלִיַּעַל כו' — **as the verse states,** *"Watch yourself, lest there be in your heart a base thing, saying, 'The seventh year, the year of remission is near,' and you look meanly at your brother the pauper and you do not give to him"* (*Deuteronomy* 15:9), וּבְלִיַּעַל הִיא עֲבוֹדַת אֱלִילִים וְכו' — **and "a base thing" is idol worship** (*Kesubos* ibid.; *Sanhedrin* 111b).

וְהַמְסַפֵּר בְּגְנוּת חֲבֵרוֹ הִיא לָשׁוֹן הָרַע — **And 2.) One who speaks disparagingly about his fellow,** *Lashon Hara,* הַשְּׁקוּלָה כַּעֲבוֹדָה זָרָה וְגִלּוּי עֲרָיוֹת וּשְׁפִיכוּת דָּמִים — commits a sin **equal to idol worship, forbidden relations and murder** (*Arachin* 15b).

וְכָל הַכּוֹעֵס כְּאִלּוּ עוֹבֵד עֲבוֹדָה זָרָה — **And 3.) Getting angry is tantamount to idol worship** (*Zohar* 1, 27b).

וְכֵן מִי שֶׁיֵּשׁ בּוֹ גַּסוּת הָרוּחַ — **And 4.) So is a person who has an inflated ego** (*Sotah* 4b).

וְכָהֵנָּה רַבּוֹת בְּגְמָרָא — **And there are many other such statements in the** *Talmud* (see *Berachos* 31a; *Pesachim* 118a; *Sanhedrin* 92a).

וְתַלְמוּד תּוֹרָה כְּנֶגֶד כֻּלָּן — **And 5.) The neglect of** *"Torah study is equivalent to them all"* (*Mishnah, Pe'ah* 1:1), כְּמַאֲמַר רַזַ"ל וְיִתֵּר הַקָּדוֹשׁ בָּרוּךְ הוּא עַל עֲבוֹדָה זָרָה וְכו' — **as in the teaching of our Sages, "The Blessed Holy One forgave** Israel even for **idol worship,** adultery and murder but for neglecting Torah study, he never forgave them" (*Jerusalem Talmud, Chagigah* 1:7).

The *Tanya* offers a further proof for the effect of cumulative sins, from a Jewish custom.

וְלָכֵן סִדְרוּ בְּקְרִיאַת שְׁמַע שֶׁעַל הַמִּטָּה לְקַבֵּל עָלָיו אַרְבַּע מִיתוֹת בֵּית דִּין וְכו' — **And this is** the main reason **why the custom of accepting the "four types of death penalty" upon oneself was introduced into the bed-time** *Shema* **ritual** (*Zohar* 3, 29b; *Pri Etz Chaim, Sha'ar Krias Shema she-al Ha-Mitah; Siddur Tehillas Hashem, Annotated Edition* (Brooklyn: Kehos, 2002), p. 145).

There are four methods of death penalty administered by the Jewish Supreme Court (*Sanhedrin*) for different violations: death by stoning, burning,

הַסוֹד כל הפוגם באות יו"ד של שם הוי' כאילו נתחייב סקילה והפוגם באות ה"א כאילו נתחייב שריפה ובאות וי"ו כאילו נתחייב הרג ובאות ה"א אחרונה כאילו נתחייב חנק. והמבטל ק"ש פוגם באות יו"ד ותפילין

sword, and strangulation. According to a popular custom, one is to accept these four punishments upon oneself before retiring to bed at night.

The Kabbalistic reason for this ritual will be explained below. The *Tanya*, however, suggests a more simple reason for this custom, based on what we have learned in this section.

1.) Since even minor sins have a cumulative effect, a person's soul could eventually become disconnected completely through them, as if he were liable for the death penalty.

2.) There is also the possibility that he may have violated a sin which the Sages deemed "tantamount" to a more serious sin, which carries the death penalty.

Therefore, one should accept the death penalty upon himself, so as to receive its cleansing effects spiritually, and avoid them physically.

מִלְּבַד שֶׁעַל פִּי הַסוֹד — All this is **besides the** stated, **Kabbalistic reason** for this custom.

It is customary to recite a passage "accepting the four types of death penalty upon oneself" every night. Obviously, the average person is not going to carry out so many sins *each day* that they add up to the death penalty. Therefore, there must be a further reason for this custom, which the *Tanya* will now cite, from the Kabbalah.

כָּל הַפּוֹגֵם בְּאוֹת יוֹ"ד שֶׁל שֵׁם הֲוָיָ"ה כְּאִלּוּ נִתְחַיֵּב סְקִילָה — According to the Kabbalah, **if a person "damages" the letter** *yud* **of the Tetragrammaton, it is as if he was liable for** death by **stoning,** וְהַפּוֹגֵם בְּאוֹת ה"א כְּאִלּוּ נִתְחַיֵּב שְׂרֵפָה — and if he "damages" the first **letter** *hei* of the Tetragrammaton, it is as if he was liable **for** death by **burning,** וּבְאוֹת וָי"ו כְּאִלּוּ נִתְחַיֵּב הֶרֶג — and for damaging **the letter** *vav,* it is as if he was liable for death by **the sword,** וּבְאוֹת ה"א אַחֲרוֹנָה כְּאִלּוּ נִתְחַיֵּב חָנָק — and for damaging the second **letter** *hei,* it is as if he was liable **for** death by **strangulation.**

The passage "accepting the four types of death penalty upon oneself" was introduced to be said every night, since even a relatively small violation can cause damage to one of the letters of the Tetragrammaton. The following are the examples given in the text that is recited.

וְהַמְבַטֵּל קְרִיאַת שְׁמַע פּוֹגֵם בְּאוֹת יוֹ"ד — **One who fails to say the *Shema* damages the letter** *yud* of the Tetragrammaton, וּתְפִלִּין בְּאוֹת ה"א — one who fails to

באות ה"א וציצית באות וי"ו ותפלה באות ה"א וכו'.
ומזה יכול המשכיל ללמוד לשאר עוונות וחטאי' וביטול
תורה כנגד כולן:

put on **Tefilin** damages **the** first **letter** *hei* of the Tetragrammaton, וְצִיצִית בְּאוֹת
וָי"ו — one who fails to put on **Tzitzis** damages **the letter** *vav* of the Tetragrammaton, וּתְפִלָּה בְּאוֹת הֵ"א וְכוּ' — and one who fails to **pray** damages **the** second
letter *hei* of the Tetragrammaton.

However, these are mere examples:

וּמִזֶּה יָכוֹל הַמַּשְׂכִּיל לִלְמֹד לִשְׁאָר עֲווֹנוֹת וַחֲטָאִים — **And from this an intelligent
person can correlate to other sins and transgressions.**

Any sin will have a damaging effect that will relate in particular to one of the
letters of the Tetragrammaton. For example, anger relates to the *yud* (*chochmah*), since *chochmah* powers humility and anger arises out of arrogance. Lust
damages the *hei* (*binah*), since a person should have used his *binah* to meditate on G-d's greatness and produce a desire for worship (Rabbi Shneur Zalman, *Likutei Torah, Devarim* 59a).

The *Tanya* concludes by reminding us of the seriousness of the sin of neglecting Torah study.

וּבִטּוּל תּוֹרָה כְּנֶגֶד כֻּלָּן — **And failing to study** *"Torah is equal to them all."*

פרק ח והנה אחרי העמקת הדעת בכל הנ"ל יוכל
לבקש באמת מעומקא דלבא כרוב
רחמיך מחה פשעי וכו'. כי אזי תקבע בלבו באמת
גודל הרחמנות על בחי' אלקות שבנפשו ושלמעלה
כנ"ל. ובזה יעורר רחמים העליונים מי"ג מדה"ר

CHAPTER 8

SHIFTING TO "UPPER TESHUVAH"
SECTION ONE: G-D'S COMPASSION

23RD TAMMUZ REGULAR | 28TH TAMMUZ LEAP

In Chapter Seven, the *Tanya* taught us two meditations to guide us on *"the true and authentic path to returning the lower hei… which is 'lower teshuvah.'"*

Having learned the *method* of this process in Chapter Seven, the *Tanya* will now teach us its *spiritual result*.

וְהִנֵּה אַחֲרֵי הָעֲמָקַת הַדַּעַת בְּכָל הַנַּ"ל — **Now after** carrying out **all the above** meditations in Chapter Seven **with deep contemplation,** יוּכַל לְבַקֵּשׁ בֶּאֱמֶת מֵעָמְקָא דְלִבָּא כְּרוֹב רַחֲמֶיךָ מְחֵה פְּשָׁעַי וְכוּ' — **you can genuinely ask** G-d, **from the depths of your heart, "With Your great mercy wipe away my sins, etc.,"** (*Psalms* 51:3).

This verse forms part of the *Tikun Chatzos* ritual, which Chapter Seven described as an "effective time" to carry out the recommended meditations.

The *Tanya* teaches us the spiritual result of doing this work.

כִּי אֲזַי תִּקָּבַע בְּלִבּוֹ בֶּאֱמֶת גֹּדֶל הָרַחֲמָנוּת עַל בְּחִינַת אֱלֹקוּת שֶׁבְּנַפְשׁוֹ וְשֶׁלְמַעְלָה כַּנַּ"ל — **For then,** through carrying out the **above** meditations in Chapter Seven, **you will genuinely establish great compassion in your heart for the Divine component of your soul, and** its root **above,** וּבָזֶה יְעוֹרֵר רַחֲמִים הָעֶלְיוֹנִים מִשָּׁלֹשׁ עֶשְׂרֵה מִדּוֹת הָרַחֲמִים — **and this will result in awakening Divine compassion from the Thirteen Attributes of Mercy.**

One of the meditations in Chapter Seven (Section Two) was, *"to awaken from the source of compassion, great compassion for your soul."* The result of this, we learn here, is *"awakening Divine compassion from the Thirteen Attributes of Mercy."*

G-d's Thirteen Attributes of Mercy are mentioned in *Exodus* 34:6-7: *"G-d! G-d! G-d who is compassionate and gracious, slow to anger, abundant in loving*

הנמשכות מרצון העליון ב"ה הנרמז בקוצו של יו"ד
שלמעלה מעלה מבחי' ההשפעה הנשפעת מאותיות
שם הוי'. ולכן הי"ג מדות הרחמים מנקים כל הפגמים
וכמ"ש נושא עון ופשע ונקה. ושוב אין יניקה

kindness, and true (to reward), preserving kindness (that people do) for two thousand (generations), forgiving intentional sin, rebellion, and unintentional sin, and absolving."

According to the *Talmud*, reciting this list of merciful attributes is effective in securing G-d's forgiveness, *"any time Israel sins,"* since, *"a covenant has been made with the Thirteen Attributes, that they never return empty-handed"* (*Rosh Hashanah* 17b), *i.e.*, they always are effective.

The Thirteen Attributes have a primordial energy, which is why they have the power to erase judgment. The *Tanya* now explains this point.

הַנִּמְשָׁכוֹת מֵרָצוֹן הָעֶלְיוֹן בָּרוּךְ הוּא הַנִּרְמָז בְּקוֹצוֹ שֶׁל יוֹ"ד — The Thirteen Attributes of Mercy **flow from the Divine will, which is hinted to by the "thorn" above the** *yud* **of the Tetragrammaton,** שֶׁלְּמַעְלָה מַעְלָה מִבְּחִינַת הַהַשְׁפָּעָה הַנִּשְׁפַּעַת מֵאוֹתִיוֹת שֵׁם הֲוָיָ"ה — **which vastly transcends the energetic flow from the** actual **letters of the Tetragrammaton,** and yet the "thorn" is still part of the Tetragrammaton and therefore can influence it (while still transcending it), וְלָכֵן שְׁלֹשׁ עֶשְׂרֵה מִדּוֹת הָרַחֲמִים מְנַקִּים כָּל הַפְּגָמִים — **and that is why the Thirteen Attributes of Mercy cleanse all** spiritual **blemishes** caused by sin.

As we have learned, sins damage the final letter *hei* of the Tetragrammaton, though in a more general sense they compromise all four letters. But even the sacred Tetragrammaton is just energy which has been emanated from the Divine will. Any "damage" caused to the Tetragrammaton can be rectified by the healing power of the Divine will, hinted to by the "thorn" of the Tetragrammaton's *yud* (as we have learned above). It is this power which the Thirteen Attributes of Mercy tap into.

PRACTICAL LESSONS

Even the sacred Tetragrammaton is just energy which has been emanated from the Divine will. Any "damage" caused to the Tetragrammaton can therefore be rectified by the healing power of the Divine will, through *teshuvah*.

וּכְמוֹ שֶׁכָּתוּב נוֹשֵׂא עָוֹן וָפֶשַׁע וְנַקֵּה — **As the verse states,** *"Forgiving sin and transgression... and I will cleanse"* (*Exodus* 34:18).

להחיצונים והסט"א מהשפעת ה"א תתאה כנ"ל (ובזה
תשוב ה"א תתאה למקומה להתייחד ביה"ו וד"ל).
וכן ממש למטה בנפש האלקית שבאדם שוב אין
עוונותיכם מבדילים וכמ"ש ונקה מנקה הוא לשבים
לרחוץ ולנקות נפשם מלבושים הצואים הם החיצונים

Here we see that in addition to forgiveness, the Thirteen Attributes bring about a "cleansing" of all spiritual blemishes caused by sin, including any "damage" caused to the Tetragrammaton.

וְשׁוּב אֵין יְנִיקָה לְהַחִיצוֹנִים וְהַסִּטְרָא אַחֲרָא מֵהַשְׁפָּעַת הֵ"א תַּתָּאָה כַּנַּ"ל — **Then** when this healing and rectification is complete, **the** negative **"external" forces and Sitra Achra can no longer suck energy flow from the lower hei** of the Tetragrammaton, which they had received through the sin.

As we have learned in Chapter Six, a sin causes the energy of the lower hei of the Tetragrammaton to be directed to the negative forces. Teshuvah reverses this process and restores the hei to its source.

(וּבָזֶה תָּשׁוּב הֵ"א תַּתָּאָה לִמְקוֹמָהּ לְהִתְיַחֵד בְּיוּ"ד הֵ"א וָא"ו — **This returns the lower hei** of the Tetragrammaton **to its place, to unite with** the other letters yud, hei **and vav.**

(וְדַי לַמֵּבִין) — **And this** explanation **should be enough for the intelligent** reader.

We have clarified how the spiritual forces represented by the Tetragrammaton are rectified through teshuvah. The Tanya now reminds us of the parallel situation in the Tetragrammaton energy within the penitent's soul.

וְכֵן מַמָּשׁ לְמַטָּה בַּנֶּפֶשׁ הָאֱלֹקִית שֶׁבָּאָדָם — **The same is true, precisely, with a** person's embodied **Divine Soul,** שׁוּב אֵין עֲווֹנוֹתֵיכֶם מַבְדִּילִים — after teshuvah, **"your sins separate you"** (Isaiah 59:2) **no more,** וּכְמוֹ שֶׁאָמְרוּ וְנַקֵּה — **as the** verse cited above states, **"I will cleanse,"** מְנַקֶּה הוּא לַשָּׁבִים — which means, **"He cleanses those who return to Him"** (Talmud, Yoma 86a), לִרְחֹץ וּלְנַקּוֹת **"washing" and cleansing their souls from "soiled** נַפְשָׁם מִלְבוּשִׁים הַצוֹאִים **garments"** (see Zechariah 3:4), הֵם הַחִיצוֹנִים — **which are the "external,"** negative **forces,** כְּמוֹ שֶׁכָּתוּב בַּגְמָרָא מְלַפַּפְתּוֹ וְכוּ' — as the Talmud states, "When a person sins in this world **it envelopes him** and goes before him on judgment day" (Sotah 3b), and this is the "soiled garment" removed through teshuvah.

This completes our extended discussion of "lower teshuvah" which is the process of **"restoring the last, 'lower' hei of the Tetragrammaton,"** as stated in Chapter Four.

כמ"ש בגמ' מלפפתו וכו'. ומאחר שרוח עברה
ותטהרם אזי תוכל נפשם לשוב עד הוי' ב"ה ממש
ולעלות מעלה מעלה למקורה ולדבקה בו ית' ביחוד
נפלא. כמו שהיתה מיוחדת בו ית' בתכלית היחוד
בטרם שנפחה ברוח פיו ית' לירד למטה ולהתלבש
בגוף האדם (וכמו עד"מ באדם הנופח ברוח פיו בטרם

98B

SECTION TWO: THE DEFINITION OF "UPPER TESHUVAH"

Now the *Tanya* begins its explanation of "upper *teshuvah*." All we know so far of this experience is the basic definition cited from the *Zohar* in Chapter Four that "upper *teshuvah*" is aimed at "*restoring the first, 'upper' hei of the Tetragrammaton.*"

וּמֵאַחַר שֶׁרוּחַ עָבְרָה וַתִּטַהֲרֵם — **And after,** *"a spirit passes, making them pure"* (*Job* 37:21).

After "lower *teshuvah*" is complete, which means that the negative "spirit" of sin has passed and you are completely cleansed and "pure" once again.

אֲזַי תּוּכַל נַפְשָׁם לָשׁוּב עַד הֲוָיָ"ה בָּרוּךְ הוּא מַמָּשׁ — **Then your soul can** *literally* **return to G-d,** through "upper *teshuvah*."

What is "upper *teshuvah*"? And how does it cause your soul to "literally" return to G-d?

וְלַעֲלוֹת מַעֲלָה מַעֲלָה לִמְקוֹרָהּ וּלְדָבְקָה בּוֹ יִתְבָּרַךְ בְּיִחוּד נִפְלָא — In "upper *teshuvah*" your soul is **elevated greatly to its source, to be attached to G-d, in an amazing merging experience.**

If all your sins have been atoned through "lower *teshuvah*," what could still be lacking in the soul's connection to G-d. Why is a further *teshuvah* necessary?

The *Tanya* explains:

כְּמוֹ שֶׁהָיְתָה מְיֻחֶדֶת בּוֹ יִתְבָּרַךְ בְּתַכְלִית הַיִּחוּד—The goal of "upper *teshuvah*" is to restore your soul to the level **when it was merged with G-d seamlessly,** בְּטֶרֶם שֶׁנִּפְחָה בְּרוּחַ פִּיו יִתְבָּרַךְ — *before* G-d "blew" with "the breath of His mouth" (*Psalms* 33:6), לֵירֵד לְמַטָּה וּלְהִתְלַבֵּשׁ בְּגוּף הָאָדָם — **causing** the soul **to come down here and enter a human body,** (וּכְמוֹ עַל דֶּרֶךְ מָשָׁל בְּאָדָם הַנּוֹפֵחַ בְּרוּחַ פִּיו — like, for example, a person who is *about* to blow air from his mouth, בְּטֶרֶם שֶׁיּוֹצֵא הָרוּחַ מִפִּיו הוּא מְיֻחָד בְּנַפְשׁוֹ) — where the breath is still bound inside him.

שיוצא הרוח מפיו הוא מיוחד בנפשו) וזו היא תשובה
שלימה. והנה בחי' יחוד זה ותשובה זו היא בחי'

Before "lower *teshuvah*," sins separate your soul from G-d. But even after this obstacle is removed, your soul remains separate from G-d *simply because it exists.*

As we learned in Part One, Chapter 35:

"A person's soul, even if that person is a complete tzadik, worshiping G-d with reverence and 'pleasurable love' (Song 7:7), nevertheless, that soul still does not lose its separate identity completely, which would enable it to be extinguished and literally absorbed in G-d's light, and to merge completely with G-d in absolute unity. Rather, the soul retains its separate identity, as one who is reverent of G-d and a lover of Him, but not one with Him."

"Upper *teshuvah*" is the process of transcending this consciousness, to no longer look at yourself as a separate, autonomous entity that has become, on some level, detached from its root in G-d. At a certain plane of consciousness, the soul is never fully detached; it is sill *"merged with G-d seamlessly... like, for example, a person who is about to blow air from his mouth, where the breath is still bound inside him."* Your soul can recall and regain the consciousness of its complete union with G-d before it became a separate entity.

PRACTICAL LESSONS

"Lower *teshuvah*" is a "return" in the sense that it restores you to the level prior to sin.

At "upper *teshuvah*," your soul recalls and regains the consciousness of its complete union with G-d before it became a separate entity.

You can't begin "upper *teshuvah*" without doing "lower *teshuvah*" first.

וְזוֹ הִיא תְּשׁוּבָה שְׁלֵמָה — **And this is complete,** "upper *teshuvah.*"

Teshuvah means "return." "Lower *teshuvah*" is a "return" in the sense that it restores you to the level prior to sin. "Upper *teshuvah*" is a "return" in the sense that it restores you to the level prior to your soul's departure from G-d, to become a separate entity.

After "lower *teshuvah*" all you want to do is to worship G-d. But the very fact that there is a "you" that wants to do the worship implies a certain distance and a disconnect. Through "upper *teshuvah,*" you reconnect to the root-consciousness of your soul, how it is the very same "substance" as G-d.

(Later the *Tanya* will explains how this consciousness is expressed in practical worship.)

וְהִנֵּה בְּחִינַת יִחוּד זֶה וּתְשׁוּבָה זוֹ הִיא בְּחִינַת תְּשׁוּבָה עִילָּאָה שֶׁלְּאַחַר תְּשׁוּבָה תַּתָּאָה —

תשובה עילאה שלאחר תשובה תתאה וכמ"ש בזוה"ק
בר"מ פ' נשא דתשובה עילאה היא דיתעסק באורייי'

This level of merging and *teshuvah* is "upper *teshuvah*" that follows "lower *teshuvah*."

You can't begin "upper *teshuvah*" without doing "lower *teshuvah*" first. Without "lower *teshuvah*," the negative energy of your sins will prevent you from reaching the higher consciousness of "upper *teshuvah*."

But both experiences share the same name, *teshuvah,* because they are on the same trajectory: the return of the soul back towards its original, intimate union with the Divine.

SECTION THREE: THE PROCESS OF "UPPER TESHUVAH"

Practically speaking, how is "upper *teshuvah*" achieved? The *Tanya* will lay down the fundamentals of this process here at the end of Chapter Eight and elaborate upon them in more detail in the following chapter.

וּכְמוֹ שֶׁכָּתוּב בַּזֹּהַר הַקָּדוֹשׁ בְּרַעְיָא מְהֵימְנָא פָּרָשַׁת נָשֹׂא — **As the holy *Zohar* states (*Raya Mehemna, Parshas Naso*, 3, 123a),** דְּתְשׁוּבָה עִילָּאָה הִיא דְּיִתְעַסֵּק בְּאוֹרָיְיתָא בִּדְחִילוּ וּרְחִימוּ דְּקוּדְשָׁא בְּרִיךְ הוּא וְכוּ' — **that "'upper *teshuvah*,' is to study Torah with reverence and love for the Blessed Holy One etc."**

The *Zohar* indicates that "upper *teshuvah*" is not achieved through *mitzvah* observance, but specifically through Torah study, *i.e.,* using the *intellect* to study G-d's word.

The intellect is capable of *objectivity*: it allows you to explore ideas and phenomena outside yourself. When your mind studies "G-d's word" in the Torah, you have grasped a Divine concept *outside your ego*. This experience has the power to lift you to "upper *teshuvah*," where you transcend the limitations of your egoic identity and "are merged with G-d seamlessly."

When you worship G-d through *mitzvos,* on the other hand, it might seem like you've transcended yourself, since you're not focusing on your own concerns; but a *mitzvah* cannot fully empower you to shed your ego. Think about what the word *mitzvah* means: It is a commandment *to you*. That means, *in its very definition, you exist*. So it can't empower you to reach the consciousness of when you were *"merged with G-d seamlessly, before G-d blew with the breath of His mouth causing the soul to come down here and enter a human body."*

Torah, on the other hand, is a glimpse into the "mind" of G-d. While the Torah discusses commandments addressed at you, it's energy and identity is *G-d's*

בדחילו ורחימו דקדב"ה וכו' דאיהו בן י"ה בינה וכו'
(ומעלת בעלי תשובה על צדיקים גמורים בזה היא
כמ"ש בזוה"ק פ' חיי שרה דאינון משכי עלייהו ברעותא
דלבא יתיר ובחילא סגי לאתקרבא למלכא וכו'):

word. When you study Torah *"with reverence and love for the Blessed Holy One,"* to uncover its core Divine power, Torah has the ability to lift your consciousness to the level which transcends your separate existence. You enter into the "mind" of G-d before the thought of the world ever arose!

The *Zohar* continues:

דְּאִיהוּ בֵּן י"ה בִּינָה וְכוּ' — *"So that you are a child (ben) of yud-hei, binah, etc.,"*

"Upper teshuvah" is the return of the first, upper *hei* of the Tetragrammaton which, as we have learned, is associated with *binah* (spelled *BeN Yud-Hei*).

Binah is *detached* cognition, which enables you to analyze an idea or text devoid of influence of the ego. That is why it is the crucial component of "upper *teshuvah,"* the return of the soul to its sublime, pre-ego consciousness (see *Likutei Sichos* vol. 39, pp. 92-3).

PRACTICAL LESSONS

"Upper *teshuvah*," is to study Torah with reverence and love for G-d, with a powerful desire of the heart.

(וּמַעֲלַת בַּעֲלֵי תְּשׁוּבָה עַל צַדִיקִים גְּמוּרִים בָּזֶה — **And** what is **the advantage of** those practicing "upper *teshuvah,"* **in this** experience of Torah study **over complete** *tzadikim,* who also study Torah, but not as a practice of *teshuvah*?

Obviously *"to study Torah with reverence and love for the Blessed Holy One"* is not necessarily an experience of "upper *teshuvah."* It is also an activity carried out by the "complete *tzadikim"* who are not doing *teshuvah.*

So what distinguishes a Torah study experience of "upper *teshuvah,"* and one which is not?

הִיא כְּמוֹ שֶׁכָּתוּב בַּזֹהַר הַקָּדוֹשׁ פָּרָשַׁת חַיֵּי שָׂרָה — The answer is, **as stated in the holy** *Zohar (Parshas Chayei Sarah,* 1, 129b), דְּאִינוּן מָשְׁכֵי עֲלַיְיהוּ בִּרְעוּתָא דְּלִבָּא יַתִּיר וּבְחֵילָא סַגִי לְאִתְקָרְבָא לְמַלְכָּא וְכוּ' — **that** those who practice *teshuvah,* **"are aroused with a more powerful desire of the heart and with greater intensity to come close to the King, etc."**

Torah study becomes an experience of *teshuvah* when it is carried out with, *"a more powerful desire of the heart and with greater intensity,"* with a desire to return the soul to G-d, *"to come close to the King."*

We have learned the definition of "upper *teshuvah*" and the basic method of its practice. In the following chapter, we will explore "upper *teshuvah*" in more practical detail.

פרק ט וביאור העניין כמ"ש בזוה"ק ותיקוני' בכמה
מקומות. דבינה איהי תשובה
עילאה והאם רובצת על האפרוחים וכו'. דהיינו שע"י

CHAPTER 9

LIVING AT "UPPER TESHUVAH"

SECTION ONE: REBUILDING YOUR EMOTIONAL CORE

25TH TAMMUZ REGULAR | 29TH TAMMUZ LEAP

In the previous chapter, the *Tanya* introduced us to "upper *teshuvah*," which we defined as reaching the consciousness of the soul, *"as it was merged with G-d seamlessly before G-d blew with the breath of His mouth causing (the soul) to come down here and enter a human body."*

The key to reaching this transpersonal state, we learned, was through the intellectual experience of Torah study, since the mind is capable of detachment from self and ego.

Our proof for this was a teaching of the *Zohar*: *"'Upper teshuvah,' is to study Torah with reverence and love for the Blessed Holy One."*

The opening of this chapter will examine another detail in the *Zohar's* words. Why does the Zohar stress that "upper *teshuvah*" requires not only detached "Torah study," but also "reverence and love"?

In fact, the stress on "reverence and love" seems to contradict what we have learned so far about the experience of "upper *teshuvah*." Reverence and love are *emotions* which are inevitably bound up with ego and identity. You only love or revere something *in relation to your self,* because emotions navigate the relationship between you and other things in the world.

So reverence and love would appear to be counterproductive to "upper *teshuvah*," which is aimed at *transcending* self and ego through the detachment of the mind?

The *Tanya* now addresses this issue.

וּבֵאוּר הָעִנְיָן — Let us clarify "upper *teshuvah*" further, כְּמוֹ שֶׁכָּתוּב בַּזֹּהַר הַקָּדוֹשׁ וְתִקּוּנִים בְּכַמָּה מְקוֹמוֹת — based on what is written in the holy *Zohar* and *Tikunei Zohar,* in various places, דְּבִינָה אִיהִי תְּשׁוּבָה עִילָאָה — that *binah* is "upper *teshuvah*," וְהָאֵם רוֹבֶצֶת עַל הָאֶפְרוֹחִים וְכוּ' — *"and the mother is crouched over the chicks"* (Deuteronomy 22:6).

שמתבונן בגדולת ה' בהעמקת הדעת ומוליד מרוח
בינתו דו"ר שכליים ובטוב טעם ודעת כענין שנא'

Binah (detached cognition) is the "mother of the chicks," *i.e.,* it gives birth to emotions. That's because your emotional relationship ("like" or "dislike") to something depends on your understanding of its value. For example, physical pleasure makes you feel good, so you desire it; knowledge helps you to make sense of the world, so you want it. Pain, on the other hand, is unpleasant, so you dislike it (see Part One, p. 559).

דְּהַיְינוּ שֶׁעַל יְדֵי שֶׁמִּתְבּוֹנֵן בִּגְדֻלַּת ה' בְּהַעֲמָקַת הַדַּעַת — **Meaning that** the result of the consciousness of "upper *teshuvah*," (*binah*/Torah study) is that **through contemplating the greatness of G-d in deep thought,** וּמוֹלִיד מֵרוּחַ בִּינָתוֹ דְּחִילוּ וּרְחִימוּ שְׂכְלִיִּים — **your faculty of *binah* will "give birth" to** a new emotional core of **intellectually generated love and reverence of** G-d, וּבְטוֹב טַעַם וָדַעַת — **with *"good insight and da'as"* (***Psalms** 119:66).

It is true that "upper *teshuvah*" requires the *detached-intellectual* power of *binah* to transcend ego and reach the consciousness of being *"merged with G-d etc.,"* as we learned in the previous chapter. But "upper *teshuvah*" also requires a *second phase,* discussed here, namely the *emotion-generating* power of *binah,* how it is *"the mother is crouched over the chicks."*

The *Tanya's* conviction is that, before reaching "upper *teshuvah*," since your identity is egocentric, your emotions will inevitably be self-serving. Even the desire to worship G-d will be because *you* want to be close to Him, or because *you* are seeking a reward.

PRACTICAL LESSONS

Once you reach "upper *teshuvah*" you can recreate your emotional core from a different set of values.

Once you reach "upper *teshuvah*," using your *binah,* you attain the transpersonal, ego-free consciousness (of when your soul *"was merged with G-d."*) Then you have the opportunity to *recreate your emotional core,* constructing your values, and the feelings that they produce, once more from scratch. This time, your emotions will be built from transpersonal consciousness: they will be *"intellectually generated"* and not self-serving. For example, instead of worshiping G-d because you see value in it for yourself, you will be motivated because *it's the right thing to do.*

That is the *Tanya's* message here. "Upper *teshuvah*" requires not only the release from ego through the detachment of *binah;* there must also be a second phase powered by *binah's* post-*teshuvah* re-engagement with your personality — the rebuilding of character from a new, non-egoic foundation, through the emotion-generating power of *binah.*

לאהבה את ה' אלקיך משום כי הוא חייך וכו' ולא
די לו באהבה טבעית המסותרת לבד וכו'. וכן ביראה
ופחד או בושה וכו' כנודע. אזי נקראת האם רובצת

And this explains why *"'upper teshuvah' is to study Torah* **with reverence and love** *for the Blessed Holy One."* The Torah study (*binah* detachment) must lead to a new set of (non-egoic) emotions (Based on *Likutei Sichos* vol. 39, pp. 90-95).

כְּעִנְיָן שֶׁנֶּאֱמַר לְאַהֲבָה אֶת ה' אֱלֹקֶיךָ מִשּׁוּם כִּי הוּא חַיֶּיךָ וְכוּ' — **As in the theme of the verse,** *"that you may love G-d, your G-d... because He is your life"* (Deuteronomy 30:20).

This verse supports the above idea: Your newly built emotional core needs to permeate your whole character, such that your consciousness of being *"merged with G-d"* becomes your *everyday life* (ibid., p. 94).

וְלֹא דַּי לוֹ בְּאַהֲבָה טִבְעִית הַמְּסָתֶּרֶת לְבַד וְכוּ' — **And you won't suffice with the natural, latent love** of G-d in your heart (see Part One, p. 448).

A central teaching of Part One of *Tanya* is that your soul has an inherent, dormant love for G-d, which does not have to be *acquired*; it merely has to be *awakened*.

Here the *Tanya* warns us that this experience will not bring you to the consciousness of "upper *teshuvah*." Natural, inherent love is bound with your ego. It is not compatible with the transpersonal consciousness of "upper *teshuvah*" which transcends ego.

This is despite the fact that (as we learned in Part One) natural, latent love is also awakened through a meditative process, *i.e.,* through *binah*. That's because, in the case of inherent love, *binah* does not actually *generate* the love; it only *awakens* the (ego-related) feelings that were already present, but dormant (see *Likutei Sichos* ibid. pp. 93-94; *Toras Menachem, Hisvaduyos* 5729, vol. 1, p. 192).

וְכֵן בְּיִרְאָה וָפַחַד אוֹ בּוּשָׁה וְכוּ' — **And the same is true of reverence, fear or shame** for G-d *etc.,* כַּנּוֹדָע — **as is known** (see Part One, Chapter 41).

These emotions too must be freshly generated by *binah* once you have reached the transpersonal consciousness of "upper *teshuvah*."

(The *Tanya* stresses "shame" here, a very crude and basic expression of reverence, to stress the extent to which the consciousness of "upper *teshuvah*" ought to reach all of your personality, even its lowest faculties).

אֲזַי נִקְרֵאת הָאֵם רוֹבֶצֶת עַל הָאֶפְרוֹחִים וְכוּ' — **Then,** when you have produced a new emotional core *from binah* **it is called,** *"the mother is crouched over the chicks etc."*

עַל הָאֶפְרוֹחִי' וְכוּ'. וְהִנֵּה עִיקַר הָאַהֲבָה הִיא אִתְדַּבְּקוּת
רוּחָא בְּרוּחָא כמ"ש יִשָּׁקֵנִי מִנְּשִׁיקוֹת פִּיהוּ וְכוּ' כַּנּוֹדָע.
וע"ז נֶאֱמַר וּבְכָל נַפְשְׁךָ שֶׁהֵם הֵם כָּל חֶלְקֵי הַנֶּפֶשׁ שֶׁכֶל
וּמִדּוֹת וּלְבוּשֵׁיהֶם מַחֲשָׁבָה דִּבּוּר וּמַעֲשֶׂה לְדָבְקָה כֻּלָּן

SECTION TWO: WORSHIP AT THE LEVEL OF "UPPER TESHUVAH"

In this section, the *Tanya* offers some practical illustrations of various modes of worship at the level of "upper *teshuvah."*

The key emphasis will be a shift away from the consciousness of separateness. Prior to "upper *teshuvah,"* you may be utterly devoted to G-d, but you view it as a relationship existing between two entities, you and G-d. Your worship aims to bridge the divide that separates you.

At "upper *teshuvah,"* your consciousness is one of being *"merged with G-d seamlessly as before G-d blew with the breath of His mouth causing (the soul) to come down here and enter a human body."* At this level, "you" are not separate from G-d; rather, all your soul powers and worship are an *expression of G-d* which you channel (Based on *Likutei Sichos* ibid., pp. 94-95).

וְהִנֵּה עִקַּר הָאַהֲבָה הִיא אִתְדַּבְּקוּת רוּחָא בְּרוּחָא — **Now the main type of love** at "upper *teshuvah"* is not the worship of another entity, but a *"merging of spirit with spirit"* (*Zohar* 1, 184a), so that you become a *channel of expression* of G-d in this world, כְּמוֹ שֶׁכָּתוּב יִשָּׁקֵנִי מִנְּשִׁיקוֹת פִּיהוּ וְכוּ' — **as the verse states, "let him kiss me with kisses of the mouth"** (*Song* 1:2), כַּנּוֹדָע — **as is known** (see Part One, p. 587).

The "kiss" is a metaphor for being *"merged with G-d seamlessly."* Once you are merged with Him, you become a beacon of G-d in the world.

וְעַל זֶה נֶאֱמַר וּבְכָל נַפְשְׁךָ — **And that is why the verse states,** *"You shall love G-d... with all your soul"* (*Deuteronomy* 6:5), שֶׁהֵם הֵם כָּל חֶלְקֵי הַנֶּפֶשׁ — **meaning, with all the parts of your soul,** שֵׂכֶל וּמִדּוֹת — **the intellectual and emotional powers,** וּלְבוּשֵׁיהֶם מַחֲשָׁבָה דִּבּוּר וּמַעֲשֶׂה — **and their "garments," of thought, speech and action,** לְדָבְקָה כֻּלָּן בּוֹ יִתְבָּרֵךְ — **to** *attach* **them all to G-d.**

"Love" here doesn't mean that you are drawn to G-d. It means that you are (already) *attached* to G-d.

As a result, everything you do is an expression of G-d, channeling His presence and energy.

The *Tanya* offers examples of this style of worship in all the areas mentioned above: emotions and intellect; as well as the soul's "garments" of thought, speech and action.

בו ית' דהיינו המדות במדותיו ית' מה הוא רחום וכו'.
והשכל בשכלו וחכמתו ית' הוא עיון התורה דאורייתא
מחכמה נפקא. וכן המחשבה במחשבתו ית' והדיבור
בדבר ה' זו הלכה וכמ"ש ואשים דברי בפיך ודברי
אשר שמתי בפיך. והמעשה הוא מעשה הצדקה
להחיות רוח שפלים כמ"ש כי ששת ימים עשה ה'
וכו' כנודע במ"א. וזו היא אתדבקות דרוחא ברוחא

99A

דְּהַיְינוּ הַמִּדּוֹת בְּמִדּוֹתָיו יִתְבָּרֵךְ — **This means that your emotional powers** are attached to and channel **G-d's emotional powers,** מָה הוּא רַחוּם וְכוּ' — *"Just as He is merciful and kind, so you must be merciful and kind"* (*Jerusalem Talmud, Pe'ah* 1:1).

וְהַשֵּׂכֶל בְּשִׂכְלוֹ וְחָכְמָתוֹ יִתְבָּרֵךְ — **And,** so too, **your intellect** is attached **to** and channels G-d's **intellect and** *chochmah,* הוּא עִיּוּן הַתּוֹרָה — **through** your delving **into the Torah,** דְּאוֹרַיְיתָא מֵחָכְמָה נָפְקָא — for *"the Torah emerged from chochmah"* (*Zohar* 2, 85a).

We turn to the "garments" of thought, speech and action

PRACTICAL LESSONS

At "higher *teshuvah*," "you" are not separate from G-d; all your soul powers and worship are an expression of G-d which you channel.

וְכֵן הַמַּחֲשָׁבָה בְּמַחֲשַׁבְתּוֹ יִתְבָּרֵךְ — **And so too, your thoughts with G-d's thoughts,** which is also through Torah study.

וְהַדִּבּוּר בְּדַבַר ה' זוּ הֲלָכָה — **Your speech with** *"the word of G-d, which is halachah (Jewish Law)"* (*Talmud, Shabbos* 138b), וּכְמוֹ שֶׁכָּתוּב וָאָשִׂים דְּבָרַי בְּפִיךָ — **as the verse states,** *"I have placed my words in your mouth"* (*Isaiah* 51:16), וּדְבָרַי אֲשֶׁר שַׂמְתִּי בְּפִיךָ — *"and my words which I have placed in your mouth"* (*Isaiah* 59:21).

וְהַמַּעֲשֶׂה הוּא מַעֲשֵׂה הַצְּדָקָה — **And your actions** are attached to G-d and channel His action, which is **charity,** לְהַחֲיוֹת רוּחַ שְׁפָלִים — *"to revive the spirit of the lowly"* (ibid., 57:15).

כְּמוֹ שֶׁכָּתוּב כִּי שֵׁשֶׁת יָמִים עָשָׂה ה' וְכוּ' — **As the verse states,** *"For in six days did G-d make* the heavens and the earth" (*Exodus* 20:11), כַּנּוֹדָע בְּמָקוֹם אַחֵר — **as is explained elsewhere** (*Tanya, Igeres Ha-Kodesh* sec. 17).

G-d's "action" of making the world gave life to all its inhabitants, similar to the act of charity which "revives spirit."

וְזוֹ הִיא אִתְדַּבְּקוּת דְּרוּחָא בְּרוּחָא בְּתַכְלִית הַדְּבֵקוּת וְהַיִּחוּד — **And** all the above

בתכלית הדביקות והיחוד כשהיא מחמת אהבה וכו'.
ולפי שפגם הברית בהוצאת ז"ל ואצ"ל בעריות או
שאר איסורי ביאה דאורייתא או דרבנן (כי חמורים
ד"ס וכו') פוגם במוח לכן תיקונו הוא דיתעסק באורייתא

are examples of *"merging of spirit with spirit"* **with complete attachment and merging** at the level of "upper *teshuvah*."

כְּשֶׁהִיא מֵחֲמַת אַהֲבָה וְכוּ' — **Because** "upper *teshuvah*" **is** a worship **through love** and awareness of deep connection, not out of mere obedience to another being.

SECTION THREE: A SPECIAL TYPE OF "UPPER TESHUVAH"

In the following chapter, we will continue the above discussion of practical worship at the level of "upper *teshuvah*."

For the rest of this chapter we will return to an earlier question which has been left unanswered. In Chapter Four, the *Tanya* cited a teaching of *Reishis Chochmah* that "lower *teshuvah*" is ineffective for the sin of emitting seed in vain and "upper *teshuvah*" is required in this case. We will now clarify this point.

וּלְפִי שֶׁפְּגַם הַבְּרִית בְּהוֹצָאַת זֶרַע לְבַטָּלָה — **The sexual sin of emitting seed in vain,** וְאֵין צָרִיךְ לוֹמַר בַּעֲרָיוֹת — **and certainly the more severe forbidden sexual relations (***arayos***),** אוֹ שְׁאָר אִסּוּרֵי בִּיאָה דְּאוֹרָיְיתָא אוֹ דְּרַבָּנָן — **or other** less severe **forbidden sexual relations, Biblical or Rabbinic,** (כִּי חֲמוּרִים דִּבְרֵי סוֹפְרִים וְכוּ') — Rabbinic prohibitions having a special importance since *"the words of the Scribes are even more stringent than the words of the Torah"* (*Talmud, Eruvin* 21b; see Part One, p. 105), פּוֹגֵם בַּמּוֹחַ — all the above cause **damage to the brain,** spiritually speaking (*Reishis Chochmah, Sha'ar Ha-Kedushah* ch. 17), לָכֵן תִּקּוּנוֹ הוּא דְּיִתְעַסֵּק בְּאוֹרָיְיתָא דְּמֵחָכְמָה נָפְקָא — **therefore they are rectified** by "upper *teshuvah*" that requires **the study of Torah, which** *"emerged from chochmah,"* i.e., a "brain" energy.

As the *Tanya* taught at the end of the previous chapter, from the *Zohar*, "'Upper *teshuvah*,' is to study Torah with reverence and love for the Blessed Holy One." Ordinarily, as we have learned, "upper *teshuvah*," is a deep bonding with G-d that occurs only *after* atonement is complete, through "lower *teshuvah*." "Upper *teshuvah*" is a *post-repentance* return to G-d.

We learn here that atonement for sexual sins constitutes an exception to this rule. Since these sins *"damage the brain,"* their atonement must be brain-relat-

דמחכמה נפקא. וז"ש בתנא דבי אליהו אדם עבר
עבירה ונתחייב מיתה למקום מה יעשה ויחיה אם היה
רגיל לקרות דף אחד יקרא ב' דפים לשנות פרק
א' ישנה ב' פרקים וכו'. והיינו כמשל חבל הנפסק
וחוזר וקושרו שבמקום הקשר הוא כפול ומכופל.
וככה הוא בחבל נחלתו וכו'. וזש"ה בחסד ואמת

ed, requiring the "upper *teshuvah*" experience, "*to study Torah with reverence and love for the Blessed Holy One.*"

In other words, in this particular case, the method of "upper *teshuvah*" (Torah study) is required as a supplement to "lower teshuvah" (atonement).

(*Reishis Chochmah* does not mean to say that the *full consciousness* of "upper *teshuvah*" is required for atonement. Rather, the experience of Torah study is a "merging of spirit with spirit" with G-d, so it inevitably has some of the qualities of "upper *teshuvah*" consciousness — see *Toras Menachem* ibid., p. 196).

The *Tanya* brings a proof that Torah study atones for these types of sins.

וְזֶהוּ שֶׁכָּתוּב בְּתַנָּא דְּבֵי אֵלִיָּהוּ — **As stated in** *Tanna de-bei Eliyahu*:

אָדָם עָבַר עֲבֵרָה וְנִתְחַיֵּב מִיתָה לַמָּקוֹם — **"If a person transgresses and is liable for the death penalty on High,"** מַה יַּעֲשֶׂה וְיִחְיֶה — **"what should he do in order that he should live?"**

אִם הָיָה רָגִיל לִקְרוֹת דַּף אֶחָד — **"If he usually would read a single page** in a To-rah study session," לִשְׁנוֹת פֶּרֶק — יִקְרָא שְׁנֵי דַּפִּים — **"he should read two pages,"** אֶחָד — **"If he would study one chapter,"** יִשְׁנֶה שְׁנֵי פְּרָקִים וְכוּ' — **"he should study two chapters, etc."** (see *Leviticus Rabah* 25:1).

The *Tanya* explains the significance of this remedy, "*he should read two pages.*"

וְהַיְינוּ כְּמָשָׁל חֶבֶל — **This is like** our **analogy of the rope (*chevel*)** cited above as an illustration of the soul's connection to G-d.

הַנִּפְסָק וְחוֹזֵר וְקוֹשְׁרוֹ — If the rope **was cut** through sin **and then retied**, through *teshuvah*, שֶׁבִּמְקוֹם הַקֶּשֶׁר הוּא כָּפוּל — **in the place of the knot**, the re-tied strands are **doubled** וּמְכֻפָּל — and they are **redoubled** to make sure the knot lasts.

וְכָכָה הוּא בְּחֶבֶל נַחֲלָתוֹ וְכוּ' — **The same is true with** the soul, "*His allotted (chevel) inheritance*" (*Deuteronomy* 32:9).

In the case of sexual sins, both "lower" and "upper *teshuvah*" are required, a point hinted to by the "double and redoubled knot" (*Toras Menachem* ibid.).

יכופר עון וכו' ואין אמת אלא תורה וכו'. ועון בית
עלי בזבח ומנחה הוא דאינו מתכפר אבל מתכפר
בתורה וגמ"ח כדאי' בספ"ק דר"ה:

The *Tanya* offers another proof.

וְזֶהוּ שֶׁאָמַר הַכָּתוּב בְּחֶסֶד וֶאֱמֶת יְכָפַּר עָוֹן וְכוּ' — And that is why the verse states, **"Through kindness and truth, a sin is atoned etc.,"** (*Proverbs* 16:6), וְאֵין אֱמֶת אֶלָּא תוֹרָה וְכוּ' — and **"'truth' (here) refers to nothing other than Torah"** (*Talmud, Brachos* 5b).

Here we see that sometimes Torah study (i.e., "upper *teshuvah*") is required as part of the atonement process, to ensure that *"a sin is atoned."*

The *Tanya* presents a final proof.

וַעֲוֹן בֵּית עֵלִי בְּזֶבַח וּמִנְחָה הוּא דְּאֵינוֹ מִתְכַּפֵּר — And the verse states, *"I have sworn unto the house of Eli, that* **the sin of Eli's house will not be atoned through sacrifice nor offering** *forever"* (*1 Samuel* 3:14), אֲבָל מִתְכַּפֵּר בְּתוֹרָה וּגְמִילוּת חֲסָדִים — but these sins, which were sexual in nature, **were atoned through Torah and acts of kindness,** כִּדְאִיתָא בְּסוֹף פֶּרֶק קַמָּא דְּרֹאשׁ הַשָּׁנָה — as stated in *Talmud, Rosh Hashanah,* chapter 1 (18a).

פרק י וְהִנֵּה תשובה עילאה זו דאתדבקותא דרוחא
ברוחא ע"י תורה וגמ"ח. היא בבחי'

CHAPTER 10

MORE ON "UPPER TESHUVAH"

SECTION ONE: ABSORBING "UPPER TESHUVAH"

26TH TAMMUZ REGULAR | 1ST AV LEAP

In this section we will discuss the theme of practical worship at the level of "upper *teshuvah*," continuing from the discussion in Chapter Nine, Section Two.

וְהִנֵּה תְּשׁוּבָה עִילָאָה זוֹ דְּאִתְדַּבְּקוּתָא דְּרוּחָא בְּרוּחָא — **Now** worship at **this** level of **"upper *teshuvah*,"** the consciousness of **"*merging of spirit with spirit*"** (*Zohar* 1, 184a), עַל יְדֵי תּוֹרָה וּגְמִילוּת חֲסָדִים הִיא בִּבְחִינַת הַמְשָׁכָה מִלְמַעְלָה לְמַטָּה — worship at this level **through Torah and acts of kindness,** brings about a **"downward flow"** of Divine energy.

Chasidic thought often categorizes a spiritual dynamic as either "downward flow" (*hamshachah milemalah lematah*) or "upward ascent" (*ha'alah milematah lemalah*). In "downward flow," your worship *channels* energy from the Divine realm into the universe. This must be preceded by "upward ascent," where you lift yourself to the level of consciousness and spiritual power at which you are able to act as a channel for the downward flow.

In the previous chapters we have discussed both of these dynamics with regard to "upper *teshuvah*." In Chapter Eight, Section Three, we learned that the consciousness of "upper *teshuvah*" is achieved through a meditative process, using the power of *binah,* to reach the consciousness of being *"merged with G-d seamlessly, before G-d blew with the breath of His mouth causing the soul to come down here and enter a human body."* This meditative work is an example of "upward ascent," lifting yourself to the consciousness of "upper *teshuvah*."

And in Chapter Nine, Section Two, we learned of the "downward flow" of Divine energy that is channeled into the universe when worship takes place at the consciousness of "upper *teshuvah*": Your thoughts channel G-d's thoughts, your speech channels G-d's speech, your actions channel G-d's actions, *etc.*

The *Tanya* reminds us of this channeling experience as it relates to Torah study.

המשכה מלמעלה למטה להיות דבר ה' ממש בפיו
וכמ"ש ואשים דברי בפיך. וימינו תחבקני בגמ"ח
דחסד דרועא ימינא וכו'. אבל אדם התחתון צריך
לילך ממדרגה למדרגה ממטה למעלה היא בחי'
תשובה עילאה ואתדבקות רוחא ברוחא בכוונת הלב

לִהְיוֹת דְּבַר ה' מַמָּשׁ בְּפִיו — When you are in the consciousness of "upper *teshuvah*," your Torah study is a channeling experience **where** you are aware **that G-d's word is literally in your mouth,** וּכְמוֹ שֶׁכָּתוּב וָאָשִׂים דְּבָרַי בְּפִיךְ — as the verse states, *"I have placed My words in your mouth"* (Isaiah 51:16).

The *Tanya* reminds us of this channeling experience as it relates to acts of kindness.

וִימִינוֹ תְּחַבְּקֵנִי בִּגְמִילוּת חֲסָדִים — When you are in the consciousness of "upper *teshuvah*," your acts of kindness are a channeling experience where G-d's *"right arm hugs me"* (Song 2:6), **with acts of kindness** (see Part One, p. 587), דְּחֶסֶד דְּרוֹעָא יְמִינָא וְכו' — since *"kindness is* G-d's *right arm"* (Tikunei Zohar 17a).

You are conscious that your act of kindness channels G-d's kindness, which is a Divine energy compared to "His right arm."

אֲבָל אָדָם הַתַּחְתּוֹן צָרִיךְ לֵילֵךְ מִמַּדְרֵגָה לְמַדְרֵגָה מִמַּטָּה לְמַעְלָה — **But** in order to reach this consciousness of "merging of spirit with spirit," and act as a channel for Divine energy, **a person in this world** who is born with a consciousness of separateness from G-d, **has to** first **ascend progressively,** through *binah* meditation (as described in Chapter Eight, Section Three; Chapter Nine, Section Two).

SECTION TWO: "UPPER TESHUVAH" AND PRAYER

Up to this point we have discussed only how the consciousness of "upper *teshuvah*" relates to Torah study and *mitzvah* observance. Now the *Tanya* describes prayer as it is carried out at this level (see *Notes on Tanya*).

הִיא בְּחִינַת תְּשׁוּבָה עִילָאָה וְאִתְדַּבְּקוּת רוּחָא בְּרוּחָא בְּכַוָּנַת הַלֵּב בִּתְפִלָּה — Having reached the consciousness of **"upper *teshuvah*,"** and **"merging of spirit with spirit,"** it will transform your experience of **focusing the heart in prayer**.

Prayer is a time of meditative work. So you might think that prayer is a method of using *binah* to **reach** "upper teshuvah," and not an experience of being *at* "upper teshuvah."

בתפלה ובפרט בק"ש וברכותיה. כדי לומר ואהבת
כו' בכל לבבך ובכל נפשך וכו' באמת לאמיתו. וכן

The *Tanya* informs us here that this is not the case. After reaching "upper *teshuvah*," your prayer experience will be different.

וּבִפְרָט בִּקְרִיאַת שְׁמַע וּבְרְכוֹתֶיהָ — **This is especially during the recital of the** *Shema* **and its blessings.**

The *Tanya* emphasizes that the experience of "upper *teshuvah*" in prayer is *"especially during the recital of the Shema,"* and not during the standing prayer *Amidah* (*Shmoneh Esrei*). Why is the experience of "upper *teshuvah*" associated with the *Shema* in particular?

Prayer has two components: a.) We present our *requests* to G-d. This takes place exclusively during the *Amidah*.

b.) It is an experience of *devotion* to G-d, as Chanah said, *"I spilled out my soul before G-d"* (1 *Shmuel* 1:15). This occurs throughout the prayer service, but is especially pronounced in the recital of the *Shema,* whose definitive theme is *mesiras nefesh*, handing yourself over to G-d.

PRACTICAL LESSONS

The consciousness of "higher *teshuvah*" is especially pronounced during moments of devotional prayer.

(From the perspective of 'b,' the devotional role of prayer, *"the remainder of the prayers are merely a 'commentary' on the Shema."* For example, when we pray for health and wealth in the *Amidah* we focus on the experience of G-d that these good fortunes bring. When you are healed, you feel close to G-d. When your financial situation improves, you sense G-d's hand. So even the *Amidah* is, in effect, a prayer to be close to G-d—Rabbi Shneur Zalman, *Siddur im Dach,* 19a).

Since prayer at the level of "upper *teshuvah*" is a devotional experience, referred to here in the *Tanya* as a *"merging of spirit with spirit,"* therefore "upper *teshuvah*" is *"especially during the recital of the Shema and its blessings"* (Based on *Toras Menachem, Hisvaduyos* 5730, vol. 2, pp. 209-213).

כְּדֵי לוֹמַר וְאָהַבְתָּ כו' בְּכָל לְבָבְךָ וּבְכָל נַפְשְׁךָ וְכו' בֶּאֱמֶת לַאֲמִתּוֹ — **So that you will say,** *"You shall love G-d your G-d with all your heart and all your soul"* (*Deuteronomy* 6:5), **with complete authenticity.**

In one of his discourses, Rabbi Shneur Zalman explains the experience of saying *Shema* with this consciousness (of "upper *teshuvah*") in more detail.

והיו הדברים האלה וכו' וכו' ודברת בם וכו' להיות דבר
ה' בפיו באמת ואין אמת וכו'. וכן לקיים כל המצות
כמ"ש אשר קדשנו במצותיו כמו הרי את מקודשת לי

*"You need to first attach your soul to 'the one G-d,' by saying Shema... with
a 'desire of the heart' (re'usa deliba), that your heart genuinely desires to attach yourself to Him.... And this is the meaning of the verse, 'You shall love G-d
your G-d,' that you should love and desire that G-d should be **your** G-d; that
you should be a vehicle of expression for Him, devoid of ego—your thoughts
expressing His thoughts, your speech expressing His speech. And also to elim-
inate and transform your (egoic) emotions, so as to express His, as is known.
For then, He will be **your** G-d" (Siddur im Dach, ibid; see Toras Menachem ibid.).*

The next verses of the *Shema* clarify how this consciousness will subsequently influence Torah study and *mitzvah* observance, so that these will also
act as *"a vehicle of expression for Him, devoid of ego."*

וְכֵן וְהָיוּ הַדְּבָרִים הָאֵלֶּה וְכוּ' וְדִבַּרְתָּ בָּם וְכוּ' — **And so too,** *"And these words... you
shall speak of them* when you sit in your house and when you go on the way"
(ibid. 6-7).

This is the next verse of the *Shema,* referring to Torah study.

לִהְיוֹת דְּבַר ה' בְּפִיו בֶּאֱמֶת — At the consciousness of "upper *teshuvah*," **G-d's
word** (Torah study) **will be "in your mouth," as an experience of truthful,** genuine **attachment** to G-d, וְאֵין אֱמֶת וְכוּ' — **and** *"'truth' (here) refers to nothing
other than Torah"* (*Talmud, Brachos* 5b).

When reciting this line of the *Shema* during prayer, we should have in mind
that the consciousness of "merging of spirit with spirit," which is being reached
at this moment, should later influence our Torah study.

Torah study should be "truthful" in that it is an experience of channeling the
word of G-d.

The remainder of the *Shema* speaks of the observance of the commandments. The *Tanya* teaches us now how to approach this from the consciousness of "upper *teshuvah*."

וְכֵן לְקַיֵּם כָּל הַמִּצְוֹות — **And so too,** we should direct the consciousness of "upper *teshuvah*," the "merging of spirit with spirit," to influence **the observance
of all the commandments (mitzvos),** so that they act as a channel for Divine
energy.

The *Tanya* reminds us of an insight that we learned in Part One which highlights how the observance of *mitzvos* is an experience of "merging of spirit with
spirit."

היא בחי' קדש העליון לשון פרישות והבדלה שאינו

99B יכול להתלבש תוך עלמין משום דכולא קמיה כלא

חשיב אלא בבחי' סובב כ"ע הוא רצון העליון ב"ה וכו'

כְּמוֹ שֶׁאוֹמְרִים אֲשֶׁר קִדְּשָׁנוּ בְּמִצְוֹתָיו — **As we say** in the text of the blessing before carrying out a *mitzvah*, *"Blessed is G-d... who has sanctified us (kidshanu) with His commandents."*

The term *kidshanu* literally means "sanctified," but it could also be read as "married" (from the term *kidushin*).

כְּמוֹ הֲרֵי אַתְּ מְקֻדֶּשֶׁת לִי — **As in** the ceremony of marriage (*kidushin*), where the groom says to the bride, *"You are sanctified (mekudeshes) to me"* (*Talmud, Kidushin* 5b; Avudraham, Morning Blessings).

The message here is: Just as marriage is an experience of merging, the same is true of a *mitzvah*.

הִיא בְּחִינַת קֹדֶשׁ הָעֶלְיוֹן — Through a *mitzvah*, you acquire **something of** G-d's **supernal sanctity.**

Merging with G-d means that, to some extent, you become like G-d; you acquire some of His "supernal sanctity."

The *Tanya* defines what "sanctity" means.

PRACTICAL LESSONS

Once you reach the consciousness of "higher *teshuvah*," your Torah study and *mitzvah* observance become experiences of attachment and merging with G-d.

לְשׁוֹן פְּרִישׁוּת וְהַבְדָּלָה — "Sanctity" **is an expression of** *separateness* **and** *distinction* (*Rashi* to *Leviticus* 19:2), שֶׁאֵינוֹ יָכוֹל לְהִתְלַבֵּשׁ תּוֹךְ עָלְמִין — the "supernal sanctity" of G-d is an energy which **cannot become embodied in the** created **worlds.**

The "supernal sanctity" of G-d is a transcendent Divine energy that is incompatible with the created universe and cannot directly interact with it.

The *Tanya* cites phrases from the *Zohar* (with which we are familiar from Part One) that depict this level of transcendent energy.

מִשּׁוּם דְּכֹלָּא קַמֵּיהּ כְּלָא חָשִׁיב — **For** this energy is so transcendent that *"in His presence, everything is considered zero"* (*Zohar* 1, 11b; see Part One p. 59).

This energy cannot *interact* with the world because its intensity *erases* the separate identity of the world, to the extent that *"everything is considered zero."*

אֶלָּא בִּבְחִינַת סוֹבֵב כָּל עָלְמִין — **Rather,** this energy *"transcends all worlds"* (ibid. 3, 225a), הוּא רָצוֹן הָעֶלְיוֹן בָּרוּךְ הוּא וְכוּ' — **since it is the Blessed Divine will** which transcends all other Divine powers.

כמ"ש בלק"א פמ"ו. וגם אחר התפלה אומרים אליך
ה' נפשי אשא דהיינו לאתדבקא רוחא ברוחא כל היום
וכו'. וכל זה ע"י ההתבוננות בגדולת א"ס ב"ה
בהעמקת הדעת בשתים לפניה ובפסוקי דזמרה כנודע.

It is this transcendent energy, the "supernal sanctity" of G-d, that you merge with when performing a *mitzvah*.

כְּמוֹ שֶׁנִּתְבָּאֵר בְּלִקּוּטֵי אֲמָרִים פֶּרֶק מ"ו — **As explained in** *Tanya,* ***Likutei Amarim,*** **Part One, Chapter 46.**

"A man marries a woman to be one with her, in a complete union, as the verse states, 'a man... clings to his wife and they become one flesh' (Genesis 2:24), and in exactly the same way, but with infinitely more intensity, is the union of the Divine Soul with the Blessed Infinite Light, when it observes Torah and mitzvos.... Since through uniting your soul with the Blessed Infinite Light and becoming absorbed in it through mitzvos, you actually attain the status and level of the Blessed Infinite One's holiness, since you are merged with, and absorbed in Him, and you are utterly one" (ibid., pp. 557-9).

This represents the consciousness of "upper *teshuvah*" when observing a *mitzvah*.

The *Tanya* comments on one more feature of the prayer service which evokes the theme of "upper *teshuvah*."

וְגַם אַחַר הַתְּפִלָּה אוֹמְרִים אֵלֶיךָ ה' נַפְשִׁי אֶשָּׂא — **And also after the** stand-ing **prayer we say, "To You, O G-d, I lift my soul"** (Psalms 25:1; *Siddur Tehillas Hashem, Annotated Edition* (Brooklyn: Kehos, 2002), p. 55), דְּהַיְינוּ לְאִתְדַּבְּקָא רוּחָא בְּרוּחָא כָּל הַיּוֹם וְכוּ' — **which is likewise** a devotional ***"merging of spirit with spirit"* all day, etc.**

The *Tanya* concludes this section by stressing that elevated conscious-ness during the *Shema* requires preparation, through devotional concen-tration in the passages that precede it.

וְכָל זֶה עַל יְדֵי הַהִתְבּוֹנְנוּת בִּגְדֻלַּת אֵין סוֹף בָּרוּךְ הוּא בְּהַעֲמָקַת הַדַּעַת — **This** consciousness of "upper *teshuvah*" during the *Shema* **is** achieved **through deeply contemplating upon the greatness of the Blessed Infinite One,** בִּשְׁתַּיִם לְפָנֶיהָ וּבִפְסוּקֵי דְזִמְרָה — **during the two blessings before** the *Shema* (*Tehillas Hashem* ibid., pp. 39-42), **and the "verses of praise" (***Pesukei de-Zimra***)** beforehand ibid., (pp. 30-38), כַּנּוֹדָע — **as is known** (see Part One, Chapter 39).

ומאחר שההתפלה היא בחי' תשובה עילאה צריך להקדים
לפניה בחי' תשובה תתאה. וז"ש רז"ל במשנה אין
עומדין להתפלל אלא מתוך כובד ראש ופרש"י הכנעה
והיא בחי' תשובה תתאה לעורר רחמים כנ"ל וכדיליף
התם בגמ' מקרא דכתיב והיא מרת נפש. אכן

SECTION THREE: "LOWER TESHUVAH" REMAINS RELEVANT

27TH TAMMUZ REGULAR | 2ND AV LEAP

You would think that once a person is capable of praying with the elevated consciousness of "upper *teshuvah*," he has already "graduated" from "lower *teshuvah*," and is no longer in need of it. The *Tanya* now informs us that this is not the case.

וּמֵאַחַר שֶׁהַתְּפִלָּה הִיא בְּחִינַת תְּשׁוּבָה עִילָאָה — **And** even **when prayer is at the level of "upper** *teshuvah***,"** צָרִיךְ לְהַקְדִּים לְפָנֶיהָ בְּחִינַת תְּשׁוּבָה תַּתָּאָה — **it must be preceded by "lower** *teshuvah***."**

Even a person who prays at the level of "upper *teshuvah*" (as described in the previous section), can still benefit from the meditation of "lower *teshuvah*" described in Chapter Seven, Section Two and Chapter Eight, Section One. Namely, *"to awaken from the source of compassion, great compassion for your soul."*

The *Tanya* brings a proof that all prayer, even on the level of "upper *teshuvah*," should be preceded by such a meditation.

וְזֶהוּ שֶׁאָמְרוּ רַזַ"ל בַּמִּשְׁנָה אֵין עוֹמְדִין לְהִתְפַּלֵּל אֶלָּא מִתּוֹךְ כֹּבֶד רֹאשׁ — **As our Sages taught in the** *Mishnah,* **"One must only initiate prayer when in a state of seriousness"** (*Berachos* 30b), וּפֵרֵשׁ רַשִׁ"י הַכְּנָעָה — **and** *Rashi* **translates** "seriousness" as **"submissiveness,"** וְהִיא בְּחִינַת תְּשׁוּבָה תַּתָּאָה לְעוֹרֵר רַחֲמִים כַּנַ"ל — **which is "lower** *teshuvah***,"** **to awaken compassion, as we have explained** (in Chapters Seven and Eight).

Submissiveness, the *Talmud* tells us, is a crucial prerequisite for prayer. Such a somber mood is associated with "lower *teshuvah*," a feeling of distance and disconnectedness from G-d, and not with "upper *teshuvah*," which is the joy of already being connected with G-d.

וְכִדְיָלֵיף הָתָם בַּגְּמָרָא מִקְרָא דִּכְתִיב וְהִיא מָרַת נָפֶשׁ — **And as the** *Talmud* **(ibid.) derives this from the verse,** *"Her spirit was bitter and she prayed to G-d"* (1 Samuel 1:10).

בברייתא שם ת"ר אין עומדין להתפלל אלא מתוך

This verse was said of Chanah the prophetess. Obviously, a person who had received prophecy must have reached the higher consciousness of "upper *te-shuvah*," and would have recited her prayers on that level. Nevertheless, before her prayers, we are told that "her spirit was bitter," indicating a somber mood of "lower *teshuvah*." This verse is therefore a good proof that "lower *teshuvah*" is required before prayer, even for a person who prays with the consciousness of "upper *teshuvah*."

But why is this the case? We have learned that "lower *teshuvah*" is a process of atonement for sins, and it must be completed before entering "upper *teshu-vah*." What, then, is the further role of "lower *teshuvah*"?

The answer to this question has already been provided in *Tanya*, Part One, Chapter 29, Section 3. There we learned that even when your past *teshuvah* remains acceptable, you can reach *"a higher level of teshuvah so that it is from deeper within the heart, and that is why King David said, 'And my sin is always before me' (Psalms 51:5)."*

Even the acceptable *teshuvah* of the past can always be upgraded (Based on *Toras Menachem, Hisvaduyos* 5730, vol. 2, *Sichas Shabbos Parshas Beshalach*, par. 16).

אָכֵן בַּבְּרַיְיתָא שָׁם — **However, a *beraisa*** in the *Talmud* (ibid.) states, תָּנוּ רַבָּנָן אֵין עוֹמְדִין לְהִתְפַּלֵּל אֶלָּא מִתּוֹךְ שִׂמְחָה — ***"The Rabbis taught: One must only initiate prayer in a state of joy."***

As we have seen, "lower *teshuvah*" has a somber mood, whereas "upper *teshuvah*" is joyous, the feeling of being connected to G-d.

The *Talmud* teaches, "One must only initiate prayer when in a state of seriousness (submissiveness)," indicating that "lower *teshuvah*" is required; but the *Talmud* also teaches, *"One must only initiate prayer in a state of joy,"* indicating that prayer also requires a mood of "upper *teshuvah*."

PRACTICAL LESSONS

Even when you reach "upper *teshuvah*," you can still continue to do "lower *teshuvah*" as well.

The *Tanya's* advice here resolves these two contradictory *Talmudic* teachings. Before prayer, we are to carry out a "lower *teshuvah*" meditation, to achieve a state of "submissiveness." And then, afterwards, the prayers themselves should be recited in a mood of "joy," *i.e.,* "upper *teshuvah*."

שמחה. ועכשיו בדור יתום הזה שאין הכל יכולין
להפוך לבם כרגע מן הקצה. אזי עצה היעוצה להקדים
בחי' תשובה תתאה בתיקון חצות כנ"ל. ומי שא"א
לו בכל לילה עכ"פ לא יפחות מפעם א' בשבוע לפני
יום השבת כנודע ליודעים שהשבת היא בחי' תשובה

SECTION FOUR: COMBINING "LOWER" AND "UPPER TESHUVAH"

Practically speaking, the *Tanya's* advice to be somber (at "lower *teshuvah"*) before prayer and joyous (at "upper *teshuvah"*) during prayer might pose a problem.

וְעַכְשָׁו בְּדוֹר יָתוֹם הַזֶּה — **But nowadays, in our** spiritually **orphaned generation,** שֶׁאֵין הַכֹּל יְכוֹלִין לַהֲפֹךְ לְבָם כְּרֶגַע מִן הַקָּצֶה — **when not everyone can instantly switch their emotions from one extreme to the other,** the above suggestion may prove difficult to implement.

In a relatively short period of time, before prayer, it may not be practically possible to switch from a mood of deep submissiveness (required for "lower *teshuvah"*), to a mood of joy (required for "upper *teshuvah"*).

Still, as we have learned, "lower *teshuvah"* is still desirable as a preparation for prayer at the consciousness of "upper *teshuvah."* The *Tanya* therefore makes the following recommendation.

אֲזַי עֵצָה הַיְעוּצָה לְהַקְדִּים בְּחִינַת תְּשׁוּבָה תַּתָּאָה בְּתִקּוּן חֲצוֹת כַּנַ"ל — **In this case,** the *"prescribed plan"* (Isaiah 14:26) **is to first achieve "lower *teshuvah"*** the previous night, **during** *Tikun Chatzos,* **as mentioned above** in Chapter Seven.

"Lower *teshuvah"* at the midnight prayer could still be considered a preparation for the morning prayer recited later on. Experiencing "lower *teshuvah"* much earlier, at midnight, would provide a longer period for the worshiper to shift from the somber mood of "lower *teshuvah"* to the joyous spirit required for prayer at "upper *teshuvah."*

The author of *Tanya,* however, was aware that nightly *Tikun Chatzos* was beyond the capabilities of some of his readership. Therefore he makes another recommendation.

וּמִי שֶׁאִי אֶפְשָׁר לוֹ בְּכָל לַיְלָה — **And for a person who cannot manage** to carry out *Tikun Chatzos* **every night,** עַל כָּל פָּנִים לֹא יִפְחֹת מִפַּעַם אַחַת בַּשָּׁבוּעַ — **he should do so at least once a week,** לִפְנֵי יוֹם הַשַּׁבָּת — **on Thursday night, preceding** *Shabbos.*

The *Tanya* explains the significance of this particular time of the week.

כַּנּוֹדָע לַיּוֹדְעִים שֶׁהַשַּׁבָּת הִיא בְּחִינַת תְּשׁוּבָה עִילָאָה — **As is known to Kabbalists**

עילאה ושב"ת אותיות תש"ב אנוש כי בשבת היא
עליות העולמות למקורם כו' ובפרט תפלות השבת
וד"ל. (ובזה יובן מ"ש שובה אלי כי גאלתיך פי' כי

וְשַׁבָּ"ת אוֹתִיּוֹת תָּשֵׁ"ב אֱנוֹשׁ — *that Shabbos* is on the level of "upper *teshuvah*," and this fact is hinted to by **the letters** of the word *Shabbos* which also spell, **"return (taSHeV) man"** (*Psalms* 90:3; *Tzava'as Ha-Rivash* (Brooklyn: Kehos, 1998), sec. 18).

This association between *Shabbos* and "upper *teshuvah*'" is not indicated explicitly in Kabbalistic sources. The *Tanya* explains why the two are thematically connected.

כִּי בַּשַּׁבָּת הִיא עֲלִיּוֹת הָעוֹלָמוֹת לִמְקוֹרָם כו' — *Shabbos* is on the level of "upper *teshuvah*" **because,** as the Kabbalah teaches, **on *Shabbos* the** energy of the **universe ascends back into its source, etc.,** (see *Etz Chaim* 40:3).

To create the universe, G-d drew energy *out* of Himself, to make a reality that has the perception of being separate from Him. On *Shabbos*, this process is reverse and the universe's energy is drawn back *into* Him.

This trajectory of return into G-d, as we have learned, is the theme of "upper *teshuvah*," that of being *"merged with G-d seamlessly, before G-d blew... the soul to come down here, and enter a human body."*

וּבִפְרָט תְּפִלּוֹת הַשַּׁבָּת — This is **particularly during the prayers of *Shabbos*.**

Prayer is a bridge connecting the world with G-d, *"A ladder set upon the ground with its top reaching the heavens"* (*Genesis* 28:12). For this reason prayer is the *actual pathway* through which the energy of the universe ascends on *Shabbos* back to its source in G-d (Rabbi Shneur Zalman, *Chayav Adam Levarech* (Brooklyn: Kehos, 2017), pp. 5-6).

Since *Shabbos* prayers are strongly connected with the consciousness of "upper *teshuvah*," if one is only able to carry out a *Tikun Chatzos* preparatory meditation once a week, it should be done on the eve of *Shabbos* (on Thursday night), when it will have the greatest effect.

In one of his discourses Rabbi Shneur Zalman compares the (spiritual) "lower *teshuvah*" (at *Tikun Chatzos*) of the eve of Sabbath to the (physical) custom of washing one's whole body before the Sabbath (*Shulchan Aruch, Orach Chaim* 260:1). To enter the "upper *teshuvah*" of *Shabbos* it is first necessary to "wash away" the spiritual "dirt" of the week, and this is done through "lower *teshuvah*" (*Chayav Adam Levarech,* ibid.).

וְדַי לַמֵּבִין — **And this will suffice for the intelligent** reader.

מֵאַחַר שֶׁמָּחִיתִי כָעָב פְּשָׁעֶיךָ הִיא הַעֲבָרַת הַסִּט"א
וּגְאַלְתִּיךָ מִן הַחִיצוֹנִים בְּהִתְעוֹרְרוּת רַחֲמִים עֶלְיוֹנִים
בְּאִתְעָרוּתָא דִּלְתַתָּא בִּתְשׁוּבָה תַּתָּאָה כנ"ל אֲזַי שׁוּבָה
אֵלַי בִּתְשׁוּבָה עִילָּאָה):

The *Tanya* concludes with one further proof that prayer at the level of "upper *teshuvah*" should be preceded by a meditation of "lower *teshuvah*."

וּבָזֶה יוּבַן מַה שֶּׁכָּתוּב שׁוּבָה אֵלַי כִּי גְאַלְתִּיךָ) — **And this also explains the** end of the **verse,** *"I have blotted out, as a thick cloud, your transgressions, and, as a cloud, your sins; return to Me, because I have redeemed you"* (Isaiah 44:22).

פֵּרוּשׁ כִּי מֵאַחַר שֶׁ"מָּחִיתִי כָעָב פְּשָׁעֶיךָ — **Meaning that since,** *"I have blotted out, as a thick cloud, your transgressions,"* הִיא הַעֲבָרַת הַסִּטְרָא אַחֲרָא — **which re-fers to the removal of the *Sitra Achra*,** through "lower *teshuvah*," וּגְאַלְתִּיךָ מִן הַחִיצוֹנִים — **and** *"because I have redeemed you"* **from the external forces,** בְּהִתְעוֹרְרוּת רַחֲמִים עֶלְיוֹנִים בְּאִתְעָרוּתָא דִּלְתַתָּא בִּתְשׁוּבָה תַּתָּאָה כַּנַּ"ל — **through arousing supernal compassion in response to your awakening from below in** "lower *teshuvah*," **as we have explained,** אֲזַי שׁוּבָה אֵלַי בִּתְשׁוּבָה עִילָּאָה) — **sub-sequently you should** *"return to Me,"* **in "upper *teshuvah*."**

The verse stresses that we are to "return" to G-d (i.e., in "upper *teshuvah*") *"because I have redeemed you,"* i.e., in response to "lower *teshuvah*," after G-d has fully atoned for our sins. The use of the word "because" suggests "lower *teshuvah*" is a preparation for "upper *teshuvah*." We do the latter after the for-mer *because* the former helps it along.

פרק יא ואמנם להיות בלבו ההכנעה היא בחי'
תשובה תתאה כנ"ל וגם השמחה
בה' שתיהן ביחד. כבר מילתא אמורה בלק"א ס"פ

CHAPTER 11

THE JOY OF TESHUVAH

SECTION ONE: FEELING JOY ALL THE TIME

28TH TAMMUZ REGULAR | 3RD AV LEAP

In Chapter Ten we learned that even when a person is able to pray at the heightened (joyous) consciousness of "upper *teshuvah*," it is still beneficial to experience (somber) "lower *teshuvah*," before the prayers.

The *Tanya*, however, was aware that *"not everyone can instantly switch their emotions from one extreme to the other."* To avoid this problem, the *Tanya* recommended carrying out the two meditations with a significant interval: "lower *teshuvah*" at the midnight prayer, and "upper *teshuvah*" during the morning prayers, several hours later.

We therefore have learned two levels of resolving this issue.

a.) Shifting from a somber mood to a joyous one *after several hours*.

b.) Those with a greater degree of emotional development can shift from a somber mood to a joyous one *right away*.

Here in Chapter Eleven we will be introduced to a third, superior level, demonstrating the highest degree of emotional development:

c.) Being somber and joyous *at the same time*.

וְאָמְנָם לִהְיוֹת בְּלִבּוֹ הַהַכְנָעָה — **But** it *is* possible **to be in a state of emotional submissiveness** and somberness, הִיא בְּחִינַת תְּשׁוּבָה תַּתָּאָה כַּנַּ"ל — namely **"lower** *teshuvah*," **mentioned above,** וְגַם הַשִּׂמְחָה בַּה' — and *also* **to be** in a state of **joy with G-d,** שְׁתֵּיהֶן בְּיַחַד — **both together.**

כְּבָר מִילְתָא אֲמוּרָה בְּלִקּוּטֵי אֲמָרִים סוֹף פֶּרֶק ל"ד — **This has already been explained in** *Tanya*, *Likutei Amarim*, **Part One, end of Chapter 34.**

We learned there: *"There is nothing to stop you being 'disgusting in your eyes, and repulsive' (Psalms 15:4), brokenhearted and ego-deflated, at the very same time you are joyous. Because being 'disgusting in your eyes etc.,'*

100A ל"ד. כמ"ש בזוה"ק חדוה תקיעא בלבאי מסטרא דא
וכו' ובצירוף עוד האמונה והבטחון להיות נכון לבו בטוח
בה' כי חפץ חסד הוא וחנון ורחום ורב לסלוח תיכף
ומיד שמבקש מחילה וסליחה מאתו ית' (כרוב רחמיך

is a reflection of your body and Animal Soul, and being joyful is a reflection of your Divine Soul and the spark of G-dliness enmeshed in it" (pp. 385-6).

It is possible to contain contradictory emotions at the same time, when you have clear boundaries. You can be somber about the selfish and sinful drive within you, the Animal Soul, and at the same time rejoice in your closeness to G-d, which derives from your G-dly soul.

The *Tanya* reminds us of the example of this experience from the *Zohar*, cited in Chapter 34.

כְּמוֹ שֶׁכָּתוּב בַּזֹּהַר הַקָּדוֹשׁ — **As the holy *Zohar* states,** that when Rabbi Shimon revealed wondrous secrets that explained the destruction of the Temple, his son, Rabbi Elazar, said that he felt, *"Tearfulness lodged into my heart on one side,"* as a result of the heightened awareness of the Temple's destruction, חֶדְוָה תְּקִיעָא בְּלִבָּאִי מִסְטְרָא דָא וְכוּ' — *"and joy lodged into my heart on the other side"* as a result of the revelation of wondrous new Torah insight (*Zohar* 3, 75a).

This, however, represents an advanced level of emotional development, which is why the *Tanya* first offered us the more basic approaches in Chapter Ten, of focusing on somberness and joy at different times.

SECTION TWO: PROOF THAT G-D ALWAYS FORGIVES

Continuing the discussion from Section One about harboring somber and joyful feelings together, the *Tanya* adds another important source of joy.

וּבְצֵרוּף עוֹד הָאֱמוּנָה וְהַבִּטָּחוֹן לִהְיוֹת נָכוֹן לִבּוֹ בָּטוּחַ בַּה' — **And to that should be added: faith and trust** in G-d, *"His heart is firm, he trusts in G-d"* (*Psalms* 112:7), that your past sins have been completely forgiven.

Even during the somber moments of "lower *teshuvah*," it is possible to also experience joy stemming from the total confidence that your *teshuvah* has been effective.

כִּי חָפֵץ חֶסֶד הוּא — You can be sure G-d has forgiven you, *"because He desires kindness"* (*Micah* 7:18), not punishment, וְחַנּוּן וְרַחוּם — **and He is *"gracious and merciful"*** (*Joel* 2:13), וְרַב לִסְלֹחַ תֵּכֶף וּמִיָּד שֶׁמְּבַקֵּשׁ מְחִילָה וּסְלִיחָה מֵאִתּוֹ יִתְבָּרֵךְ — **so He is abundantly forgiving, immediately when you ask forgiveness and**

מחה פשעי כבסני טהרני וכל עוונותי מחה וכו') בלי
שום ספק וס"ס בעולם. וכמו שאנו מברכין בכל
תפלת י"ח תיכף שמבקשים סלח לנו כו' ברוך אתה ה'
חנון המרבה לסלוח והרי ספק ברכות להקל משום

(כְּרֹב רַחֲמֶיךָ מְחֵה פְשָׁעָי כַּבְּסֵנִי טַהֲרֵנִי וְכָל עֲווֹנוֹתַי מְחֵה וְכוּ') **atonement from Him,**
— when you say, *"With Your great mercy wipe away my transgressions...
cleanse me and purify me... wipe all my sins away"* (Psalms 51:3, 4, 11), בְּלִי שׁוּם
סָפֵק וּסְפֵק סְפֵיקָא בָּעוֹלָם — **without any doubt, or shred of a doubt in the world,**
He certainly forgives you.

It is common to doubt whether one's *teshuvah* has been accepted by G-d.
Therefore the *Tanya* will devote considerable attention to this issue, offering
multiple proofs that we can be confident of G-d's forgiveness after *teshuvah*.

First, *Tanya* offers a proof from a point of Jewish Law.

וּכְמוֹ שֶׁאָנוּ מְבָרְכִין בְּכָל תְּפִלַּת שְׁמוֹנֶה עֶשְׂרֵה — **As we say each time** we recite the
Eighteen Blessings of the *Amidah* prayer, תֵּכֶף שֶׁמְּבַקְשִׁים סְלַח לָנוּ כו' — **immediately after requesting,** *"Pardon us...,"* בָּרוּךְ אַתָּה ה' חַנּוּן הַמַּרְבֶּה לִסְלֹחַ — **we**
say, *"Blessed are You, G-d, gracious One who pardons abundantly"* (Siddur
Tehillas Hashem, Annotated Edition (Brooklyn: Kehos, 2002), pp. 47-48).

וַהֲרֵי סָפֵק בְּרָכוֹת לְהָקֵל — **Now** the law states **that whenever there is a doubt**
whether a blessing ought to be said, **we rule leniently** and do not say it, מִשּׁוּם
חֲשַׁשׁ בְּרָכָה לְבַטָּלָה — **because we are concerned** not to recite a **"blessing in
vain"** (Berachos 33a; Shulchan Aruch, Orach Chaim, ch. 67).

Since a blessing contains G-d's name we need to be certain that the blessing
is in order, otherwise G-d's name will be recited in vain. If there is any doubt,
Jewish Law rules that the blessing must not be said.

A CHASIDIC THOUGHT

"When a Jew undertakes to do *teshuvah* and does it with joy, and since 'joy breaks through barriers' — it takes him out of all constraints, including the constraints of his former conduct; also the kind of conduct which, though good at the time, could often times have been even better. In all these cases there is the assurance that, *'Nothing stands in the way of teshuvah,'* increasing still further the joy in doing it."

(From a letter of the Rebbe, 18th of Elul 5738)

חשש ברכה לבטלה אלא אין כאן שום ספק כלל
מאחר שבקשנו סלח לנו מחל לנו. ואילו לא היינו
חוזרים וחוטאים היינו נגאלין מיד כמו שאנו מברכין
בא"י גואל ישראל. והרי אפי' במדת ב"ו כן שצריך
האדם למחול תיכף ומיד שמבקשים ממנו מחילה ולא

אֶלָּא אֵין כָּאן שׁוּם סָפֵק כְּלָל — **But in this case**, when saying, *"Blessed are You, G-d, gracious One who pardons abundantly,"* **there is no doubt at all,** מֵאַחַר שֶׁבִּקַּשְׁנוּ סְלַח לָנוּ מְחַל לָנוּ — **because we have** previously **requested** *"Pardon us... forgive us..."* and G-d's forgiveness at that earlier moment was a certainty!

The text of the blessing reads: *"Pardon us, our Father, for we have sinned; forgive us, our King, for we have transgressed; for You are a good and forgiving G-d. Blessed are You, G-d, gracious One who pardons abundantly."*

After saying, "Pardon us... forgive us" at the beginning of the sentence, G-d forgives us immediately. That is why we can confidently recite the blessing at the end of the line, which includes G-d's name, (*"Blessed are You, G-d, gracious One who pardons abundantly"*), because we are certain that G-d forgave us as soon as we said *"Pardon us... forgive us."*

וְאִלּוּ לֹא הָיִינוּ חוֹזְרִים וְחוֹטְאִים — **And if we would not go back and sin again,** הָיִינוּ נִגְאָלִין מִיָּד — **we would be redeemed immediately,** כְּמוֹ שֶׁאָנוּ מְבָרְכִין בָּרוּךְ — as we say in the blessing, **"Blessed are you G-d... re- deemer of Israel"** (ibid.).

G-d's immediate forgiveness would be sufficient to bring about the redemp- tion of Israel. This fails to occur, not because of any lack of forgiveness on G-d's part, but because we sin again so quickly that there is no time for all Israel to be atoned.

The *Tanya* brings a further proof that Divine forgiveness is guaranteed, from a point of Jewish ethics.

וַהֲרֵי אֲפִלּוּ בְּמִדַּת בָּשָׂר וָדָם כֵּן — **In fact, even humans are required to act in this way** of complete forgiveness to each other, שֶׁצָּרִיךְ הָאָדָם לִמְחֹל תֵּכֶף וּמִיָּד — **for you are supposed to forgive someone as soon as they ask you for forgiveness,** שֶׁמְּבַקְּשִׁים מִמֶּנּוּ מְחִילָה — וְלֹא יְהֵא אַכְזָרִי מִלִּמְחֹל — **and not be cruel and unforgiving** (*Bava Kama* 92a).

If even humans are expected to be forgiving, then we can be assured that G-d will act likewise.

The *Tanya* illustrates the extent of human forgiveness that is expected from us, according to the *Talmud*.

יְהֵא אַכְזָרִי מִלִּמְחוֹל וַאֲפִי' בְּקוֹטֵעַ יַד חֲבֵירוֹ כְּדְאִי'
בַּגמ' בְּסֹפ"ח דב"ק. וְאִם בִּיקֵשׁ מִמֶּנּוּ ג"פ וְלֹא מָחַל
לוֹ שׁוּב א"צ לְבַקֵּשׁ מִמֶּנּוּ. וְהַגִּבְעוֹנִים שֶׁבִּיקֵשׁ דָּוִד
הַמֶּלֶךְ ע"ה מֵהֶם מְחִילָה בְּעַד שָׁאוּל שֶׁהֵמִית אֶת
הַגִּבְעוֹנִים וְלֹא רָצוּ לִמְחוֹל גָּזַר דָּוִד עֲלֵיהֶם שֶׁלֹּא יָבֹאוּ

וַאֲפִלּוּ בְּקוֹטֵעַ יַד חֲבֵרוֹ — Forgiveness is required **even if a person** causes irreversible damage, such as **cutting off somebody else's hand,** כִּדְאִיתָא בַּגְּמָרָא
בְּסוֹף פֶּרֶק ח' דְּבָבָא קַמָּא — as stated in the *Talmud,* (*Bava Kama*, end of chapter 8, 92a).

Even humans are expected to grant forgiveness for a very severe, irreversible offense.

Another law states:

וְאִם בִּקֵּשׁ מִמֶּנּוּ שָׁלֹשׁ פְּעָמִים וְלֹא מָחַל לוֹ — And if the victim **was asked** by the offender for forgiveness **three times, and** the victim **refused to forgive him,** שׁוּב אֵין צָרִיךְ לְבַקֵּשׁ מִמֶּנּוּ — then there is no requirement to ask again (*Yoma,* 87a).

Here we learn that forgiveness must be granted *quickly.*

So if humans are required to forgive others, a.) for severe offenses, and b.) quickly, we can be sure that G-d will certainly do the same.

The *Tanya* offers another proof for this point from a Biblical narrative.

וְהַגִּבְעוֹנִים שֶׁבִּקֵּשׁ דָּוִד הַמֶּלֶךְ עָלָיו הַשָּׁלוֹם מֵהֶם מְחִילָה בְּעַד שָׁאוּל שֶׁהֵמִית אֶת
הַגִּבְעוֹנִים — And when Kind David asked forgiveness from the Gibeonites for Saul, who had killed some Gibeonites, וְלֹא רָצוּ לִמְחֹל — and they refused to forgive (2 *Samuel* 21:2, 6), גָּזַר דָּוִד עֲלֵיהֶם שֶׁלֹּא יָבֹאוּ בִּקְהַל ה' שֶׁהֵם רַחֲמָנִים וְכוּ'
— David decreed that Gibeonites were not permitted to "enter G-d's congre-

---

A CHASIDIC THOUGHT

"Even *teshuvah* has to be with joy, as explained in *Chasidus*. And there is good reason to be filled with joy, inasmuch G-d has been kind enough to illuminate one's mind and heart so as to see the need of doing *teshuvah*, and G-d has promised that *teshuvah* is effective."

(From a letter of the Rebbe, 28th of Marcheshvan, 5725)

בקהל ה' שהם רחמנים וכו' כדאי' בפ"ח דיבמות.
ובמדת הקדב"ה עאכ"ו לאין קץ. ומה שמשבחים ומברכים
את ה' חנון המרבה לסלוח המרבה דייקא וכמ"ש
בעזרא ורב לסלוח. דהיינו שבמדת ב"ו אם יחטא איש
לאיש ויבקש ממנו מחילה ומחל לו ואח"כ חזר לסורו
קשה מאד שימחול לו שנית ומכ"ש בשלישית ורביעית.
אבל במדת הקב"ה אין הפרש בין פעם א' לאלף
פעמים כי המחילה היא ממדת הרחמים ומדותיו

gation" (Israel) through conversion, **since one of the signs of** true **Israelites is that they are "compassionate,"** כִּדְאִיתָא בְּפֶרֶק ח' דִּיבָמוֹת — as stated in *Talmud, Yevamos,* **(Chapter 8,** 78b).

A failure to be forgiving was sufficient to prove that prospective converts did not belong in the congregation of Israel.

וּבְמִדַּת הַקָּדוֹשׁ בָּרוּךְ הוּא עַל אַחַת כַּמָּה וְכַמָּה — And if all the above is required of humans, **all the more so it is true of G-d,** לְאֵין קֵץ — **infinitely so!**

29TH TAMMUZ REGULAR | 4TH AV LEAP

G-d's forgiveness is, of course, *far greater* than human forgiveness, as the *Tanya* now illustrates.

וּמַה שֶּׁמְּשַׁבְּחִים וּמְבָרְכִים אֶת ה' חַנּוּן הַמַּרְבֶּה לִסְלֹחַ — **And** that is why **we say of G-d** in the *Amidah, "gracious One who pardons abundantly"* הַמַּרְבֶּה דָּיְיקָא — **stressing "abundantly,"** וּכְמוֹ שֶׁכָּתוּב בְּעֶזְרָא — **as in** the statement in **Ezra's** prayer, וְרַב לִסְלֹחַ — that G-d **forgives abundantly** since He is *"the G-d of forgiveness"* (*Nehemiah* 9:17).

G-d's capacity for forgiveness is greater than ours, since He forgives "abundantly."

What, exactly, is "abundant" forgiveness, and why is it unique to G-d?

אִם יֶחֱטָא אִישׁ — **Meaning that, human nature is such,** דְּהַיְינוּ שֶׁבְּמִדַּת בָּשָׂר וָדָם — **that if one person wrongs another,** לְאִישׁ — **and then the** offender **asks for forgiveness,** וּבִקֵּשׁ מִמֶּנּוּ מְחִילָה — **and** the victim **forgives him,** וּמָחַל לוֹ — **but then** the offender **repeats his offense** to the victim, וְאַחַר כָּךְ חָזַר לְסוּרוֹ — **it is very hard** for the victim **to forgive** the offender **a second time,** קָשֶׁה מְאֹד שֶׁיִּמְחֹל לוֹ שֵׁנִית — **and certainly a third or fourth time.** וּמִכָּל שֶׁכֵּן בִּשְׁלִישִׁית וּרְבִיעִית.

אֲבָל בְּמִדַּת הַקָּדוֹשׁ בָּרוּךְ הוּא אֵין הֶפְרֵשׁ בֵּין פַּעַם אַחַת לְאֶלֶף פְּעָמִים — **But G-d's "nature" is such** that there is no difference between forgiving **a first time** offender, **to** someone who has offended even **a thousand times,** כִּי הַמְּחִילָה

הקדושות אינן בבחי' גבול ותכלית אלא בבחי' א"ס
כמ"ש כי לא כלו רחמיו. ולגבי בחי' א"ס אין הפרש
כלל בין מספר קטן לגדול דכולא קמי' כלא ממש
חשיב ומשוה קטן וגדול וכו'. ולכן מעביר אשמותינו
בכל שנה ושנה וכל החטאי' שמתוודים בעל חטא מדי
שנה אף שחזר ועבר עליהם חוזר ומתודה עליהם

100B

הָרַחֲמִים מִמִּדַּת הִיא — **because** His **forgiveness is from** the *Divine* **attribute of compassion,** וּמִדּוֹתָיו הַקְּדוֹשׁוֹת אֵינָן בִּבְחִינַת גְּבוּל וְתַכְלִית אֶלָּא בִּבְחִינַת אֵין סוֹף — **and G-d's attributes are not finite and limited, but rather, without end,** כְּמוֹ — **as the verse states,** *"for His compassions never end"* (*Eichah* 3:23). שֶׁכָּתוּב כִּי לֹא כָלוּ רַחֲמָיו

וּלְגַבֵּי בְּחִינַת אֵין סוֹף אֵין הֶפְרֵשׁ כְּלָל בֵּין מִסְפָּר קָטָן לְגָדוֹל — **And compared to infinity, there is no difference at all between a small or a large number,** דְּכֹלָּא קַמֵּיהּ כְּלָא מַמָּשׁ חָשִׁיב — **for** *"in His presence, everything is considered zero"* (*Zohar* 1, 11b), וּמַשְׁוֶה קָטָן וְגָדוֹל וְכוּ' — **and** *"He equalizes small and large, etc.,"* (*Liturgy, High Holidays*).

This explains G-d's quality of "abundant" forgiveness: G-d will forgive us for a sin even if we are repeat offenders, "even a thousand times." This is because His capacity to forgive is infinite, stemming from a Divine attribute.

The *Tanya* offers a further illustration of G-d's willingness to forgive repeatedly and "abundantly."

PRACTICAL LESSONS

For G-d, there is no difference between forgiving a first time offender, to forgiving someone who has offended even a thousand times.

וְלָכֵן מַעֲבִיר אַשְׁמוֹתֵינוּ בְּכָל שָׁנָה וְשָׁנָה — **Therefore,** *"He removes our sins every single year"* (*Liturgy, High Holidays*), on the Day of Atonement, וְכָל הַחֲטָאִים שֶׁמִּתְוַדִּים בְּעַל חֵטְא מִדֵּי שָׁנָה — which is why **a sinner may confess** the same **sins annually in the** *Al Cheit* confession text, אַף שֶׁחָזַר וְעָבַר עֲלֵיהֶם — **even though he regressed and repeated the offenses** for which he had asked forgiveness the previous year, חוֹזֵר וּמִתְוַדֶּה עֲלֵיהֶם בְּיוֹם הַכִּפּוּרִים בַּשָּׁנָה הַבָּאָה — **he may still confess over them again on the Day of Atonement the following year,** וְכֵן לְעוֹלָם — **perpetually** each year, even though he ends up repeating them.

As a further illustration of G-d's forgiveness for repeat offenses, the *Tanya* offers us the example of our confessions on the Day of Atonement. Even though we committed many of the sins that we atoned for last year, G-d nevertheless forgives us again this year when we confess.

ביוה"כ בשנה הבאה וכן לעולם. ובכל שנה ושנה
לאו דוקא אלא כמו כן בכל יום ויום ג"פ מברכי' בא"י
חנון המרבה לסלוח וכמארז"ל תפלה כנגד תמידין
תקנוה. ותמיד של שחר הי' מכפר על עבירות הלילה
ותמיד של בין הערביים על של יום וכן מדי יום ביום
לעולם. אלא שיוה"כ מכפר על עבירות חמורות.
והתמיד שהוא קרבן עולה מכפר על מ"ע בלבד. וכן

אֶלָּא כְּמוֹ וּבְכָל שָׁנָה וְשָׁנָה לָאו דַּוְקָא — And this cycle occurs **not only every year,** אֶלָּא כְּמוֹ
כֵן בְּכָל יוֹם וָיוֹם שָׁלֹשׁ פְּעָמִים מְבָרְכִים — **rather it** could even be **every day, as we
say three times a day in the blessing,** בָּרוּךְ אַתָּה ה' חַנּוּן הַמַּרְבֶּה לִסְלֹחַ — *"Blessed are you, G-d... who gracefully and abundantly forgives."*

G-d will forgive us multiple times in the same day for repeat offenses of the
same sin, if we do *teshuvah* in between. That is why we ask for forgiveness in
the prayers three times daily.

The *Tanya* brings a further proof of this point.

וּכְמַאֲמַר רַז"ל — **And as our Sages taught,** תְּפִלָּה כְּנֶגֶד תְּמִידִין תִּקְּנוּהָ — *"The or-
der of daily **prayers were introduced corresponding to the sacrifices"** (Talmud,
Berachos 26a), וְתָמִיד שֶׁל שַׁחַר הָיָה מְכַפֵּר עַל עֲבֵרוֹת הַלַּיְלָה — **and the morning**
Tamid **sacrifice would atone for the sins of the night,** וְתָמִיד שֶׁל בֵּין הָעַרְבַּיִם עַל
שֶׁל יוֹם — **and the afternoon** *Tamid* **sacrifice, for the sins of the day,** (Numbers
Rabah 21:21), וְכֵן מִדֵּי יוֹם בְּיוֹם לְעוֹלָם — **and so too each day, perpetually.**

The order of daily sacrifices was likewise based on the need for continual
atonement for sins, even if they were repeat offenses.

If there is atonement every day, why then do we need a special "Day of
Atonement"?

אֶלָּא שֶׁיּוֹם הַכִּפּוּרִים מְכַפֵּר עַל עֲבֵרוֹת חֲמוּרוֹת — **Only, the Day of Atonement would
atone for serious transgressions,** וְהַתָּמִיד שֶׁהוּא קָרְבַּן עוֹלָה מְכַפֵּר עַל מִצְוֹת עֲשֵׂה

A CHASIDIC THOUGHT

"Teshuvah embraces and permeates every aspect of the repenter's being, from the innermost
core of his soul down to his every-day conduct
and experience."

(From a letter of the Rebbe, Days of Selichos 5720)

התפלה בזמן הזה עם התשובה כנ"ל. ואין זה אחטא
ואשוב. כי היינו דוקא שבשעת החטא היה יכול לכבוש
יצרו אלא שסומך בלבו על התשובה ולכן הואיל
והתשובה גורמת לו לחטוא אין מספיקין וכו'. ואף

בִּלְבַד — whereas the *Tamid*, which was a Burnt Offering, would atone only for the neglect of **positive commands** (as we learned in Chapter One).

וְכֵן הַתְּפִלָּה בַּזְמַן הַזֶּה עִם הַתְּשׁוּבָה — **And this is the role of prayer nowadays, accompanied by** *teshuvah*, כַּנַ"ל — **as above.**

Just as a sacrifice would bring atonement in Temple times if it was accompanied by *teshuvah*, the same is true of our daily prayers for atonement: they are always effective so long as they are accompanied by *teshuvah*.

SECTION THREE: WHY DAILY ATONEMENT IS ACCEPTABLE

We have learned: *"If a person says 'I will sin now and I will repent for it later on,' he will not be given the opportunity to repent"* (*Talmud, Yoma* 85b; see Part One, Chapter 25).

How, then, can the *Tanya* argue (in Section Two) that it is acceptable to atone for multiple offenses of the same sin on a yearly or even daily basis?

וְאֵין זֶה אֶחֱטָא וְאָשׁוּב — The above does not fall under the *Talmud's* prohibition of **sinning with** the intention of **doing** *teshuvah* later on, כִּי הַיְינוּ דְוְקָא שֶׁבִּשְׁעַת הַחֵטְא הָיָה יָכוֹל לִכְבּוֹשׁ יִצְרוֹ — **for the** *Talmud* **speaks of a case where the person could have overcome his evil inclination at the time of the sin,** אֶלָּא שֶׁסּוֹמֵךְ בְּלִבּוֹ עַל הַתְּשׁוּבָה — **but, instead, in his heart, he relied on** subsequent *teshuvah*.

וְלָכֵן הוֹאִיל וְהַתְּשׁוּבָה גּוֹרֶמֶת לוֹ לַחֲטֹא — **Therefore, since it is the** *teshuvah* that led him to justify his **sin,** אֵין מַסְפִּיקִין וְכוּ' —*"he will not be granted the opportunity to repent"* (ibid.).

The *Tanya* provides us with an important clarification of the *Talmud's* teaching. The prohibition against saying, *'I will sin now and I will repent for it later,''* refers to a specific case where the person sins *on the basis* that he will be able to atone later.

However, saying *Al Cheit* every year on the Day of Atonement, and "forgive us" three times a day in the prayers, does not fall into this category, since we do not say, "I will sin now and I will repent for it later," *at the time of sinning*.

The *Tanya* will now clarify the second part of the *Talmud's* statement, *"he will not be granted the opportunity to repent."*

גם זאת אין מספיקין דייקא. אבל אם דחק ונתחזק
ונתגבר על יצרו ועשה תשובה מקבלין תשובתו. אבל
אנו שמבקשים בכל יום סלח לנו אנו מקדימין לבקש
והחזירנו בתשובה שלימה לפניך דהיינו שלא נשוב
עוד לכסלה וכן ביוה"כ מבקשים יהי רצון מלפניך

וְאַף גַּם זֹאת אֵין מַסְפִּיקִין דַּיְיקָא — **And, even** if a person does sin on the basis that he will be able to atone later, **the** *Talmud's* **stress is "he will not be** *given the opportunity* **to repent,"** meaning that *teshuvah* won't come easily to him, not that it is impossible, אֲבָל אִם דָּחַק וְנִתְחַזֵּק וְנִתְגַּבֵּר עַל יִצְרוֹ וְעָשָׂה תְּשׁוּבָה — **but if he squeezes and strengthens himself, overcoming his evil inclination, and repents,** מְקַבְּלִין תְּשׁוּבָתוֹ — **then his** *teshuvah* **will be accepted.**

The *Tanya* offers another argument why reciting "forgive us" three times a day does not fall under the category of *"I will sin now and I will repent for it later."*

אֲבָל אָנוּ שֶׁמְּבַקְשִׁים בְּכָל יוֹם סְלַח לָנוּ — **But when we say every day,** *"forgive us,"* אָנוּ מַקְדִּימִין לְבַקֵּשׁ וְהַחֲזִירֵנוּ בִּתְשׁוּבָה שְׁלֵמָה לְפָנֶיךָ — **we first request,** in the text of the *Amidah*, *"and return us in complete teshuvah before You,"* דְּהַיְינוּ שֶׁלֹּא נָשׁוּב עוֹד לְכִסְלָה — **meaning that we** commit **not to return to the same "foolishness"** and sin **again,** וְכֵן בְּיוֹם הַכִּפּוּרִים מְבַקְשִׁים — **and likewise on the Day of Atonement we say,** יְהִי רָצוֹן מִלְפָנֶיךָ שֶׁלֹּא אֶחֱטָא עוֹד — *"May it be Your will that I do not sin again."*

Above we argued that saying *"Pardon us… for we have sinned"* three times a day does not create a cycle of *"I will sin now and I will repent for it later,"* because the confession did not occur *at the time of the sin,* and therefore did not motivate it.

The *Tanya was* willing to admit that there is a cycle of sinning followed by repentance, but the cycle is not "prohibited" since the sin was not carried out in reliance upon the repentance.

A CHASIDIC THOUGHT

"A feeling of depression and anxiety is not helpful to true *teshuvah*, but rather on the contrary, for true and sincere *teshuvah* is followed by a feeling of happiness and closeness to G-d, and sincere determination to observe the Torah and *mitzvos* and serve G-d with joy and gladness of heart."

(From a letter of the Rebbe, 18th of Kislev, 5719)

שֶׁלֹּא אֶחֱטָא עוֹד מַסְפִּיקִין וּמַסְפִּיקִין כְּמַאֲמָרַזַ"ל הַבָּא
לְטַהֵר מְסַיְּיעִין אוֹתוֹ הַבָּא דַּיְיקָא מִיַד שֶׁבָּא וְאִי לְזֹאת
גַּם הַסְּלִיחָה וְהַמְּחִילָה הִיא מִיַד. וּמ"ש וְחַטָאתִי נֶגְדִּי
תָמִיד אֵין הַמְּכֻוָּן לִהְיוֹת תָּמִיד עֶצֶב נִבְזֶה ח"ו דְהָא

Here the *Tanya* presents a further argument, that the cycle itself is not something real. The fact that we ask G-d to *"return us in complete teshuvah before You,"* means that our true intent is to never sin again, *"that we should not return to the same foolishness"* (see Rabbi Yehoshua Korf, *Likutei Biurim*).

מַסְפִּיקִין וּמַסְפִּיקִין — And since this is the case, G-d will **grant** us **the opportunity** to repent **again and again.**

The *Tanya* cites a final proof that G-d's forgiveness is immediate.

כְּמַאֲמַר רַזַ"ל הַבָּא לְטָהֵר מְסַיְּיעִין אוֹתוֹ — **As in the teaching of our Sages,** *"When one comes to purify himself, one is assisted* from heaven" (*Talmud, Shabbos* 104a), הַבָּא דַּיְיקָא — **and the emphasis here is** *"when one comes,"* מִיַד שֶׁבָּא — **meaning,** *immediately* **when he comes,** וְאִי לְזֹאת גַּם הַסְּלִיחָה וְהַמְּחִילָה הִיא מִיַד — **and if so, the forgiveness and atonement will also be immediate.**

As soon as *"one comes to purify himself,"* at the very same moment, *"one is assisted from heaven"* and granted atonement.

SECTION FOUR: RECALLING YOUR SINS

1ST AV REGULAR | 5TH AV LEAP

In Sections Two and Three, the *Tanya* has proven at great length that G-d forgives our sins immediately, as soon as we repent. This should be a source of joy, even amid the somber mood of "lower *teshuvah.*"

In this section we will pose a challenge to this idea, from a verse which is included in the bed-time and midnight prayer texts.

וּמַה שֶׁכָּתוּב וְחַטָאתִי נֶגְדִּי תָמִיד — **And as for what the verse states,** *"My sin is opposite me always"* (*Psalms* 51:5), this does not contradict what we have learned above.

The *Tanya* has demonstrated amply that Divine forgiveness is immediate, and we should be joyous at the thought that we are free of sin after *teshuvah.* How is this to be combined with the feeling that, *"My sin is opposite me always"*?

אֵין הַמְּכֻוָּן לִהְיוֹת תָּמִיד עֶצֶב נִבְזֶה חַס וְשָׁלוֹם — **The intention** of this verse **is not that we should always be depressed and loathing of ourselves,** G-d forbid,

כְּתִיב בְּתְרֵי' תַּשְׁמִיעֵנִי שָׂשׂוֹן וְשִׂמְחָה וְכוּ' וְרוּחַ נְדִיבָה
תִּסְמְכֵנִי וְכוּ' וּמִשּׁוּם שֶׁצָּ"ל כָּל יָמָיו בִּתְשׁוּבָה עִילָּאָה
שֶׁהִיא בְּשִׂמְחָה רַבָּה כַּנַּ"ל אֶלָּא נֶגְדִּי דַּיְיקָא כְּמוֹ וְאַתָּה
תִּתְיַצֵּב מִנֶּגֶד מִנֶּגֶד סָבִיב לְאֹהֶל מוֹעֵד יַחֲנוּ וּפֵרֵשׁ"י מֵרָחוֹק.
וְהַמְכֻוָּן רַק לְבִלְתִּי רוּם לְבָבוֹ וְלִהְיוֹת שְׁפַל רוּחַ בִּפְנֵי
כָּל הָאָדָם כְּשֶׁיִּהְיֶה לְזִכָּרוֹן בֵּין עֵינָיו שֶׁחָטָא נֶגֶד ה'.

101A

תַּשְׁמִיעֵנִי שָׂשׂוֹן וְשִׂמְחָה וְכוּ' — דְּהָא כְּתִיב בַּתְרֵיהּ, — **for the verse states afterwards,** וְרוּחַ נְדִיבָה תִּסְמְכֵנִי וְכוּ' — **"Let me hear tidings of joy and gladness... sustain me with a generous spirit"** (*Psalms* 51:10, 14).

וּמִשּׁוּם שֶׁצָּרִיךְ לִהְיוֹת כָּל יָמָיו בִּתְשׁוּבָה עִילָּאָה שֶׁהִיא בְּשִׂמְחָה רַבָּה כַּנַּ"ל — **Because a person ought to be all his days in "upper** *teshuvah*" **which is very joyous, as we have learned** in Chapter Ten.

The very same *Psalm* stresses the importance of joy. And, as we have learned, "lower *teshuvah*" is supposed to lead to "upper *teshuvah*," which is the joy of feeling connected to G-d.

But if it is not meant to depress us, what does the verse *"My sin is opposite me always"* imply?

אֶלָּא נֶגְדִּי דַּיְיקָא — **Rather the emphasis is** *"My sin is* **opposite** *me (negdi),"* כְּמוֹ וְאַתָּה תִּתְיַצֵּב מִנֶּגֶד — **as in the verse,** *"You stand opposite (mineged)"* (2 *Samuel* 18:13), מִנֶּגֶד סָבִיב לְאֹהֶל מוֹעֵד יַחֲנוּ — *"mineged, around the Tent of Meeting camp"* (*Numbers* 2:2), וּפֵרֵשׁ רַשִׁ"י מֵרָחוֹק — **and** *Rashi* **translates** *mineged,* **"from far."**

The term "opposite" (*negdi*) implies "from far." We shouldn't forget our history of sin, but it should be kept psychologically distant. When we do recall our prior sinful behavior, we ought to feel detached from it.

Practically, what does this mean? What is the point of recalling your sins, only to feel detached from them?

וְהַמְכֻוָּן רַק לְבִלְתִּי רוּם לְבָבוֹ — **And the intended message** of the verse *"My sin is opposite me always"* **is only** *"that one's heart not be arrogant"* (*Deuteronomy* 17:20), וְלִהְיוֹת שְׁפַל רוּחַ בִּפְנֵי כָּל הָאָדָם — **to be** *"humble in spirit before every person"* (*Mishnah, Avos* 4:10), כְּשֶׁיִּהְיֶה לְזִכָּרוֹן בֵּין עֵינָיו שֶׁחָטָא נֶגֶד ה' — **when there will be** *"a reminder between your eyes"* (*Exodus* 13:9) **that you have sinned against G-d.**

The *teshuvah* process could easily lead a person to become self-righteous and arrogant. He may begin to look down on others who are not *Ba'alei Teshuvah,* and feel superior to them.

ואדרבה לענין השמחה יועיל זכרון החטא ביתר שאת
בכדי לקבל בשמחה כל המאורעות המתרגשות ובאות
בין מן השמים בין ע"י הבריות בדיבור או במעשה
(וזו עצה טובה להנצל מכעס וכל מיני קפידא וכו')
וכמארז"ל הנעלבים ואינן עולבין שומעי' חרפתם ואין

It is to counteract this feeling that the verse says, *"My sin is opposite me always."* Not to imply that we still carry the sin, for it has certainly been forgiven. Rather, the message to the *Ba'al Teshuvah* is to (personally) recall that he once sinned, so as not to become self-righteous and arrogant from his later spiritual successes.

The above explanation clarified why recalling past sins does not pose an obstacle to being joyous (at "higher *teshuvah*"). Now we will learn another insight, why the activity could actually *help* us to be joyous.

וְאַדְּרַבָּה לְעִנְיַן הַשִּׂמְחָה יוֹעִיל זִכְרוֹן הַחֵטְא בְּיֶתֶר שְׂאֵת — **And, on the contrary, in terms of joy, remembering the sin will actually be helpful,** בִּכְדֵי לְקַבֵּל בְּשִׂמְחָה — **in order to accept joyfully any** unfortunate כָּל הַמְאֹרָעוֹת הַמִּתְרַגְּשׁוֹת וּבָאוֹת **events which later erupt and come** (see *Kesubos* 8b), בֵּין מִן הַשָּׁמַיִם בֵּין עַל יְדֵי הַבְּרִיּוֹת — **whether they are acts of G-d, or** even **men** (since everything is orchestrated by G-d), בְּדִבּוּר אוֹ בְּמַעֲשֶׂה — **in speech or action.**

When a person suffers *any* misfortune, he can always say to himself: "This came to me to bring about an even deeper atonement for my earlier sins," (as we learned in Chapter One, that atonement will sometimes require suffering). As a result, instead of the natural tendency to become depressed by misfortune, by recalling *"my sin is opposite me always,"* a person can feel a sense of joy that his atonement is being completed.

(וְזוֹ עֵצָה טוֹבָה לְהִנָּצֵל מִכַּעַס וְכָל מִינֵי קְפִידָא וְכוּ') — **And this is a good way to avoid getting angry and all types of resentment, etc.**

Anger is founded on judgment, that a certain action was wrong. But if you learn to perceive every misfortune as a gift of atonement (since *"My sin is opposite me always"*), you will not judge any occurrence as inappropriate. On the contrary, the misfortune was very much in order, to give you the benefits of full atonement and cleansing.

וּכְמַאֲמַר רַזַ"ל — **As in the teaching of our Sages,** הַנֶּעֱלָבִים וְאֵינָן עוֹלְבִין — who praised *"those who are humiliated yet do not humiliate back,"* (in action), שׁוֹמְעִים חֶרְפָּתָם וְאֵין מְשִׁיבִים — *"who hear insults to them and do not respond,"* (in speech), עוֹשִׂים מֵאַהֲבָה וּשְׂמֵחִים בְּיִסּוּרִים וְכוּ' — *"who act out of love and are joyous amid suffering"* (*Talmud*, *Shabbos* 88b).

The *Tanya* cites another Talmudic teaching which illustrates this point.

משיבי' עושים מאהבה ושמחי' ביסורי' וכו' וכל המעביר על מדותיו מעבירי' לו על כל פשעיו:

וְכָל הַמַּעֲבִיר עַל מִדּוֹתָיו מַעֲבִירִין לוֹ עַל כָּל פְּשָׁעָיו — And *"whoever overcomes his feelings* of resentment, *all his sins are overlooked"* (*Talmud, Rosh Hashanah* 17a).

This teaching clarifies that overcoming feelings of resentment is actually *part of the teshuvah process* by which *"all his sins are overlooked"* (*Toras Menachem,* 5730, volume 3, p. 459).

We will continue to discuss the process of being "joyous amid suffering" in the following chapter.

פרק יב וטעם השמחה ביסורי הגוף לפי שהיא טובה גדולה ועצומה לנפש החוטאת למרקה בעה"ז ולהצילה מהמירוק בגיהנם (בפרט בדורותינו אלה שאין ביכולת להתענות כפי מספר כל הצומות שבתיקוני תשובה מהאר"י ז"ל הצריכות למירוק הנפש להצילה ממירוק בגיהנם)

CHAPTER 12

ATONEMENT IN THIS WORLD
SECTION ONE: ACCEPTING SUFFERING JOYOUSLY

2ND AV REGULAR | 6TH AV LEAP

In the previous chapter the *Tanya* advised us to be "joyous amid suffering," in the knowledge that suffering brings about full atonement and cleansing. We continue now to elaborate on this point.

וְטַעַם הַשִּׂמְחָה בְּיִסּוּרֵי הַגּוּף — **The reason why we ought to accept suffering of the body joyously,** לְפִי שֶׁהִיא טוֹבָה גְּדוֹלָה וַעֲצוּמָה לַנֶּפֶשׁ הַחוֹטֵאת — **is because it is an incredibly great benefit to the sinner's soul,** לְמָרְקָהּ בָּעוֹלָם הַזֶּה — **to cleanse it in this world,** וּלְהַצִּילָהּ מֵהַמֵּרוּק בַּגֵּיהִנּוֹם — **so as to save it from the** harsher **cleansing of Purgatory (Gehinom).**

Suffering brings benefits both in this world and the next. It cleanses your soul so that you can end your life with the same purity with which it began; and suffering will spare you from the more painful suffering of Purgatory.

As the Sages taught: *"A person should take joy in suffering more than in his good fortune. For even if a person has good fortune all his life, he will not be atoned for his sins. What brings atonement for his sins? It is suffering"* (*Mechilta, Bachodesh* chapter 10).

(בִּפְרָט בְּדוֹרוֹתֵינוּ אֵלֶּה — **This is particularly relevant in our times,** שֶׁאֵין בַּיְכֹלֶת — **when we do not** לְהִתְעַנּוֹת כְּפִי מִסְפַּר כָּל הַצּוֹמוֹת שֶׁבְּתִקּוּנֵי תְּשׁוּבָה מֵהָאֲרִ"י זַ"ל **have the** physical **ability to carry out the number of fasts prescribed by** *Arizal* for *teshuvah* discussed in Chapter Two, הַצְּרִיכוֹת לְמֵרוּק הַנֶּפֶשׁ לְהַצִּילָהּ מִמֵּרוּק בַּגֵּיהִנּוֹם) — **which are necessary for cleansing the soul and saving it from the** harsher **cleansing of Purgatory.**

The extensive fasting recommended by *Arizal* is an effective method of cleansing the soul. Since this is not practical for most people nowadays, suffer-

וכמ"ש הרמב"ן ז"ל בהקדמה לפי' איוב שאפי' יסורים
של איוב ע' שנה אין להן ערך כלל ליסורי הנפש
שעה אחת בגיהנם כי אש א' משׁשים וכו'. אלא לפי
שעוה"ז חסד יבנה וביסורין קלין בעוה"ז ניצול מדיני'
קשים של עוה"ב כמשל הילוך והעתקת הצל בארץ
טפח לפי הילוך גלגל השמש ברקיע אלפים מילין

ing acts as a replacement method for the necessary cleansing of the soul, and therefore we should accept it with joy.

The *Tanya* cites proof for the great benefits of avoiding the suffering of Purgatory.

וּכְמוֹ שֶׁכָּתַב הָרַמְבַּ"ן ז"ל בַּהַקְדָּמָה לְפֵרוּשׁ אִיוֹב — **As Nachmanides writes in the introduction to his commentary on** *Job,* שֶׁאֲפִלּוּ יִסּוּרִים שֶׁל אִיוֹב שִׁבְעִים שָׁנָה אֵין לָהֶן עֵרֶךְ כְּלָל לְיִסּוּרֵי הַנֶּפֶשׁ שָׁעָה אַחַת בַּגֵּיהִנוֹם — **that even the sufferings of Job for seventy years do not compare at all to the suffering of the soul in Purgatory for one hour.**

כִּי אֵשׁ אֶחָד מִשְּׁשִׁים וְכוּ' — **We see this also from the** *Talmud's* **comment that** physical **fire is a mere sixtieth of the** intensity of the **fire of Purgatory** (*Talmud, Berachos* 57b).

Why is spiritual cleansing in this world easier?

אֶלָּא לְפִי שֶׁעוֹלָם הַזֶּה חֶסֶד יִבָּנֶה — **Rather,** *"(this) world is built on kindness"* (*Psalms* 89:3), וּבְיִסּוּרִין קַלִּין בָּעוֹלָם הַזֶּה נִצוֹל מִדִּינִים קָשִׁים שֶׁל עוֹלָם הַבָּא — **so with moderate suffering in this world** of "kindness," **a person will be saved from the harsh judgments of the next world.**

PRACTICAL LESSONS

A relatively small degree of suffering in this physical world will relieve you from a great deal of suffering in the next, spiritual world.

This world is built on the energy of *chesed* (kindness), whereas the next world is built on *din* (judgment). By relieving oneself of judgment in this world, the punishment is received through an energy of *chesed* and is therefore lighter (*Derech Mitzvosecha* 143a).

SECTION TWO: AN ILLUSTRATION

The *Tanya* offers us a physical illustration.

כְּמָשָׁל הַלוּךְ וְהַעְתָּקַת הַצֵּל בָּאָרֶץ טֶפַח לְפִי הִלּוּךְ גַּלְגַּל הַשֶּׁמֶשׁ בָּרָקִיעַ אַלְפַּיִם מִילִין וְכוּ' — **You could compare it to the movement of a shadow on earth, which is displaced** just **one handsbreadth when the sun itself moves thousands of miles in the sky.**

וכו'. ויתר על כן לאין קץ הוא בנמשל בבחי'
השתלשלות העולמות מרום המעלות עד עוה"ז
הגשמי. וכנודע ממ"ש בזוה"ק מענין עליות עולמות
העליוני' באתערותא דלתתא בהקרבת עוף אחד בן
יונה או תור ע"ג המזבח או קומץ מנחה. וכן הוא
בכל המצות מעשיות כנודע מהאריז"ל. וז"ש רז"ל
ע"פ והתקדשתם והייתם קדושים אדם מקדש עצמו

1018

A small movement on the earth translates to a huge movement in the heavens. That is why a relatively small degree of suffering in this physical world relieves a person of a great deal of suffering in the next, spiritual world.

The *Tanya* points to a limitation of the analogy.

וְיָתֵר עַל כֵּן לְאֵין קֵץ הוּא בַּנִּמְשָׁל — This difference in scale is true of the spiritual **reality even more so, infinitely,** בִּבְחִינַת הִשְׁתַּלְשְׁלוּת הָעוֹלָמוֹת מֵרוֹם הַמַּעֲלוֹת עַד עוֹלָם הַזֶּה הַגַּשְׁמִי — when we speak of the difference in scale of **the incremental** flow of energy **through the worlds, from the greatest** spiritual **heights down to this physical world.**

The sun and its shadows are both physical objects. When we apply the analogy to teach us the impact of a physical act on the spiritual realms, the difference in scale is incomparably greater.

וְכַנּוֹדָע מִמַּה שֶׁכָּתוּב בַּזֹּהַר הַקָּדוֹשׁ — As we know from what the holy *Zohar* states (1, 64b), מֵעִנְיַן עֲלִיּוֹת עוֹלָמוֹת הָעֶלְיוֹנִים בְּאִתְעָרוּתָא דִלְתַתָּא בְּהַקְרָבַת עוֹף — about the effect of an "awakening below" through the offering of one bird sacrifice אֶחָד בֶּן יוֹנָה אוֹ תּוֹר עַל גַּבֵּי הַמִּזְבֵּחַ of *"a dove or pigeon"* (*Leviticus* 1:14) on the Altar, how it influences and elevates the spiritual worlds, אוֹ קוֹמֶץ מִנְחָה — or even a plant sacrifice from a handful of meal (*ibid.* 2:2), וְכֵן הוּא בְּכָל הַמִּצְוֹת מַעֲשִׂיּוֹת — and the same is true of all the practical commandments, כַּנּוֹדָע מֵהָאֲרִיזַ"ל — as is known from *Arizal* (see *Etz Chaim* 39:2).

A fundamental principle of the Kabbalistic world view, articulated by the *Zohar* and *Arizal*, is that small acts of worship in the physical world have enormous ramifications in the spiritual realms.

The *Tanya* applies this principle to explain why suffering ought to be joyous. Joy comes from the awareness that a relatively small amount of suffering in this world redeems the soul from a larger amount of suffering in the next, spiritual world.

וְזֶהוּ שֶׁאָמְרוּ רַזַ"ל עַל פָּסוּק וְהִתְקַדַּשְׁתֶּם וִהְיִיתֶם קְדוֹשִׁים — And this is the meaning of our Sages' comment on the verse, *"You should sanctify yourselves and be holy, for I am G-d, your G-d"* (*Leviticus* 20:7), אָדָם מְקַדֵּשׁ עַצְמוֹ מְעַט מִלְּמַטָּה

מעט מלמטה מקדשין אותו הרבה מלמעלה וכו'
(וכמ"ש לעיל בענין אשר קדשנו במצותיו וכו' בחי'
סוכ"ע וכו') וככה ממש הוא בענין שכר ועונש

מְקַדְּשִׁין אוֹתוֹ הַרְבֵּה מִלְמַעְלָה וְכוּ' — the Sages explained, **"When a person sanctifies himself to a small extent below, he will be sanctified a great deal from above"** (see *Talmud, Yoma* 39a; Part One, p. 316).

This *Talmudic* teaching is a support for the Kabbalistic world view, indicating a disproportionate response "from above" to a "small extent" of worship "below."

(וּכְמוֹ שֶׁבֵּאַרְנוּ לְעֵיל בְּעִנְיַן אֲשֶׁר קִדְּשָׁנוּ בְּמִצְוֹתָיו וְכוּ' בְּחִינַת סוֹבֵב כָּל עָלְמִין וְכוּ') — **As we explained above,** Chapter 10, **in our comments on** the phrase *"who sanctified us with His commandments,"* referring to the disproportionate, Divine **light which transcends all worlds** that a person accesses from a relatively small *mitzvah* act).

The disproportionate response from above in the Kabbalistic world view refers specifically to *mitzvah* observance. But the *Tanya* now clarifies that it is applicable in our case too, of suffering.

וְכָכָה מַמָּשׁ הוּא בְּעִנְיַן שָׂכָר וָעֹנֶשׁ — **So too, precisely,** the above principle applies in **the case of reward and punishment,** כְּמַאֲמַר רַזַ"ל שָׂכַר מִצְוָה מִצְוָה וְכוּ' — **as our Sages taught, "The reward for a mitzvah is the mitzvah"** (see *Mishnah, Avos* 4:2), וּכְמוֹ שֶׁנִּתְבָּאֵר בְּמָקוֹם אַחֵר — **as we have explained elsewhere** (Part One, p. 459).

The reward for a *mitzvah* is not a secondary offshoot of worship; it is a direct reflection of the *mitzvah* energy itself: *"The reward for a mitzvah **is the** mitzvah."*

A CHASIDIC THOUGHT

"Life's trials, tragedies and difficulties actually bring us closer to our goal, our *raison d'etre;* they are part of the Divine system of toil and endeavor enabling us, finite mortals, to reach the highest levels of rewards and goodness—which can only be earned by meaningful 'labor' and effort. It follows that one must not allow the difficulties of life's trials (or even one's failure from time to time) to overcome the double joy of being G-d's children and of having received His promise *'Your people are all righteous.'"*

(From a Letter of the Rebbe)

כמארז"ל שכר מצוה מצוה וכו' וכמ"ש במ"א. ודעת
לנבון נקל ומשכיל על דבר ימצא טוב:

Since this is the case, it follows that the spiritual dynamic of *mitzvos* (that a small act in this world produces a disproportional spiritual response), also applies to the dynamic of reward and punishment.

This is proof that a small amount of suffering in this world will relieve a person of a greater suffering in the next world.

This concludes our discussion.

וְדַעַת לְנָבוֹן נָקֵל — And *"knowledge for the understanding is easy"* (Proverbs 14:6), וּמַשְׂכִּיל עַל דָּבָר יִמְצָא טוֹב — *"One who is wise with a word finds good"* (*ibid.* 16:20).

This citation from *Proverbs*, here at the end of *Igeres Ha-Teshuvah,* hints to the central theme of this work: the power of *teshuvah* to repair all four letters of the Tetragrammaton.

"One who is wise," hints to *chochmah,* the *yud*;

"For the understanding (navon)," hints to *binah,* the *hei.*

"Good" hints to *yesod* (*Zohar* 1, 60a), which contains all six energies hinted by the *vav;*

"A word," hints to *malchus,* the power of speech, alluded to by the last *hei.*

The key to this process is through "knowledge" (*da'as*), which is the bridge between intellect and emotion, (which is why the verse stresses this point first).

The verse,*"Knowledge for the understanding is easy"* hints to the *Tanya's* central message, that when we apply our *da'as,* through immersive meditation using *binah* ("understanding"), worship will be "easy."

This is a fitting conclusion to the *Tanya,* a text aimed, *"to clarify well how (authentic worship) is very much **within reach,'"*** (Author's Title Page, Part One, p. 3; Based on *Toras Menachem* 5729, vol. 1, pp. 73-74; *Sichos Kodesh* 5732, vol. 2, p. 21-24).

GLOSSARY

Adam kadmon. "Primordial man," the all-encompassing, general will to create the Universe which arose in the 'mind' of G-d prior to the entire creative process.

Amidah. "Standing prayer," also known as *Shmoneh Esrei*, the climax of each prayer service which is recited in silent devotion while standing.

Arizal. A Hebrew acronym for *Adonenu Rabbi Yitzchak Zichrono Livracha* "our master Rabbi Yitzchak of blessed memory," referring to Rabbi Yitzchak Luria (1534-1572), who founded the highly influential and authoritative school of Lurianic Kabbalah.

Asiyah. "Action," the lowest of the four supernal worlds, having both a spiritual and physical component.

Atzilus. "Emanation," the highest of the four supernal worlds, adjacent to the infinite source of creation.

Ba'al Shem Tov. "Master of the Good Name," an appellation given to Rabbi Yisrael ben Eliezer (1698-1760), the founder of Chasidism.

Ba'al Teshuvah (pl. *Ba'alei Teshuvah*). "Master of penitence," one who "returns" from a non-observant lifestyle to become a Torah observant Jew.

Beriah. "Creation," the second highest of the four supernal worlds.

Besht. Hebrew acronym for the *Ba'al Shem Tov.*

Binah. "Cognition," in the human soul, it is the power of precise, rational thought which forms the second stage of the intellectual process, following from *chochmah*. In its heavenly source, *binah* is the second of the ten *sefiros.*

Chabad. A Hebrew acronym of *chochmah, binah* and *da'as*, the three intellectual *sefiros*. It also refers to the school of Chasidic thought founded by Rabbi Shneur Zalman of Liadi, which emphasizes the role of mindful contemplation in worship.

Chasid (pl. *chasidim*). A devotee of the Chasidic movement.

Chasidism. A spiritual revivalist movement beginning in the southern Kingdom of Poland (today western Ukraine) in the 18th century, based on teachings of the *Ba'al Shem Tov.*

Chasidus. Chasidic teachings.

Chesed. "Kindness," a *sefirah* representing love, abundance, generosity and revelation. It stands in opposition to the *sefirah* of *gevurah.*

Chiluf. The "switching" of Hebrew letters that takes place during the creation process.

Chochmah. "Inquiry," in the human soul, it is the precognitive power of inspiration and creativity, which feeds *binah,* the second stage of the intellectual process. In its heavenly source, *chochmah* is the first of the ten *sefiros* which acts as a "window" to the Blessed Infinite Light.

Da'as. "Recognition," the third intellectual *sefirah,* following from *chochmah* and *binah. Da'as* does not add any new information; rather, it fosters an attachment to the existing idea, to render it "real" and relevant.

Din. Judgment energy which is the source of negative spiritual forces.

Elokim. Literally "judge," is one of G-d's names appearing extensively in the Bible, often denoting a Divine force of *gevurah* (see *gevurah*).

En-Sof. "Without end," a term in the Kabbalah used to refer to G-d.

Exodus Rabah. The section of *Midrash Rabah* on the Book of Exodus. (See "*Midrash Rabah*").

Gematria (pl. *Gematrios*). The numerical value assigned to Hebrew letters and words.

Genesis Rabah. The section of *Midrash Rabah* on the Book of Genesis. (See "*Midrash Rabah*").

Gevurah. "Severity," one of the ten *sefiros* signifying, fear, discipline, restraint and judgment. It stands in opposition to the *sefirah* of *chesed.*

Halachah. Jewish law.

Havayah. See Tetragrammaton.

Hishtalshelus. The unfolding "chain" of spiritual worlds through which G-d powers the universe.

Igeres Ha-Kodesh. Fourth section of *Tanya*, appended posthumously, containing letters by the author.

Igeres Ha-Teshuvah. Third section of *Tanya*, discussing the concept of repentence.

Is'hapcha: The approach of "transforming" negative forces completely.

Kabbalah. Jewish esoteric wisdom which has been received from a reliable source.

Kavanah (pl. *Kavanos*): "Intention," thoughts and feelings that accompany prayer and the performance of *mitzvos*.

Kelipah (pl. *Kelipos*). "Peel," a Kabbalistic term referring to negative and evil forces. *Kelipah* conceals the presence of G-d just as peel hides a fruit.

Kelipas Nogah. "Bright *kelipah*," a negative energy that contains some good and has the possibility of being transformed to holiness.

Keser. "Crown," the highest of the *sefiros*, acting as a medium between the Blessed Infinite Light and the other sefiros.

Kelos Ha-Nefesh. "Languishing of the soul," an intense passionate state, where the soul desires the extinction of its own separate identity, so as to merge with G-d.

Makif. "Surrounding [light]," a Divine energy which cannot be confined within limited, defined vessels and is only present in a disengaged fashion.

Malchus. "Sovereignty," the tenth and lowest of the *sefiros*, identified in Kabbalah with the feminine, *Shechinah*, the palpable presence of G-d on earth.

Ma'amarei Admor Ha-Zakein. Chasidic discourses by the author of Tanya, Rabbi Shneur Zalman of Liadi. 27 volumes.

Mechilta. Halachic Midrash of the Tannaic period to the Book of Exodus.

Midrash. Homilies and commentaries on the Torah by the *Talmudic* Rabbis.

Midrash Rabah. A major collection of homilies and commentaries on the Torah, ascribed to Rabbi Oshiah Rabah (c. 3rd century), perhaps assembled during the early Geonic period. First printed in Constantinople 1512

Mishnah. Fundamental collection of the legal pronouncements and discussion of the *Tanna'im*, compiled by Rabbi Yehudah ha-Nassi early in the third century. The *Mishnah* is the basic text of the Oral Law.

Mishneh Torah. See *Rambam*.

Misnagdim. Hostile opponents to the Chasidic movement.

Mitzvah (pl. *mitzvos*). "Commandment," the Divine commandments articulated in the Torah.

Nefesh. Lowest of three levels of the soul, responsible for basic body intelligence.

Neshama. Highest of three levels of the soul, responsible for self-conscious intelligence.

Octogrammaton. An eight-lettered Divine name formed by alternating the letters of Havayah and Adonai.

Rabenu Bachaye. Rabbi Bachaye ben Asher (1263-1340) of Saragosa, Spain. Author of a popular Torah commentary which incorporates literal, allegorical and Kabbalistic interpretations, often cited in Chasidic discourses.

Ramak. Rabbi Moses Cordovero, Kabalist of 16th century Safed. Student of Rabbi Yosef Caro. Author of numerous works, including *Pardes Rimonim,* a classic work which explains fundamental concepts of Kabbalah

Rambam. "Maimonides," acronym for Rabbi Moshe ben Maimon, (1135-1204) leading Torah scholar of the Middle Ages. His major works are *Sefer ha-Mitzvos, Commentary to the Mishnah, Mishneh Torah* (*Yad Ha-Chazakah*), a comprehensive code of Jewish law, *Moreh Nevuchim,* "Guide for the Perplexed," a primary work of Jewish philosophy.

Rashbam. Acronym for Rabbi Shmuel ben Meir, *Talmud* and Torah Commentator, who supplemented *Rashi's* (his grandfather's) commentary on the *Talmud* (c. 1085-1174). Brother of Rabeinu Tam.

Rashi. Acronym for Rabbi Shlomo Yitzchaki (1040-1105), author of fundamental commentary to the Bible and Talmud.

Ratzon Ha-Elyon. "Higher will," the inner will of G-d.

Raya Mehemna. "The Faithful Shepherd," a section of the *Zohar* which discusses the Kabbalistic significance of the commandments.

Rebbe. Spiritual leader of a Chasidic group.

Ruach. Second of three levels of the soul, responsible for emotional intelligence.

Sefirah (pl. *Sefiros*). A network of ten "energies" or "potencies" in the human soul. These mirror the ten heavenly *sefiros,* the Divine forces through which G-d influences the universe.

Shaloh. Acronym for *Shnei Luchos Habris,* "The two tablets of the Covenant", an encyclopedic compilation of ritual, ethics, and mysticism by Rabbi Isaiah Horowitz (1560-1630).

Shechinah. The "Divine presence" which is palpable and manifest on earth.

Shulchan Aruch. Universally accepted Code of Jewish Law encompassing all areas of practical *halachah,* by Rabbi Yosef Caro (1488-1575).

Sifri. Halachic Midrash on the books of Numbers and Deuteronomy.

Sitra Achra. "Other side," that which does not belong to the side of holiness.

Sovev-Kol-Almin. "Encircles-all-worlds," a Divine light and energy that is incompatible with the created worlds because it is too intense to engage with the worlds and become enmeshed with them.

Talmud. Comprehensive term for the *Mishnah* and *Gemara* as joined in the two compilations known as *Babylonian Talmud* (6th century) and *Jerusalem Talmud* (5th century).

Temurah. The "exchanging" of Hebrew letters that takes place during the creation process.

Tetragrammaton. Sacred Divine Name which is never pronounced, consisting of four letters, *yud-hei-vav-hei.* Often referred to by spelling it in reverse as *Havayah.*

Tikunei Zohar. Section of the Zohar containing an extended commentary to the Torah portion of *Bereshis.*

Tiferes. "Beauty," the sixth of the *sefiros* which harmonizes the influences of *chesed* and *gevurah.*

Tohu. "Chaos," an intense, disorderly Divine energy which precedes *tikun,* the "corrected" heavenly system of interconnected *sefiros.*

Tzadik (pl. *tzadikim*). Literally, "a righteous person." In the *Tanya* the term refers to a person who has transformed their Animal Soul to good.

Tzimtzum. "Diminishment," a process described in Lurianic Kabbalah through which the Infinite Light of G-d was diminished to enable the creation of a finite universe.

Yalkut Shimoni. Comprehensive Midrashic anthology, covering the entire Bible, attributed to Rabbi Shimon Ha-Darshan of Frankfurt (13th century).

Yetzirah. "Formation," the third of four supernal worlds.

Yesod. "Foundation," the ninth *sefirah,* which connects the energies above it with the tenth *sefirah, malchus.*

Yichud Ha-Elyon. "Integration of Divine attributes," a harmonization of the channels through which G-d's influence flows down into the worlds.

Yichuda Ila'ah. "Upper Unification," a term used by the Zohar to describe the desired consciousness when reciting the first line of the *Shema.*

Yichuda Tata'a. "Lower Unification," a term used by the Zohar to describe the desired consciousness when reciting the second line of the *Shema*

Zohar. Primary text of Kabbalah, containing the teachings of Rabbi Shimon ben Yochai and his disciples in the form of a commentary on the Torah. First published in the late 13th century by Rabbi Moshe de Leon (c. 1250–1305), in Spain.

לעילוי נשמת

אבי הרה"ג הרה"ת ר' **שלום דובער** הכהן ע"ה הכ"מ

בן הרה"ג הרה"ת ר' **מרדכי זאב** הכהן ז"ל

גוטניק

ראב"ד דק"ק מעלבורן יע"א

נפטר כ"ה אייר תשע"ח

ואמי הרבנית **דבורה** ע"ה

בת הרה"ח **אברהם** ע"ה

גוטניק

נפטרה כ"ג אלול תשע"ה

נדפס ע"י

הרה"ח הרה"ת ר' **מאיר** שיחי' הכהן **גוטניק**

וזוגתו **שינדל טעמא** תחי'

בניהם ובנותיהם